In the
High Pyrenees

A New Life in a Mountain Village

BERNARD LOUGHLIN

PENGUIN BOOKS

For my wife Mary Rogan and our children
Maeve and Eoin.

PENGUIN BOOKS

Published by the Penguin Group
Penguin Books Ltd, 25 St Stephen's Green, Dublin 2, Ireland
Penguin Books Ltd, 80 Strand, London WC2R ORL, England
Penguin Group (USA) Inc., 375 Hudson Street, New York, New York 10014, USA
Penguin Books Australia Ltd, 250 Camberwell Road, Camberwell, Victoria 3124, Australia
Penguin Books Canada Ltd, 10 Alcorn Avenue, Toronto, Ontario, Canada M4V 3B2
Penguin Books India (P) Ltd, 11 Community Centre, Panchsheel Park, New Delhi – 110 017, India
Penguin Books (NZ) Ltd, Cnr Rosedale and Airborne Roads, Albany, Auckland, New Zealand
Penguin Books (South Africa) (Pty) Ltd, 24 Sturdee Avenue, Rosebank 2196, South Africa

Penguin Books Ltd, Registered Offices: 80 Strand, London WC2R ORL, England

www.penguin.com

Published by Penguin Ireland 2003
Published in Penguin Books 2004

3

'Tarantella' by Hilaire Belloc is reprinted by permission of PFD on behalf of the Estate of
Hilaire Belloc. Copyright © 1970 by the Estate of Hilaire Belloc; the lines from 'L'Estaca'
by Lluís Llach are quoted by permission of Andréas Claus Management; the lines from
'Epic' by Patrick Kavanagh are quoted by kind permission of the Estate of the late
Katharine B. Kavanagh, through the Jonathan Williams Literary Agency; the lines from
The Green Children, the opera composed by Nicola LeFanu, are from Kevin Crossley-
Holland's libretto, quoted by permission of the librettist; the lines from 'Cavalls. Vista
panoràmica dels Pirineus' by Ronny Someck are from *En papier de vidre*, by Tamir
Greenberg and Ronny Someck (Edicions Proa, Enciclopèdia Catalana SA, Barcelona
2000), and are quoted by permission of the publisher and author.

Printed in England by Clays Ltd, St Ives plc

Contents

Do you remember an Inn,
Miranda?
Do you remember an Inn?
And the tedding and the spreading
Of the straw for a bedding,
And the fleas that tease in the High Pyrenees,
And the wine that tasted of the tar?

Hilaire Belloc, 'Tarantella'

Prologue:
A Juggernaut in Burg, April 1999

I am standing with Oppen, the Little Shepherd, at the Head of the Ridge, the entrance to the village of Farrera. He is looking for sheep. I am watching for a removals van bringing our traps from Ireland.

We are facing north. The village of Burg is at the other side of the wide valley below us. We are at 1,365 metres of altitude in the Catalan Pyrenees. It is April 1999. The line of peaks that fills the western horizon is snow-covered end to end from the storm of two days ago. There is muddy, half-melted ice underfoot. The sky is overcast. It is cold enough to make me sorry I am not wearing warmer clothes.

In an attempt to make conversation, I am asking the Little Shepherd stupid questions about sheep. How much does a lamb go for these days? What age are they sold at? How many bales of hay does one sheep eat in the course of a winter? Why do they wag their tails when they go to the toilet?

As he makes his terse replies, Oppen takes a CD of *Il Trovatore* out of his pocket and puts it into the Walkman he has hanging round his neck. He adjusts his earplugs. I try to think of another sheep question. We both gaze down the mountain.

At that moment a white juggernaut crawls into sight round one of the tight bends on the road below Burg.

— That must be the lorry with our furniture.

— *No passarà*, Oppen states with all the authority of a man who has spent twenty-five years in these mountains.

It will not pass.

— *No podrà girar enlloc*, he continues.

It won't be able to turn anywhere.

— *No passarà*, he repeats.

Just in case I hadn't heard him the first time, I suppose.

As I went racing down the road in the car, slowing here and there for patches of ice, I looked at all the bends, the field beside the bridge over the Burg river, the steep path up to the mayor's cowshed – trying to find somewhere the square-shouldered behemoth I could see still bulling its way up towards Burg might turn.

I slewed to a halt in front of the lorry – a lowering Mercedes with a three-legged badge big as a paella dish on the grille – just as it was hulking through the gap at the entrance to Burg between the Bonicois' high house and the even higher stone wall opposite. I got out of the car waving my arms.

— Whoa! I shouted up to the man in the cabin. Whoa!

Ana de Bonicoi was looking out of an open window on the second floor of her house at the sheer white side of the truck's trailer that was filling her vision like a blank film screen. Jacint de Bonicoi was out in the road behind me, waving too, and shouting Whoa! in Catalan, which is *Whoa!!!!!!!!!*

I climbed up the passenger side of the cabin and put my head through the window the driver had rolled down.

— Hello, Joe, I said as I shook his hand.

I knew his name because he had phoned me on his mobile a couple of times already that morning to ask for directions, the last time from Ribera in the valley of Cardós, which was the wrong valley altogether.

— I was expecting a removals van, I said.

— I only picked up the load in Dieppe. I don't even know what's in it. I haven't looked. Furniture, is it?

— Yeah, and not very much of it either. It couldn't be filling a quarter of the space there is back there.

From my spiderman's perch on the side of the cabin, 'back there' was a long acre, 'down there' to the ground was a dead man's drop, and there was no 'over there', just the stone wall of the Bonicois' house pasted on the driver's window like wallpaper.

— I don't know where we're going to turn this thing, I continued. And there's no way it will get up to where we live, over there.

At the other side of the Burg valley the ridge on which Farrera sits was framed by the snowy mountains.

— You'll have to try to get on up. You're blocking the road here. We might be able to do something at the other end of the village. It's the only place I can think of.

I got the car out of the way, then walked in front to guide Joe as he manoeuvred the lorry through the barns and houses of Burg to the steep hill in front of the municipal offices, once the village school, beside the half-built social centre whose ground floor was serving as garage for a tractor, a hay baler, a plough, a harrow and couple of cattle trailers.

Joe stopped and got down from the cab. He was in his twenties, tall, fresh-faced, Irish-country-looking, dressed in a yellow Trip To Tipp T-shirt and blue shorts, with wide sandals on his feet and no socks. Despite the cold there was a sheen of sweat on his forehead.

— When I started up the road from that last village down there a man started waving and shouting, but I couldn't understand what he was saying. Now I know, he said, with the embarrassed grin of a footballer who has just scored an own goal.

— Forestry lorries go up and down here all the time, some-times with really big loads of tree trunks, but I had no idea

when you phoned you were driving a yoke this size. I suppose
there's no way it could be reversed back down the mountain?

— Not a hope in hell.

— Then how the Jesus are we going to get it turned?

— I'll try backing her rear end in there, he said, pointing
to the entrance of the tractor shed under the social centre.

He climbed back up into the cabin. When he gunned the
engine the hinged flap on the upright exhaust pipe clicked
open like the whistle on a steam train. He drove the lorry
further up the road, its wheels churning through the slush.
He put it into reverse. When the back of the trailer came
level with the concrete ramp, he locked the steering hard.
The rear pair of wheels seemed to get a grip. Then the next
set left the ground and spun without traction. He gave the
engine more juice. The cabin jerked and wallowed, but the
trailer did not budge. He pulled out on to the road and started
over again, dropping back and locking hard. The rear wheels
began to mount the ramp until the steel protector bar across
the back scraped then dug into the concrete, stuck, with the
front wheels only inches from the edge of a steep field that
ended in the Burg river, far, far below. Joe, grim and silent,
looked down at me and joined his two hands in a steeple of
prayer on the sill of his open window. He gingerly inched
the lorry back up the road, then reversed it once more. On
the turn this time a hydraulic cable snapped. There was a
wheezing of air-brakes as the lorry settled to its knees like a
tired dromedary.

El Bernat, the mayor's father, came ambling up. He stood
rocking back and forth on his heels, appraising the situation,
his eyelids languidly lowering and then struggling to open
again.

— Why not drive her up to the Bonys and turn her there?
he suggested, with a slur as if he was drunk, only he wasn't

drunk, just very, very tired from all his years of standing about in fields minding cattle.

— Because she won't get past the bridge and there's snow on the Bonys, I answered, shouting a little.

— What about turning her in Farrera?

— He'll never get to Farrera. There are patches of snow and ice all the way.

This time shouting quite loudly.

As Joe was fixing the hydraulics Lluís Llobet arrived in his car from the direction of Farrera, followed by two more cars that stopped behind his. Josep Maria, the taxi man who brings the children to and from school, stopped below the lorry. No one could pass, everybody blocked from going about their normal business by the Irish people's furniture van that was not a furniture van but a mammoth, autobahn-cruising, kilometre-crunching, heavy-metal Merc with Offaly number plates and right-hand drive, and something of a sensation, for the children were all kneeling up on the bench seats in the back of the school jeep to get a good look at it. Josep Maria was grinning and waving at me.

As I dashed up and down telling the people in the cars we were going to make one more attempt to get the truck in off the road, I was speculating to myself about what it would take to dismantle it section by section and carry it back down the mountain to reassemble somewhere flat.

Joe came out from behind the hydraulics housing, wiping his hands on a cloth.

— I'll give her another go, he announced.

He drove the lorry up the road and then took the widest, most daring angle, with the outer one of the paired right front wheels actually hanging over the Field of the Abyss at one point, and this time he managed to get the rear end of the trailer up to the door of the tractor shed and most of the cabin in off the road, so that the waiting cars could pass, their occupants waving and smiling at us in gratitude for the spectacle.

Joe dropped an overnight bag out of his lorryman's loft and climbed down after it. He rooted to find a jumper that he put on over his T-shirt and then a pair of long trousers that he pulled on over his shorts, all the while looking at the tracks the truck had left in the mud and slush of the road, the steep slope up to the social centre, and the awkward angle this hill made with the road. When he was dressed he shook his head and stated, calmly and factually,

— We've got her in there now but I don't know how we're going to get her out. There's no way I'll get her turned back down the road.

He walked round and opened the door of the trailer to let me see our furniture. It was packed way up at the far end, wrapped in blankets of shoddy, seeming to have shrunk since the last time I had seen it in ceiling-high wooden storage crates in a damp shed in Newtownmountkennedy, County Wicklow.

Our plan had been for the removals van – for we had always assumed it would be a van – to arrive placidly on the *plaça* of Farrera and sit there for long enough for us to unpack our belongings and put them into the garage and attic of l'Era de Casa Joan, John's Haggard, the house we were renting while we braced ourselves to renovate our own house, Casa Felip. We had lived in Casa Felip for a rough-and-ready year in the mid 1970s and then bought it in 1989, since when we had only spent summer holidays under its shot roof, imagining the snug home it might be if we ever had the money to fix it up.

Now we would have to transport everything the two kilometres from Burg to Farrera. I left Joe to his hydraulics and drove back up there, the estate car's rear end waggling over the icy bits like a duck's arse on a frozen pond.

At John's Haggard I told my wife, Mary, what had happened. She was not surprised. So far, so typical, she said. We would have to do the best we could. I would take the dumper we had recently bought down to Burg. She would ask a couple who owed us a favour to come down in their open-backed truck to give us a hand. She and our son, Eoin, would bring down the car.

All through the late afternoon and into the evening we made trips up and down, the bucket of the dumper, the back of the car and the flat bed of the truck packed with boxes of books, bubble-wrapped paintings, a hallstand, chests of drawers, a sideboard, a green dresser, five beds, three sofas, four tables, a couple of dozen chairs, assorted lamps, cartons of clothes and other bric-à-brac: the magic porridge pot of possessions that had erupted out of the two rucksacks, one small suitcase and an infant in a Moses basket that were all the goods and chattels, chick and child we had had when we left Farrera twenty-five years before.

As we worked, people from Burg came to look at the monster that had landed in their midst. Sergi de Bernat, the mayor's nine-year-old son, walked once right round it, from nose to tail, a small beachcomber measuring a stranded whale.

— She's big, hey! She's a big one all right. She's the biggest was ever up here, that's for sure, he beamed at us.

By the time it was dark we had about half the furniture out of the lorry. Joe, who was meant to be already halfway back to Barcelona to collect another load, had been on and off the mobile phone to his boss in Edenderry, County Offaly. When I said there was nothing more we could do for now and he would have to spend the night with us, he phoned his boss and told him that, then stood with the mobile phone to his ear, just listening, his face getting redder and redder.

Over dinner Joe told us he was from a farm in Tipperary. I

told him an old joke of my father's about a man who goes to dump the carcass of a rare animal, a rarey, that ends with 'it's a long way to tip a rarey'. He laughed. This was his first time in Spain. He had slept the night before at the truckers' halt at Jorba on the National Route 2. In the restaurant there somebody had explained to him the Roman numeral system used for main roads in Spain. What he had thought was the National Route 11 he had discovered was in fact the NR II or NR 2. He had never heard of Roman numerals before. The trucks parked up together for security, he said. He never locked his loads because locks only attracted the thieves. The lorries being in a pack deterred them. The only problem was in truck parks in cities where the whores would be battering on the windows all night. He didn't speak any foreign languages. He had been to Paris, Brussels, Berlin, Rome, Bucharest, Budapest, but he had never seen any of the sights. He stuck to the motorways. For loads like this one he found his way by map and much use of the mobile phone. The mobile phone cost him a fortune: three hundred quid a month, sometimes. It was his only way of staying in touch with home.

After dinner I went out on to the balcony to inspect the night sky. It was starless and ponderous. I told Joe I didn't like the look of it. It might snow again.

While Mary and I went to bed, Joe and Eoin sat up over a couple of bottles of beer discussing football. I heard Eoin asking Joe questions about the trucker's life. Maybe he wants to be a trucker too, as I once did.

At seven o'clock in the morning we heard Joe stirring. I got up and looked out the window.

— Joe, I shouted down as he came out of the bathroom. It snowed!

I heard him gulp.

We had breakfast – rashers, sausages, two eggs each, with

potato farls Mary had made – and tried to make light of the situation, while Joe glanced out the window every now and then as if it were not snow falling past it but bars growing on it, imprisoning him here for the rest of his days.

— If I tell them at home I was in Spain in April and it was snowing they won't believe me.

After breakfast Joe and Eoin climbed up on the dumper with me to go down to Burg. The dumper has four-wheel drive. It needed every one of them.

As we offloaded the remainder of our stuff from the back of the lorry into the dusty ground floor of the social centre among the agricultural machinery, the menfolk of Burg gathered to give us advice. El Bernat was there, still talking about the Bonys. Jacint de Casa Bonicoi wanted us to be sure the lorry did not hit his telephone line on the way down. Paquito de Casa Toni was sucking a sweetie lollipop, one of the Chupa-Chups he seems to have substituted for a tobacco habit, and saying he didn't think we would ever get it turned. Cheerful Ramonet de Casa Savissà was as sanguine about our chances as his hair was dried-blood red, saying aye, surely, you'll get her out if you just keep at it. Francesc de Casa Estudiant (brother-in-law of a man, now deceased, who had gathered herbs for a living, and had also been known to read books, an activity so remarkable it had changed the name of his house) wondered if we could detach the rig from the trailer and then pull the trailer out with a tractor. Young Sergi de Bernat was also there, as if he had taken the day off school. He looked like he hoped the lorry might stay there for ever so that he could just come every day and marvel at it.

Around noon it stopped snowing. The sun came out. The snow melted fast in the sudden spring heat. By two o'clock in the afternoon there was no snow left in Burg.

Joe, who was pretty determined, I could see, to get back to

his life on the open road, first of all tried to turn the truck downhill, but the torque, as he called it, was not tight enough. He then ran it up the road again, the wheels spinning in the washes of mud, to try to get the back of it further into the corner under the verandah of the social centre, against the retaining wall. He improved the position by only a few inches, still not enough for the lorry to turn.

— If we could get a tractor to push the back of the trailer in against the wall, we might be able to do it, he told me when he climbed down from the cabin.

I went to find the mayor, Jordi de Bernat, who was looking at cattle in a byre in the lower part of the village. He said he would come up with his tractor and see what he could do.

When he arrived, we attached the chains he had brought with him to the motor end of the lorry to try to pull its nose downhill. Even with the big, blue, brand-new TORO tractor roaring at full throttle, the rig would not budge. The men were all shouting contradictory instructions. Paquito was muttering a shower of scatological Communion-host oaths through the side of his mouth not occupied by Chupa-Chup. I could feel the cold fog of old feuds in the air.

— Tell him to try shunting the back wheels of the trailer towards the wall, Joe shouted down from the cabin.

I translated this. None of the Burg men thought it would work.

— The trailer is lighter than it looks. Tell him that, Joe insisted.

I repeated this to Jordi de Bernat. He shrugged his shoulders.

— Well, we'll try, he assented.

He brought his tractor round through the back street of the village so that it faced the side of the trailer. As Paquito and I held up a thick plank across the two rear wheels, Jordi de Bernat brought the solid metal nose of the tractor up to the plank and nudged, and dunted, and then pushed with all the tractor's power until the trailer moved, by inches at first, then a couple of feet with the next shove, until finally its back wheels slurped through the mud right up to the wall.

Joe started the lorry's engine. It bellowed into life as if it too was ravenous for the road. He slowly eased out the front of the rig, the wheels locked tight, the outside front-left one skirting the edge of the Field of the Abyss, for a heart-stopping instant seeming to be poised over the void, and then the juggernaut was moving downhill, once more in thrall to the gravitational pull of far-off Offaly.

When the lorry was completely out, Joe stopped it. He jumped down from the cabin to shake the mayor's hand. Jordi de Bernat, who shrugs a lot, heaved a 'sure I knew we would get it out of there, we built this village with our own hands, we've been living here for a thousand years, there's nothing we can't do, just try us, now what's next?' lift of his shoulders, and smiled modestly. All the other men were grinning. Only Sergi looked crestfallen. As if we had just snatched away his future.

I ran down through the village in front of the lorry to watch for obstacles. The passenger-side mirror only whiskered the Bonicois' house this time. I used a long stick to hold their telephone line clear of the trailer's roof. When he was safely past, I signalled at Joe to stop. I climbed up into the cabin. From up there, Joe's little world felt snug as a tree house: the bunk bed behind the curtains at the back, the fridge under the dashboard where he had told us he kept his food, the CB radio receiver, the CD and radio deck, a big bar of chocolate on the hump between the driver's seat and the passenger seat, and the two bottles of *cava* in fancy tin boxes Mary had given him lying on the seat beside me.

— We'll miss you, Joe.

— Thanks for everything. It was an experience.

I signed the paper he handed me to say we had received our goods in good order. I shook his hand, thanked him again, and climbed down.

As I watched the back of the trailer disappear down the road, and then walked slowly back up through Burg, it was as though Joe's juggernaut had been the last lift out of here and I had just waved it on.

As if now, with our traps here, there is no way back.

I
Love Affair,
with Mountains

And the cheers and the jeers of the young muleteers
(Under the vine of the dark verandah)?
Do you remember an Inn, Miranda,
Do you remember an Inn?

Hilaire Belloc, 'Tarantella'

The Generalísimo's Parting Gift

I had first gone to Farrera on the twenty-first of November 1975, the day after the Caudillo of Spain, Generalísimo Francisco Franco, died.

I heard about the dictator's death on the afternoon of the twentieth, when Toni Strubell, the Catalan Englishman whose flat I was sharing in the old part of Barcelona, came home. He casually greeted the two men who were doing renovations, closed the door between my bedroom and where they were working, then embraced me and danced me silently round the bed, giddy with glee and the champagne he had been quaffing in the forenoon with his grandfather, who had spent almost forty years in exile after the Spanish Civil War.

After we had finished our mute dance of death, Strubell opened the doors again, talked briefly to the workmen, and went back out. Later he explained that he had not mentioned Franco's demise to them because he had not wanted them to leave our toilet a hole in the floor, the shower disconnected and the kitchen a mess, because if they had heard the news they would have downed tools and gone off for the four days of public mourning that had already been declared.

That evening, when Toni and I went out together to see what was stirring, there was no dancing in the streets, exactly, but rather a festive seething up and down the Ramblas: a fizzing and bubbling of cries, laughter, greetings, meetings of eyes, smiles; an air of levity and liberation. In the Plaça Catalunya flurries of waving of the Catalan flag provoked not very determined baton charges from the paramilitary police, who were out in force on every corner, it seemed, though they looked as if the heart had gone out of them and they were only doing it out of habit.

Among the throng we met Richard Betts, a cousin of Strubell's, also of English and Catalan parentage. Richard told us he was going to the mountains for the Generalísimo's posthumous holiday. I asked if I could go with him. I had no idea where these mountains were but had no other plans either: except maybe to take a train going in any direction out of the city and get off wherever the conductor asked me to pay, as I had already done twice, as experiments in random choice, during the two months I had been living in Barcelona. Even La Garriga, a dusty town to the north where I had slept out in the woods, had been interesting, just because it was Spain.

The next morning I left the city with Richard in his SEAT 600. We headed north-west, with me tracking the journey on the map I had bought. As we drove, Richard talked in his soft, slightly foreign-seeming, public-school-accented English. He had been educated partly in England and partly in Catalonia. His mother was married to a Spanish diplomat, who was not Richard's father. They were posted to Bogota. They wanted him to go to medical school but he was not so sure.

In the back of the car he had his recently deceased grandfather's bee-keeping equipment: a smoke-puffer, a centrifuge for spinning out the honey from the combs, a hood and mask, and two beehives in flat, square sections. He said that in the old days all the families in the village where we were going had kept bees. Nobody kept bees there any more but in the spring and summer there were lots of flowers. He was going to find a good spot to set up the hives, then bring up two swarms in the spring. In a bad winter he might have to give them sugar but in good years he would get pounds of honey.

As we tootled along in the tiny car, never leaving the inside lane, being overtaken by everything else, he told me about places along the way. Montserrat – a nobbly, yellowish eruption of a mountain that looked to have been been made up elsewhere then flown in and set down on the plains which surrounded it – was holy to the Catalans because of the Black Virgin who was venerated in the monastery there. Cervera, through whose narrow streets we passed at a crawl, had been an ecclesiastical and university town. During the Civil War hundreds of priests, nuns and seminarians had been killed there by the anarchists. Some of the towns in defensive-looking huddles we saw from the road looked as if they too had had their battering in the war and had not quite recovered yet. Winter wheat thrust plastic-green out of cloddy brown earth in unfenced, stone-terraced fields scraped down from scrubby hilltops where low bushes grew amid the fissures of fierce erosion. This region was called La Segarra. It had been a bread basket of cereal-growing since Roman times. The long, low, red-brick buildings with no glass in their windows were piggeries whose inmates were fattened on the grain stored in the tall silos beside them. A smell of bacon-flavoured slurry pervaded the car, making me hungry and sick all at once.

As we crested the brow of a hill we had ascended in a series of loops, mountains appeared all along the northern horizon. The Pyrenees? I asked Richard. The brownish ones in front were the Pre-Pyrenees, he said. They had been formed after the Pyrenees proper. The Pyrenees were the higher, snow-covered ones behind. An hour or so later, as we approached the towering, now reddish, weather-rounded bluffs of these Pre-Pyrenees, vultures wheeled in the blue sky above us. I craned forward in the seat to watch them.

— So you're an ornithologist, like Toni? Richard asked.

— More of a lazy bird-watcher, I replied. We don't have

vultures in Ireland. Nor eagles, either. We killed them all. It's wonderful to see so many of them here.

Richard stopped the car by the side of the road so that I could look at the birds through my binoculars. Their harsh calls of ugly souls reincarnate echoed above the sound of water rushing through a gorge below us. More of them launched themselves off stained ledges above us as we walked along the road a little way to look at a weeping, seeping, verdigrised cliff face of stalactites and stalagmites that was like a cave turned inside out. Richard said this formation had inspired the phantasmagorical sculptures of Gaudí's Sagrada Família, which I had seen for the first time the week before. The map called it the Canyon of Hell.

On the other side of a series of tunnels we motored through a wide bowl of a valley encircled by mountains. Richard said this had been a lake dammed by the upthrusting of the Pre-Pyrenees, until the water had cut its way out through Gaudí's gorge. What was left was called a *conca*, a shell, because that was the shape it had if you looked at it from above. The only ways out were through the defile where we had stopped or by roads that climbed the walls of the shell. In the distance, beyond ploughed fields of ochre-coloured alluvial soil, on the other side of a single-gauge railway line, there was a big reservoir emptied to its muddy bottom as if its dam too had burst.

As the Pyrenees themselves grew around us, the roads got narrower and twistier. This region was called the Pallars Sobirà, Richard explained. It was one of the most remote places in Spain. The people here spoke their own dialect of Catalan. There were not many of them left. The villages we could see sitting on outcrops of rock above the river or clinging to forested slopes were mostly abandoned. In many of them no one lived all the year round any more. In the village we were heading for there were only three native families left. They were all old. An outsider called Joan Martí had rented a house there for five years. He had kept cows and sheep. Now he too had left. A friend of Richard's had bought the house where he had lived. With other friends he was going to set up a commune.

I was very interested in communes, I told him. I would like to join one myself one day. I had a friend who lived in the Findhorn Community on the Solway Firth in Scotland. Had he ever heard of it? No, he hadn't. It had been set up in a caravan park by a retired British Army officer. His wife got messages from God. They grew giant vegetables in the gardens they had made on a disused dump. They didn't use artificial fertilizers but vibed with the plants' devas to encourage them to grow. Some of their cabbages weighed forty pounds. They had to be lifted out of the gardens with cranes and cut up with chainsaws.

We passed through close-packed towns backed against the walls of the valley of a fast-flowing river which was swollen and troubled by smaller rivers and streams tumbling out of side valleys. For most of the time we had the road to ourselves. We had to stop at one point to let a red bus pass. This was the bus to Barcelona which made the journey twice a day in both directions, Richard said. As it passed I could see the name of the bus company written on the side: ALSINA GRAËLLS, with an umlaut. I hadn't known Catalan had umlauts.

Around five in the afternoon, having been on the road for eight hours, we drove up a single-track dirt road that doubled back on itself as it climbed, until there was a sheer drop to the valley floor on our right. After passing through the village of Burg (had there been Germans here? I wondered), then weaving round a series of curves above a woodland that withheld the view, revealed it again, hid it again, and then showed a diorama of range upon range of sculpted white peaks to the far west like the opening of a cowboy picture in Panavision and Cinemascope, we stopped under a hand-painted tin sign hung on the corner of a stone barn that said FARRERA.

We got out of the car and walked down a steep path strewn with loose stones. At the bottom, across a small paved square, we passed through double wooden doors that gave directly into animal stalls on the ground floor of a square-faced house. At the back of the stalls we climbed up stairs that had been cut out of a wall of rock. Through a creaking door at the top we emerged into a living space divided down the middle by a glass and wood partition under a low, wood-beamed ceiling. The room within was a narrow kitchen with a wide chimney over an open fireplace. The room without had a table with benches along each side, a sideboard with a record player, a scatter of records and some books, and a door at the end that gave out on to a balcony.

Richard introduced me to everyone there, five women and four men, though with my little Spanish and no Catalan it took me a while to sort out who was who. A woman called Maria Dolores, who worked sometimes as an interpreter, she said, became Our Lady of Refuge for tongue-tied me, feeling my lack of the language like a bag over my head. She took me out on to the balcony at the end of the main room to show me the view: the village spread out over the hillside below us, a valley of fields and forests beyond it, and the snowy summits to the west, all bathed now in the martian light of dusk that also lit the Mediterranean beauty of her face, or at least what I thought had to be meant by Mediterranean beauty: Roman nose, Greek chin, Egyptian brow, Thracian curls, Libyan lips. She held my gaze with her frank, amused, olivaceous eyes as we conversed in what I remember as a fragrant, warm, confidential colloquy, even though it was quite chilly out on the balcony in a fretful breeze that seemed an aspect of the falling dusk. She told me about the village, how old it was – at least a thousand years – how few people now lived there, how many had lived there once, and how all the houses had names, though these were not usually the names of the people who now lived in them. The house we were in was called Casa Maria, named for its original owner, so long dead and gone that no one even remembered who she had been. The maiden aunts of the man who looked like Jesus Christ had bought the house for him. The others were friends who had known one another for years.

When we went back in, the rest of them talked to me in English, of which some of them had a smattering, or Castilian, which I had been learning from *Hugo's Teach Yourself Spanish in Three Months*. They talked to one another in Catalan, of which I understood hardly a word, though I had liked what I had heard of it, from Strubell and others, for its being softer and more sibilant than Spanish, more French-sounding, without any of the sandy Arabic *jotas* on which I had been choking for weeks.

As we sat round the smoky fire drinking an acrid herbal mix with hot water poured over it and honey stirred in, there was a discussion about communes. They were very earnest about starting one, though no one seemed very clear how it might work. As Maria Dolores translated for me what they said, she added, *sotto voce*, they were all very naive, was that not the word? A fellow called Jordi Petit, sharp-tempered and impatient as if he had truths to impart that were obvious and brooked no contradiction, said there would be nothing new about a commune here. People in villages like this had lived in a communal way for centuries. Each family had had its own house and its own land but they had always helped one another with the seasonal tasks. At one time there had been over 300 people living in the village. Now there were only seven or eight left. The commune could exploit the land that was not being used. They did not actually own any land yet. It was hard to buy land because even after they emigrated the natives held on to it, with the idea that they might return or that it might be worth money one day. It was worth next to nothing now.

For dinner, served in the *menjador*, the eating room, the one with the balcony door, an enormous round loaf of white bread with a thick crust was taken out of a deep drawer at the end of the table and cut up into wedges. There was a bean stew and a big pot of starch-sticky rice. After dinner, Richard went out to buy milk from one of the locals. When he came back, the milk was boiled over the fire to sterilize it. Jordi Petit said there was a lot of brucellosis and tuberculosis in the local herds. When the milk had come to the boil we had a bowl each, into which we dunked wedges of bread covered with apricot jam out of a kilo jar. This dessert left me feeling replete, if slightly anxious about my legs swelling up or the alveoli of my lungs starting to bleed.

Later, as I laid out my sleeping bag on the floor of the *menjador*, I noticed a tall glass bottle in the corner with a sign taped to it inviting visitors to put in money. A few coins lay at the bottom of it. They were gone the next day when I dropped in my own contribution. It too had disappeared by the afternoon.

One of the first ones whose name I did get was Oppen. He was stocky in stature, dishevelled in appearance, clownish-glum in manner. Even then it struck me that he was different from the rest of them, like a man waiting for the party to be over so that he could get on with his work. He joined in the continuous, high-spirited badinage, was the centre of it sometimes, and

you could see everybody liked him, but there was a seriousness
to him the others did not seem to have. He told me his mother
was Spanish and his father German. His whole name was Rafel
Oppenheimer i Salinas. When I tried him out in German, his
was even more rudimentary than mine. He had never lived in
Germany. His family had always spoken Castilian at home. At
school everything had been in Spanish. He had learned Catalan
in the street.

After breakfast the next day he took me through a low
door at the back of the *menjador* to an adjoining high-roofed,
open-fronted barn to show me the battery of cages he had set
up to rear rabbits to sell at the local market. They were fat,
brown rabbits with very long ears. As I helped him to fill the
inverted bottles that trickled water into their feeding pans,
Oppen told me, in the mixture of Spanish, German and
English we had struck up, that they needed careful watching
lest the females ingest their young, or the males maul one
another, or their sores not heal. He treated their wounds with
purple stuff out of a dirty-looking bottle. He said his first batch
had all died over a few days for no apparent reason. He wanted
to make enough money from the rabbits to buy some sheeps
and start a herd. How, he asked, do English-speaking people
distinguish sheeps from ships, ships from chips and sheet from
shit? I told him we just did. I got him to repeat the words after
me. He feigned not to get it. He was not going to give up his
little joke that easily.

Later that morning Richard asked me to give him a hand
taking the beehives out of his car and carrying them up to an
abandoned barn in a part of the village called El Castell. He
thought that would be an ideal situation for the bees: high up,
so they could fly straight out without getting entangled in
people's hair, under the shade and shelter of the half a roof
that remained on the building, and not too far from the fields

and gardens where the flowers would appear in the spring. He said bees liked to feel their hives were settled, so he would leave them there over the winter and bring up the swarms in April or May.

A man called Jordi Viñas, tall, long-haired and bearded, known, Maria Dolores told me, as el Jordi Gran to distinguish him from el Jordi Petit, arrived later that day. He was wearing a multi-hued kaftan and flower-embroidered bell-bottom jeans under a black overcoat, like a laicized priest who had not yet been able to afford a full set of civvies. We helped him to bring down packages of flat paper kits of toy houses from a van he had parked behind Richard's car. These play houses were to be assembled and packed into cardboard cartons: piecework for which they would be paid by the completed carton delivered to the wholesaler.

Even though I had money from my teaching job in Barcelona, I wanted to show willing, like the aspiring communard I was, so for two days I sat with the rest of them round the big table in the *menjador* and folded the toy houses; hours and hours of flip, flop, tuck, slip, glue, press, stack. There was a camaraderie about it, a hubbub of talk and laughter. Oppen did not assemble any little boxes but was in and out of the room all the time, stopping occasionally to lean against the sideboard and josh with the others, who got brighter and more boisterous when he appeared. He had a shy, wry way with the girls, as if he would really like to have had one of them for a special friend but did not know how to get beyond jokes. I didn't think any of them were having sexual relations just then, except Richard and his raunchy girlfriend Magda, but I had the feeling that some of them had had sex with some of the others at some time in the recent past, in various modalities. Maria Dolores told me that the son-of-god lookalike, Carles Carbó, was nicknamed Rompebragas – Pantyhose-breaker, she said. I told her I thought Knicker-breaker would be a better translation. She liked that expression and chortled over it for ages, throwing glances at Carles as if he were sporting flitters of the knickers he had ripped as trophies wound into his long, lustrous, Düreresque locks.

As we worked at the little boxes, flip, flop, tuck, slip, glue, press, stack, I couldn't get the song out of my mind, 'Little boxes, little boxes . . . and they're all made out of ticky-tacky, and they all look just the same'. I sang what I remembered of it.

— Ah, Nina y Federico, Magda cried. And they all sang '*Puf, el drac màgic*' in a rollicking chorus. That was the only line I understood.

On my third day in Farrera, to get away from the little boxes, I went out for a walk. I felt exhilarated as soon as I stepped outside the door of Casa Maria. Inside it had been warm and convivial. Outside it was cold and bracing. Beyond the village I clambered up a stream valley, following a path that wound between trees leaning over on their roots, then losing it where water frothed and surged around tangles of branches swept down by floods and jammed against boulders. I picked my way across the pebbly, bouldery glar of the river's steep banks, intent on heading upwards, until I emerged into an upland valley with paths that followed the contours round slanted meadows bounded by tumbled drystone walls. Many of the fields ended in washes of slatey erosion on the banks of streams. In hollows there were clumps of deciduous wood-land, with here and there thickets of prostrate, thorny juniper bushes, and forests of pine higher up. Scattered groups of cows with their calves grazed the tough-looking, close-cropped vegetation. Further away the landscape was shades of brown and black between smears and swathes of snow.

After a while, as I toiled upwards, stopping frequently to

draw breath, Farrera disappeared, and then there were only mountains, more and more of them appearing the higher I got. Having plodded up to a pass through deeper and deeper snow, determined to see what lay beyond it, scaling the last bit more or less on my hands and knees, I stood at the top looking towards the east, where I had been told Andorra was. Out that way there was no house or shelter or sign of man, just pine forests marching stiff and erect up to a craggy peak off which the wind was blowing plumes of snow.

The place where I was standing had to be the Coll de So, the Pass of Sound, which I had seen on a map in Casa Maria. Where there is always a wind, Oppen had told me, because wind finds the lowest and shortest way over mountains.

I sheltered from the wind under a west-facing cliff and smoked a cigarette. It made me dizzy, agog as I already was with wonder at where I had got myself now, an amazed, side-hugging little voice in my head going, 'The Pyrenees, the Pyrenees!', and me, a wee lad from Belfast, here in the midst of them.

I took a different route back, along the northern side of the valley, jumping and sliding on the sides of my boots through snowdrifts and then down slopes of scree, like Jack Kerouac bouncing down from his summer of fire-watching on Desolation Mountain.

From an eminence overlooking the village, the houses and barns were all black and grey and dark brown with stone and slate and weathered wood. Below it and here and there throughout it were terraced gardens, their walls overrun with ivy. I saw one man working in a sloping plot below the track that ran along the bottom of the village. That must be the Marsal they had talked about, the only man who still worked in the old way, they had said. A bundled-up woman was herding five big brown cows back to the village from the fields above the stream where I had started my walk. She must be the Conchita from whom Casa Maria bought its milk.

It was almost dark by the time I got back to Casa Maria, where they were still flipping, flopping, tucking, slipping, gluing, pressing and stacking the little boxes. They seemed shocked that I had gone as far as I had, with the snow there must be up there, as if I had risked my life. It occurred to me that none of them were particularly outdoors people. No one else had been out of the house further than to collect milk all the time I had been there. As I told her about my ramble, Maria Dolores looked at me with a twinkling scepticism, as if she suspected I had taken something hallucinogenic, for I was gabbling and garrulous, even essaying a few words in Catalan:

— *Ha molta neu adalt.*

Is much snow up.

That evening, after much discussion, and everyone helping, peeling and cleaning vegetables, washing up, stirring and peering into pots, setting out the motley array of plates and knives and forks on the table from which the little boxes had been cleared, filling wine from a barrel out the back into the *porró* thing they had been trying to teach me to use (you hold it up by its big spout and aim the smaller, thinner spout at your mouth, and then, as you wipe the spilt biddy from the front of your shirt, smile bravely as they break their hearts laughing at you), the dinner finally appeared on the table sometime around eleven o'clock, as on previous nights, without anybody seeming to think that was in any way late.

Afterwards we smoked joints made from a lump of oily black hashish with whitish streaks of opium through it. It was the first dope I had smoked in Spain. I was instantly stoned, and slightly paranoid too, for I knew that under Franco's laws the mandatory minimum sentence for possession of hash was seven years and a day, with no remission. Some tentative tappings and soundings started a session of jamming and noise-making between a guitar strummed and plucked by the son-of-god, Carles Carbó; a saxophone played by Joan, pronounced Joe-Ann, he had told me; a metal tray banged and beaten by Magda, Richard's girlfriend; tins and bottles rattled by her three cousins, all of them curly-haired, frivolous and vivacious; Jordi Petit rasping the prongs of a fork over the holes of a colander; Jordi Viñas, head down, intently battering a bongo; comb and paper demurely vibrated by the lips of Maria Dolores; Oppen using his knuckles on an upturned metal casserole dish; Richard on a harmonica; and me, chanting made-up blues and bits of Irish songs as I ullulated my delight at finding this magical place and the gay tribe of fellow nomads who had pitched their tents in it.

Boy and Girl Next Door

Just after Christmas of the year Franco died, Mary Rogan came to live with me in the flat I was sharing with Toni Strubell in Carrer de la Palla (hereinafter referred to as Straw Street) in Barcelona.

Mary and I were boy and girl next door, at one remove.

My uncle and aunt, Frank and Mairéad Blaney, lived in the house beside Mary's family's in St Agnes Drive in Andersonstown, the agglomeration of housing estates on the western fringes of Belfast where I also lived, only a few streets away. I may have met Mary then, when visiting the Blaneys, though I have no memory of it. When I was fifteen or sixteen I saw her one time I went with my father to deliver to her house a consignment of the holy pictures he made. They were to be collected by her aunts, who had a newspaper shop and Catholic repository in Broughshane Street in Ballymena. When she came out of the kitchen, from which an aroma of baking scones followed her, I thought she looked like one of the madonnas my father framed. Every morning after that, from the top deck of the Falls Road trolley-bus, I would scan the crowds of winegum-red-uniformed girls going into St Dominic's Convent School in hopes of catching a glimpse of her.

On New Year's Eve 1966 I met Mary at a party in her friend Eleanor Garvey's house. She was sixteen, I was seventeen. She was sitting on a sofa in the living room, wearing a red tartan miniskirt with a Celtic brooch pinning its fold above her long legs in high brown-leather boots. I sat beside her. We talked all evening, and then kissed, to the Beatles singing 'I Wanna Hold Your Hand' on Eleanor's Dansette record-player, as I had a sensation of my soul undoing itself from my body and floating above us in semi-detached bliss.

Before we left the party we arranged to meet at Casement shops a couple of nights later. Mary was late and came with a friend. She told me she could not go out with me because her father said she was too young to be going out with boys. She had to study for her A-levels.

Two years later, when we met again at the zebra crossing in front of the Students' Union at Queen's University, in my second year, her first, Mary was wearing a grey tweed maxi-coat. It had a wide collar that framed her long, dark, silky hair and round face, in which I thought I saw traits of Cherokee. Her smile seemed to say she still liked me, or at least was curious to know what I might be like to like.

On our first real date we saw Ibsen's *A Doll's House* in the Dramsoc Hut.

Thus began the Belfast episode of our love story, against a background of bombs during the day, gun battles almost every night, riots, tear gas, rubber bullets, Saracen armoured cars prowling the streets like recently-landed spacecraft, police jeeps that overnight, it seemed, grew metal grilles over their windows and donned plastic skirts, wailing sirens, racing ambulances, an air of Cyprus, Aden, Amritsar: a filmic happeningness that was exciting as long as you were watching it from a distance, or hearing its crumps and thuds and crackles from afar, or walking through the aftermath, knowing the war hadn't got you yet, and you were still at the pictures.

Since then we had worked in Switzerland, she as an au pair and I as a dishwasher; travelled to Greece together, sleeping under olive trees in a Swiss army sleeping bag big enough for two; knelt in freezing clay to harvest grapes in autumnal France; been chambermaids in the Majestic Hotel in Chamonix, Mont Blanc; ridden on the Marrakesh Express; and spent a *Wind in the Willows*, 'Owl and Pussycat' summer as bargees on the River Shannon – for all that neither rivers nor true love always run smoothly, especially at their outsets.

Now Barcelona was to be a new beginning for us.

When Mary arrived in Straw Street, flushed from the journey, smiling, all my brutishness forgiven, again, Toni Strubell – matinée-idol good-looking, his dashing Englishness flirting with an arch, ironic Spanishness – greeted her with kisses on both rosy cheeks. With ample gesticulations that almost grazed the walls he showed her the extent and elegance of the appointments in our narrow apartment. In the bare kitchen at the back he apologized for there being no cooker, for he had heard what a good cook Mary was. He might buy one soon.

In that out-of-doors-at-all-hours city, we would not miss it, for he never did get one.

A year before, Mary and I had spent a night walking these same streets of the Gothic Quarter, not knowing it was called the Gothic Quarter, waiting for the boat to Valencia we were to catch at five in the morning on our way to Morocco. Late in the evening we had stopped for a drink in a bar-cum-restaurant that stayed in my memory as a paragon of eating houses. I remembered the wide door, as if it had once been some kind of shop or store, the vaulted ceilings, and how over everything inside there had been a fur of grease and tobacco tar: on the walls, dribbling in oily runnels down the sides of old bottles on the high shelves that ran round the room, darkening paintings and posters, hanging in cobwebby strands from the ceiling, with more of it swirling in the smoky air, agitated by a halting fan. But I had not remembered the bar's name nor retained any clear idea of where it was. In my first weeks back in the city, while living in a *pensión* on the Via Augusta near where I was teaching in the Dublin School of English, I had gone down to the old part of the town night after night to look for this hostelry of hostelries, but did not find it.

Then, the night I moved into Toni Strubell's flat in Straw Street, it had just turned up round the corner, a hundred metres from our front door. El Portalón it was called on the wooden sign that hung above the broad doors that were still folded back, revealing an interior that was even more dusky, picaresque and *délabré* than I remembered it: the embodiment of all my fancies of what a quixotic Spanish tavern should be, for I was reading *Don Quijote* at the time and thought this could well have been where the Squire and Sancho had put up on their visit to the city that, according to Cervantes, was '*archivo de la cortesía, albergue de los extranjeros, y en sitio y belleza única*' – repository of courtesy, inn for foreigners, and in situation and loveliness unique.

After Mary arrived, we ate in El Portalón almost every day, sometimes both lunch and dinner, often with Toni Strubell, and nearly always with our Irish friend Colm Tóibín, who adopted it and us as his locals. We came to know by sight and occasional converse the furniture-makers, fuel-dealers, carpenters, picture-framers, basket-makers and other artisans who worked in the surrounding streets, many of which carried the names of the trades which had been or still were practised in them. We were usually joined by Miquel Ángelo, who worked as a *matador de cucarachas*, cockroach-killer, and every day had a salad of sliced tomatoes with rings of onion and a scatter of olives drenched in oil and vinegar, while we made our choices from the menu on the blackboard: *botifarra* sausage with fried beans; lentil stew; soup with chick peas, cuds of fat and wedges of cabbage stalk; seared meat with chips; kidneys in sherry sauce; or trout Basque style, stuffed with ham and cheese. Mary, who was a vegetarian at the time, had a more limited choice, but did not starve either.

Colm, boyish (twenty-one then to Mary's twenty-five and my twenty-six), bearded and bookish, never without a volume of poetry about his person, was breathlessly enthusiastic about everything – the Fellini season at the Filmoteca, the cheap Sunday-morning concerts at the Palau de la Música, the paint-ings of Joaquín Mir, the singing of Victória de los Angeles – to the point where he would sometimes be overwhelmed by his stammer (whose gradual subduing we would witness dur-ing these years) in his haste to tell us about his latest discoveries. He was from Enniscorthy, County Wexford, and talked about it and its personages a lot – Mrs Murphy Flood's Scrabble evenings where his mother once laid out the four letters for the female pudenda and then had to get the dictionary to prove to the other ladies that the word existed, for they had never heard of it; Big Dinners Quinn's detailed recitals of the menus of meals he had out; the dialect of Forth and Bargy, a remnant of the Norman invasions; the yearning in the harvest season of the farmboys at the boarding school he had attended in Wexford town, who would stand at the windows of the dormitory in the moonlight looking over the walls at the fields in the distance – all with the novelist's ability he already had to make his home place an entertaining moral universe. He talked about his family too, in a guarded, thousand-miles-between-him-and-them-and-all-harm but withal dutiful and affectionate way, which endeared him to Mary, who has always been a family person, and something of a small-town person too, with her roots and antecedents in Ballymena, County Antrim.

Colm had studied history at university in Dublin. He followed Spanish and Catalan politics closely and often discussed them with Toni Strubell, who had launched himself – with what we came to know was his characteristic impetuosity – into the political ferment in the streets, where you never knew when you would bump into a crowd waving Catalan flags and chanting slogans like '*Viola, demissió, per feixista i cabró*' (Viola – the mayor of Barcelona who had been appointed by Franco *a dedo*, by the pointing of the dictator's finger – resign, why don't you, fascist and bollocks that you are.)

Toni was a member of Esquerra Republicana, the leftist, republican, Catalanist party that had been outlawed during the Franco years. When the red – as for emergencies – phone he had installed in the flat rang, he would have an urgent, brisk conversation in Catalan, then pull on his coat and stride out into the fray, wherever he had been told it was going to take place that day, for he never missed a demonstration or a postering, at which he became a dab hand with the brush and bucket he kept at the ready at the front door.

At the time the Catalan flag was still banned. Its red stripes on a yellow ground represent the four trails of blood that Count Ramón Berenguer (or Guifré El Pilós – Wilfred the

Hairy – depending on the version to which you subscribe)
had smeared down a banner with the fingers of his right hand
dipped into a wound on his side as he expired on the field of
battle. One night a few weeks before Franco died, Strubell
had wrapped a Catalan flag as big as a sheet round his upper
body under his clothes to smuggle it past the police and
bouncers at the door of a Lluís Llach concert to which he
brought me. When Llach announced that he was going to
sing '*L'Estaca*', a protest song about a rotten old stake that was
blocking everybody's way, Toni stood up in the seat beside
me, took off his jacket and jumper and shirt, and unfurled the
flag to wave it with fervour at the chorus:

> *Si jo l'estiro fort per aquí*
> *i tu l'estires fort per allà,*
> *segur que tomba, tomba, tomba,*
> *i ens podrem alliberar.*

> If I haul strongly this way
> and you haul strongly that way,
> it will surely fall, fall, fall,
> and we will all be free.

Toni was also involved with a group campaigning to save
wetlands near Girona that were important wintering grounds
for migratory birds. I had met him through a woman who had
known him at Oxford. She had thought we would get on
because we were both bird-watchers. He knew birds by their
English, Latin, Spanish and Catalan names. As a licensed ringer
he had captured and ringed birds in Oxfordshire woods and
in the Guadarrama mountains north of Madrid. He had
worked on the Coto Doñana, the nature reserve on the estuary
of the Guadalquivir south of Seville. For two student summers
he had travelled in the Rif and the Atlas mountains in Morocco

trying to verify the presence there of a residual population of Spanish imperial eagles, which were down to a last seventy or eighty pairs in Europe. He had not found any.

He was a grandson of Dr Josep Trueta, who had been a surgeon on the Republican side in the Civil War. The widespread adoption of Dr Trueta's method of eliminating all dead tissue from wounds, washing them and immobilizing the affected limbs in plaster, with no daily swabbing, cut the rate of deaths from gangrene from the 10 per cent it had been in the First World War to less than 1 per cent in the Second World War. He also discovered ways to treat the reversal of the blood system in the kidneys after traumatic injury, which had been the cause of thousands of fatalities among those apparently not so badly wounded. Dr Trueta had gone into exile in England after the Republican defeat, becoming Professor of Orthopaedic Surgery at Oxford. His only daughter married an Englishman. Their children, Toni and his brother Miquel, were brought up between Oxford and Catalonia.

As well as bringing Spain's past to life – touch the hand of the man who touched the hand of the man who saved thousands of Republican soldiers from death – Toni became our guide and mentor in the underground of the Catalan language and culture that was hidden beneath the Castilian façade forty years of Francoism had painted over Barcelona: even if most of the paint turned out to have been only distemper.

Through his grandfather's book, *The Spirit of Catalonia*, we learned about Catalanism, the deep-rooted sense of themselves as a people among the peoples of the rest of the Spains – a plural the more purist among them sometimes use – that has endured with the Catalans since they had their own Mediterranean imperium stretching as far as Aragon in the west, Provence in the north and Sardinia in the east. In its mercantile glory days, Catalonia had rivalled Venice as a trading power. This had imbued the Catalans with a sense of their privileges and prerogatives that made them irksome to royal Spain for many centuries, and a raw itch to its fascist successor. As we would see, this Catalanism had only been waiting for the death of Franco to emerge back into the light of day from its safe hiding in the bosom of the Catalan bourgeoisie, where it had been sheltered and nurtured ever since the Civil War.

And in those effervescent days of *el destape* – the taking of the cork out of the bottle, as the blinking into the light after the long cellarage of Francoism was called – when first a peek of half a nipple on magazine covers, next a whole nipple, then two bare, brazen breasts, and finally full frontal nudity made a striptease mockery of the dead dictator, all kinds of sexualities emerged from the back streets of the Barrio Chino into the public glare of the Ramblas – transvestites in gorgeous gowns and daggerish stilettos, broken-down prostitutes with smeared lipstick and smoke-stained voices, men meeting other men – as everything became possible in a Spain which had had to dissemble and hide so many facets of itself for so many fascist years.

In the sometimes panicky, rumour- and portent-filled atmosphere of those first months without the Caudillo, it was as though a striped canopy of the Catalan flag had been thrown over Barcelona, bathing the city in a theatrical light that played upon the relics of its bloody history: the monument to the heroes of the Napoleonic war opposite the door of the cloister of the cathedral; the bullet-scarred façade of the church of Saint Felip Neri where the victorious Nationalists had executed hundreds of their enemies in the enclosed square to the sound of the water falling into the fountain under its acacia trees; the raised bronze letters of JOSÉ ANTONIO PRIMO DE RIVERA – PRESENTE on the wall of the bishop's palace; the daubings and graffiti of the factions and parties that were taking up where they had left off after the Civil War; and all the other signs we learned to read.

Voyeurs and *flâneurs* as we were, living on the street (*la calle*, that southern place or state of being in which you do not so much walk as bathe) and wandering night after night through the alleys, sinks and souks of the old town under the reddish-yellow light of that imagined tent, Mary, Colm and I marked our maps of *terra* ever more *cognita et amata* in a peregrination that usually started in El Portalón and often ended in El Drugstore on the Ramblas that stayed open twenty-three hours a day, where all the street people eventually drifted, *y nosotros también*, until Colm would say 'I'm going off now', and we would go our separate sexual ways.

On the eighteenth of March 1976 the three of us went to Farrera together on the red Alsina Graëlls bus from the Ronda Universitat. It took seven hours, with a pee stop at La Panadella and a change of buses in La Pobla de Segur, and left us at Llavorsí when night had already fallen.

I can't remember what I had told Mary and Colm about the place before we went, beyond that we needed to buy food to bring with us, as we did. They sat together on the back seat of the jeep-taxi we hired to go to Farrera, looking worried, their apprehension growing perceptibly as the jeep jounced on the tortuously climbing, muddy road, slippery from recent rain. The jeep got stuck in a rut between Burg and Farrera. We had to get out and help the taxi man to push it free.

We entered Casa Maria by the barn door, groped for a light switch, found none, and had to light our way with matches up the stone stairs to the kitchen. When we found the switch for the light and its bare-bulb glare fell upon the bleak, untidy austerity, I could feel Mary and Colm thinking – for in their

short acquaintance they had already come to share a wariness
of my tendency to take up with bad company, veer off, get
lost and plough on regardless — how typical it was of me to
bring them up these dark, cold mountains, in the middle of
March, after a night and a journey such as we had just had, for
the evening before we had been to a St Patrick's Day party in
the Hotel Colón with rich- and sleek-looking Spanish people
called O'Connell, Farrell, O'Donnell, descendants of the old
Wild Geese, who had looked on with well-bred astonishment
as the new Wild Geese of the English-teaching migrations
grazed and guzzled their way through a case of Jameson
whiskey. We weren't any of us the better of it yet.

After a while, responding to our calls, Oppen appeared
from upstairs with wisps of straw sticking out of his matted
hair and an out-at-the-elbows jumper over rumpled stripy
pyjamas. His greeting was gruff. Mary and Colm sat together
on the bench beside the ashes of a dead fire while we tried to
make conversation and explain our unannounced presence.
As Oppen listened, he candidly examined the boxes of gro-
ceries we had brought: fruit, vegetables, meat, bread, chocolate, butter, for the Irish must always have butter, and wine.
We told him he should help himself. We had brought it for
all of us. His hunger was unabashed. He ate things directly
from their packets.

The alms bottle in the *menjador* was empty. It looked to
have been empty for some time.

The morning of the nineteenth of March dawned blue and
clear, but bone-chillingly cold. In Carles Carbó's room at the
front of the house beside the upstairs balcony Mary and I lay
deep in the pile of blankets she had procured from Oppen the
night before, one of her skills being bed-making, learned from
her mother, who was a nurse. Colm slept in an unwindowed
room at the back of the house, where he dreamed he was a

driver on the metro in Barcelona burrowing from station to station, light to light, through blackness into more blackness. When we did finally get up and go downstairs, Oppen was eating a bowl of the muesli we had brought.

The rest of the would-be communards had left, Oppen explained, though some of them might be back soon when they had earned some money in the factories of Switzerland. For the moment Oppen was there on his own with his rabbits, the first few sheep he had bought, and a smooth-haired dog called Maya, a stray someone had brought from Barcelona, along with her black, hairy pup Clea, bred out of one of the local dogs. Oppen showed us how Clea had two claws instead of one on her front ankles. This was a sign of a born sheepdog. He was going to train her himself.

I see that first visit with Mary and Colm hardly at all as an event in its own right any more, simply because I forget the details, or get them mixed up with other times we were there, such as the time we were staying in the same room and Mary and I were arguing about something, probably about whether we should be there at all (for Mary has always had more doubts about that than me), she sitting on the bed, me by the open window, and a scops owl landed on the clothes line that was stretched from the balcony a few feet away, from which it stared balefully at me as if to say 'Would you ever stop tormenting that poor woman?'

I do remember that Oppen treated Mary with the same lorn jocosity I had seen him display towards the other girls of my first visit. When he tasted her cooking, he became almost genial. She managed to bake a cake in the poky, inconstant oven. Oppen ate most of it. Cake would become a running joke with them, for years and years.

After breakfast that first day, I took Mary and Colm up to

see the beehives Richard had set up in the ruined barn on El
Castell. The rest of the roof had collapsed and flattened them.

Later, when I asked about Maria Dolores, Oppen told me
she had committed suicide, did I not know? A love affair gone
wrong, he said.

Birds of Passage

Back in Barcelona, we went with Carles Carbó to a *fiesta mayor*
in his *barrio*, where we danced behind an oompah-oompah
band in an inferno of firecrackers and squibs under a thunder-
shower of streamers and confetti thrown from the balconies
of flats. At Zeleste, the club where the musical cork was being
drawn from Franco's bottle, we met Joan the saxophonist,
who was playing there with the group he had formed. One
day on the Ramblas we bumped into Magda's cousins, the
Castelar sisters, and discovered that Mariona was going to train
as a classical singer, Helena was joining a theatre company and
Marta was getting married. None of them was likely to be
living in Farrera again.

Colm moved from Castelldefels to share Richard's mother's
flat on Capitán Arenas with him. When a woman came one
day a week to clean it, he would close the door of his room
and stay in there until she left, refusing to let her touch his
disarray of books, records, clothes in piles and bags of fruit.
He sometimes bought oranges by the five-kilo sack and ate
them all in one sitting, fructivoracious Irish boy as he was,
making up for years of vitamin C deprivation.

Towards the summer Mary and I began to think of moving
to somewhere else in Spain. Andalusia was discussed. Then
we learned that a house in Farrera, Casa Felip, could be rented

for a year for the equivalent of £90. We decided we would go to live there when the term finished at the Dublin School of English. Our grubstake would be the 25 per cent of my wages they had been keeping by for me in lieu of holiday pay, since we did not pay tax, social security, pension contributions, or anything else of an official sort in the fiscal free-for-all of Franco's Spain, whose ethos still prevailed, in which nothing was what it seemed and the Dublin School of English was registered as a travel agency.

At the beginning of June Mary and I went to Farrera on the Alsina, as we had discovered it was familiarly called by those who used it, whose luggage lockers held the provisions we had laid in from wholesalers: fifty-kilo sacks of dried lentils, peas and beans, cases of tinned tomato paste, boxes of canned sardines, pasta in tall brown-paper bags. These were to be our stores for a high-altitude voyage with the moon as our balloon.

Casa Felip was set back into the mountainside over three storeys of barn and byre which farmers from Burg were using to store hay and keep cattle. Mary and I took the bedroom that had been closed off with a wooden partition from the otherwise completely open top floor of the house, where the Andorrà family, from whom we were renting it, had once all slept. There was no electricity. We bought big white candles in blue paper packets of fifty, and learned to live by their light.

In the 1950s the Andorràs had built on a red-brick and pebble-dash block of two rooms at the front of the house over the entrance to the barn, to rent to a *carabiner* and his family, one of those billeted in such villages to keep the peace for Franco and patrol against smugglers from Andorra. This cabin-like extension had been divided into a kitchen with an open fire on a raised concrete platform under a chimney hood and a bedroom with a balcony that looked over the village towards the west. This was where Tony Dumphy and Barbara Gamble would sleep, friends from university days in Belfast who came to join us for a year out from the careers as journalists on which they were embarked in London.

Barbara, unrepentantly urban, with the resilience of a Belfast Royal Academy girl who was determined to have a good time on her holidays, took everything in her loping stride: the primitive living conditions, where her all-over washes in the basin with the one cold tap at the back of the house were object lessons in the ablutive absolute; the staple diet of lentils, for which she would develop a life-long abhorrence; Spanish, which she systematically learned until she arrived at her chosen plateau; English classes she and I organized between us, in Sort, the capital of the region (I marched her to the bus on the first day by the supposedly shortest walking route – dressed in her lady teacher's long skirt, heeled shoes and smart jacket – through thorny thickets in the valley below Farrera, where I got us so lost that I ended up carrying her over the river on my back); the novel she started that was published some years later; an all-devouring reading programme; crocheting that she had learned from her grandmother and now took up again, finding that once she started she couldn't stop.

Tony and I spent most of the summer hauling firewood from a forest along a stream about a quarter of a mile from the village. We used a bowsaw to cut up fallen trees, mostly elms, first victims of the Dutch elm disease that would ravage the village woods, hedges and field boundaries, where quicks of elm had been planted to reinforce walls that the dead weights of the mature trees were now causing to collapse. We transported the sectioned trunks back to the village on a wheelbarrow. By September we had the dark store room at the back of Casa Felip piled high with fuel for the winter to come.

When he first arrived in Farrera, Tony was often pale and

short of breath. A few times he looked like he might faint from the effort of hauling wood, great smoker as he was – as we all were, except Mary, who was only an occasional dainty puffer. Yet as the summer went on Tony's street tyke's chest and footballer's trunk straightened and broadened and strengthened, like a last spurt of growth. He and I told ourselves we could drink as much as we liked of the rough wine that was delivered to the door in a fifty-litre plastic barrel for the equivalent of £6 and smoke as many as we wanted of the untipped, stumpy, black Celtas we bought by the carton of 2,000 for six pesetas a packet of twenty, because with all our exertions out on the mountain, the good air, the healthy food, we were sweating and working the toxins out of our systems.

From the day we arrived we were part of the nebulous not-quite-commune, the flux of friends and friends of friends that whirled around Casa Maria. It would be full of people for weeks on end. Then there would be just Oppen on his own, again. Oppen was already a constant, having decided the first time he came to Farrera that he would settle there: he went back to Barcelona, collected his few belongings, returned, and stayed for ever. Carles Carbó came and went, each new arrival celebrated with festive stews of rice into which he mixed the slabs of salted cod his mother always gave him as a viaticum.

Throughout that year we would have a stream of visitors of our own. Colm came up from Barcelona for weekends, bringing boxes of fruit, braces of chickens, strings of sausages, bottles of Torres brandy and other delicacies with which to enliven our frugal fare. Toni Strubell came with his Basque girlfriend, Karmentxu Pastor, whom he had met on the night ferry from Genoa when he was collecting exhausted migratory birds from where they had flopped on the deck under the lights. He had brought Karmentxu – a fiery Pasionaria with long, straight, hennaed hair under a black beret, only tomboy sister of five brothers, one of whom would die in a climbing accident on Everest – and five sockfuls of swallows, goldcrests and willow-warblers back to Straw Street. He released the birds from the roof but cleaved to Karmentxu, whom he would marry soon afterwards. At the nightly music sessions we had in the kitchen of Casa Felip they sang duets in Basque or Catalan:

> *Muntanyes regalades*
> *són les del Canigó,*
> *car tot l'estiu floreixen,*
> *primavera i tardor.*

> Wonderfully apparelled mountains
> are those of the Canigó,
> for all the summer they blossom,
> and in spring and autumn.

The taxi bringing my sister Marian from Llavorsí got stuck and could not get beyond Burg, after a storm had washed away part of the road. We had to go down and porter her luggage up on our heads. A peeled-headed Englishman called Nigel from Peele in Devon, whom I had met one day in Sort and invited back to Farrera with me, sang 'You'll wonder where the yellow went when you brush your teeth with Pepsodent, Pepsodent!' when pressed to do his turn at the come-all-ye's. A bird-watcher friend of Toni Strubell's and his American girlfriend, who was a Gillette heiress, stayed for a week but brought nothing with them, not so much as a free razor blade, though we did see seven or eight hundred honey buzzards on migration when we went out for a walk with them one day, on which spectacle we feasted for weeks. Our old friend Conor O'Clery, then the northern editor of the

Irish Times, came with his four children for Easter. The first night they were there a sudden cold snap poured in around them where they slept on straw in the open-fronted barn, until we moved them up to the kitchen, where they kept the fire burning all night.

There were sometimes intense discussions about whether we would fight in another civil war if the dark forces that still lurked in the Spanish political undergrowth were to try to smother the nascent democracy, and about the war at home in Ireland, which was going through one of its most murderous phases. Even from our mountain remoteness, where we had no television or radio and saw a newspaper only rarely, we knew enough to appreciate the peaceful, reasoned way the Catalans were negotiating and winning their autonomy. There was only one violent act that I can remember, when Viola, the loathed *feixista i cabró* mayor of Barcelona, was strapped back to back with his wife on two chairs and a bomb put under them. Unlike Ireland, where so many dirty deeds were being done in the name of Britishness and Irishness, Catalonia, post-Franco, was reinventing Catalanness through work, imagination and money. The Catalans are the Protestants of Spain. Here in the mountains, the Catalan heartland, we saw their work ethic all around us, where people talked about *la feina*, the job, the task in hand, with a reverence and insistence that often made us feel very unProtestant indeed, having no real work to do.

Sacred Sheeps

It was bitterly cold in Farrera for much of that winter.

We spent Christmas there, with Oppen as our guest for the dinner we had on the twenty-fifth, rather than on the evening of the twenty-fourth, as the Spanish do, for we were Irish after all, or British, as Barbara might have thought of herself, and English in the case of Tony Dumphy. We had ice from icicles in our gin and tonics. After dinner, Oppen, who had been out all day on the mountain with his sheep, rumly sang:

> *A vint-i-cinc de desembre,*
> *fum, fum, fum.*
> *A vint-i-cinc de desembre,*
> *fum, fum, fum.*
> *Ha nascut un minyonet*
> *ros i blanquet, ros i blanquet;*
> *fill de la Verge Maria,*
> *ha nascut a una establia,*
> *fum, fum, fum.*
>
> *Aquí dalt de la muntanya,*
> *fum, fum, fum.*
> *Aquí dalt de la muntanya*
> *fum, fum, fum.*
> *Si n'hi ha dos pastorets*
> *abrigadets, abrigadets;*
> *amb la pell i la samarra,*
> *mengen ous i botifarra,*
> *fum, fum, fum.*

On the twenty-fifth of December,
smoke, smoke, smoke.
On the twenty-fifth of December,
smoke, smoke, smoke.
A little child has been born,
ruddy and white, ruddy and white;
son of the Virgin Mary,
born in a little stable,
smoke, smoke, smoke.

Up here on the mountain,
smoke, smoke, smoke.
Up here on the mountain,
smoke, smoke, smoke.
If there are two wee shepherds,
hopped up, hopped up,
with furs and woollen cloaks,
they eat eggs and sausages,
smoke, smoke, smoke.

As we sat, eyes streaming, in the smoke from our own fire.

In January Oppen had to do his military service. He was conscripted into the Second Regulars on the Chafarinas Islands near Melilla in the south of Spain. Tony Dumphy undertook to look after his thirty sheep for him, occasionally relieved by me.

By the time he went to the military service – called *la mili* in Spanish by its victims, with always a sense that it is *la puta mili*, the fucking military service – Oppen was already known locally as El Pastoret, the Little Shepherd. From '*el puto ejército de la puta cola*', the fucking army of the fucking queue, where you queued for breakfast, lunch and dinner, for target practice, for grenade-throwing, for everything, he would say, Oppen pined for his sheep and his mountains. He sent us a photograph of himself in baggy green uniform on one of the islands. There was a lighthouse in the background. In the rocky foreground he was stretching out his hand to some sheep.

Minding Oppen's sheeps was a sacred trust.

The herd all had everyday names, *la puta azul*, *la puta verde*, *la puta blanca*, the *puta* this, *puta* that and *puta* the other thing, whoresmelts of wilful beasts every one of them, while he entered their official names, often those of women he knew, into a big ledger of ovine couplings, births, deaths and sales, in which Tony inscribed the names he gave to that year's lambs as they were born.

When you were out with the sheep, once you learned to be one step ahead of their tendency to disperse willy-nilly, you adapted your pace to theirs. We herded them through the areas in which Oppen had already established some grazing rights, or at least tolerances: up one side of the Farrera valley to Juverri, where there were communal pastures like high downs rolling away towards Andorra, and then back through the Pass of Sound, in a round it would take a livelong day to complete.

The ewes were big, broad-faced, unhorned, fawn-coloured, floppy-eared – not at all like the low, black-faced, curly-horned, piebald, pointy-eared, wiry creatures of the Irish hills. In the intervals when they were grazing, heads down, often in a row, in that nipping, eager way sheep have, jostling one another for space, sometimes allowing the muscle-bound *macho* to mount and tup them from the ample store in the stuffed sock of his dangling scrotum, you could look around you and gaze godwards – Cathar herdsmen as we felt we were, needing no intermediary between us and the Lord above.

Everywhere you looked there was something new to see: a succulent plant growing out of a crack in a rock, lichens bearding the branches of trees, insects that rose and rasped round your every step, flowers that bloomed in their successions and then seeded. Our *Guide to the Wild Flowers of Europe* and *Guide to the Birds of Europe* became grimy and bulging from so much leafing through them to identify geraniums, pinks, stonecrops, saxifrages, alpine accentors, shrikes, vultures, eagles, hawks, falcons, tits, finches. As Tony and I laid down a stratum of bird-watching on the geology of our long friendship, Mary painted watercolours of flowers that she hung around the kitchen of Casa Felip, where we would find them again, years later, as if pressed and preserved between pages of the book of our past.

I did not, in truth, help Tony very much with the sheep, for Tony was mostly happy to do it himself. He came to know every one of Oppen's sheep by name, history and foibles. After a day out on the mountain with them he would come back to Casa Felip brimming over with stories of where he had been and what he had seen, trying as he was, he said, to memorize the landscape stone by stone, tree by tree, path by path, so that he would have it in his mind for ever. He talked about the sheep as the animals with the golden hooves that had been clearing ground for man for millennia. On the couple of meadows Oppen owned Tony would erect a temporary stockade, called a *pleta*, where the sheep would be closed in for a number of nights so that they could graze the herbage close and fertilize it with their droppings, moving the corral as often as was necessary for the whole field to be chequered yellow, brown and green from the cropping and dunging it had received.

On some evenings, hearing bleating and bells from behind the house, we would go up to watch the senior shepherd, El Besolí, bring down his big herd from the high pastures where they grazed in summer transhumance from the lowlands. Besolí was in his seventies then, a stocky, dark-faced man dressed in a suit of black corduroy, a white shirt open at the neck and a tight-fitting waistcoat. The pleated cummerbund he wore across his stomach under the waistcoat was an extra pocket from which he would fish out his knife, bits of string to tie fences, a newspaper folded down to a small pad, or a packet of the Ideales he smoked. This blackest and twiggiest of tobacco came rolled loose in cigarette papers which had to be undone, re-rolled, licked, twisted off at one end, then smoked in quick, hard puffs before they disintegrated again. After standing quiet and patriarchal on a rocky outcrop surveying his promised land, his Canaan, smoking his Ideal, Besolí would grind out the butt with his boot, and then – his whistles and calls sending a couple of skinny, mongrel-looking dogs skirling hither and thither – come down the last stretch, erect and commanding, step by steady step, at the head of the herd. When he held his staff out diagonally from him the sheep stopped obediently in a line behind it and his pets would come nuzzling up to his pockets for the bits of bread and cubes of sugar with which he regaled them. If he had brought the sheep down for salt, as he did every month or so, he and his helpers – who came to include Tony – would scatter the lick from big white sacks over tables of flat rocks. When he gave the whistle to the dogs to let the sheep go, they would come racing down to lap up the salt as eagerly as if they knew they had a mineral deficiency.

In the spring of 1977, when Besolí came back from the lowlands with his flock, Tony helped him more and more. They would sometimes go up the mountain together, or meet in the pastures below the Pass of Sound, where the two herds would regard one another with suspicion, Besolí's a woolly army, Oppen's a little band of sisters sticking close together.

As the old man's aide-de-camp Tony was often invited to Besolí's house for meals. One evening, after being out on the mountain all day helping Tony to look after Oppen's sheep, an old friend from Belfast, Gerard Lenaghan, was included in this invitation.

Over dinner, just to make conversation, Gerard asked Besolí, in his elementary Spanish,

— *Y sus putas, Señor Besolí, como van?*

And how are your whores doing, Mr Besolí?

Peasants Pleasant and Unpleasant

During that year in Farrera we observed peasant life with interest but detachment, for we never succumbed to the belief that we could live that way. We knew from books we read and what we saw around us that we were seeing the final subsidence of the epic flood that had carried the agrarian revolution out of the valleys of the Tigris, Euphrates and Nile of ten thousand years ago, to strand its last converts here at this high tidemark of cereal-growing, and the cows, pigs, horses, sheep, goats, chickens and rabbits that had been swept along with them.

After Oppen left for *la mili*, there were only Carles Carbó living more or less on his own in Casa Maria (where he was visited by a camera crew from the brand-new Catalan TV station wanting to know what it was like living in a commune, and Carles said, 'What commune? Me? Here? On my own?'), awaiting his own call to *la mili*, from which he would escape by crouching in a corner for two months refusing to eat or speak or queue or take orders from anyone; the three Manresàs, Joan, Angeleta, and Maria, an orphaned distant cousin, in their house; Conchita, Juanito and their mother in Casa Poblador; Marsal and Generosa in Casa Marsal; two gloomy fellows squatting in a house on El Castell like furtive, dirty-faced cavemen; and ourselves in Casa Felip – among all the other houses that had been left shuttered and dark when their inhabitants decamped to easier lives in the lowlands.

The Manresàs lived in their *casa pairal* at the western extremity of the village. A *casa pairal*, meaning an ancestral house of consequence, is a bastion of prosperity built up over generations by families of peasants, which is what the natives of these mountainy redoubts, who were only ever imperfectly feudalized, call themselves – *pagesos*, meaning owners and workers of their own land. The house itself, Casa Manresà, was an imposing structure of four floors under a wave-ruffled lake of slated roof, with a big covered balcony at the front that overlooked a slabbed yard with doors off it into stores and animal stalls. It stood among a cluster of stone-built hay barns, byres and haggards that they also owned, including the A-framed, open-fronted alpha and omega of threshing sheds, La Bastida, which heaved heavenwards beside the church like a side chapel dedicated to the God of Corn.

Years before we lived there the Manresàs' two daughters had both married and moved away to the main valley, leaving Joan and Angeleta to look out from their balcony – the set for a Lorca play of grudges and score-settlings – at the fields and gardens they no longer had the strength themselves nor the indentured manpower to maintain. El Manresà was not able to work much himself any more yet he was always vigilant lest someone else's animals encroach on his land. El Araña, the Spider, Tony called him. When we met him round the village – a grubby handkerchief knotted at the four corners on his head, eyes bloodshot, wine stains round his mouth – he would expostulate to us about Oppen's sheep having strayed

into one of his patches or some other incursion or infraction
we had committed. We were never sure how angry he really
was, for he usually had what I, perhaps wrongly, took to be a
wicked sense of humour at play around his stubbled face: I
would hear years afterwards that he had said one day he was
going to take down his gun and clear all the hippies – *els jipis*,
pronounced with the hard Spanish j – out of the place.

And who could blame him? On full-moon nights, when
we had been carousing late, we would climb up into the belfry
of the church to look out at the fields and the forests washed
a thousand shades of grey, the slate roofs of the village below
us like molten outpourings from the mountain, as the valley
resounded with the screeches and wails of predators made
ruthless and prey made restless by the lunatic lamp in the sky
high, high above. One of these times we rang the heavy
bronze bell with the hammer-headed clapper on its knotted
cord and then put our heads up into it as it vibrated like a
second skull. Manresà confronted us the next day. The bell
should only be rung for emergencies, he shouted, his red face
right up into mine, so close I could see the flecks of dried snot
on his head-hanky. We had woken him up. He hadn't known
what was happening. We had better not do it again.

— You're a crowd of *gamberros*, he roared at us as he
marched off.

We looked up *gamberro* in the dictionary when we got
home. Teddy boy, it said.

Marsal's real name is Josep Puyals. After he married Generosa
of Casa Marsal, he inherited the name of the house when
Generosa's father died, whose name had not been Marsal
either. Thus rebaptized by the sweat of his own brow, Marsal
is never known by any other name. Generosa called him
Marsal. His children call him Marsal. He calls himself Marsal.

A tin sign over the door of their house announced TELÉ-
FONOS in the plural, even though there was only one, the
only one in the village. We went there sometimes in the
evenings to make calls whose cost Generosa reckoned up in a
complex arithmetic based on the number of units the green-
eyed counter in the corner showed we had used multiplied
by so many pesetas and then divided by some other number
depending on whether the call was at a peak period or not.
Afterwards we would sit with them on the bench within the
open fireplace or on low chairs in front of it, as Generosa
encouraged us to stay, plying us with glasses of muscatel or
brandy, glad for Marsal to have someone with whom to
reminisce.

— *Ens feu companyia*, they would say.

You make company for us.

When he got started, if he was not too exhausted from the
day's labours that often left him drained and sweating, his face
puce, hardly able to speak, reminding me of the way my own
father had spent himself in his work, Marsal would talk about
the only time he had ever been out of the valley, the three
and a half years he had spent in Franco's army doing his
military service immediately after the Civil War. He had been
posted to Pals on the Costa Brava. He would say that Pals was
the only place he knew that was as beautiful as Farrera, not
knowing what had happened to Pals in the intervening years
of mass tourism. He blamed the *rojos*, the reds, and *la gent
d'esquerres*, the leftists, for starting the war. He could wax quite
wroth on the subject, so we learned to divert him away from
it, even though his Catalan dialect and his Pallarese accent
were sometimes so opaque to us we only got the drift of what
he was saying, and often not even that much. He never let
that deter him.

★

At night we went with a miniature churn with a tight-fitting lid to buy milk from Conchita de Poblador in the low-ceilinged, cobweb-hung, dimly lit byre where her five cows were chained at mangers into which she forked down hay through slats from the barn above. The cows were chocolate- and beige-coloured, broad-beamed in the rear, with wide, curly foreheads and spreading, black-tipped horns; big-eyed, long-lashed, patient and seigneurial. She called them La Marquessa, the Marchioness; Perla Guapa, Lovely Pearl; Esquirolet, Little Squirrel; La Vaca Blanca, the White Cow; and Tele, who had been so named when the first television set arrived in the village simultaneously with her birth.

Conchita was dumpy and fussy, wrapped in layers of clothes that culminated in a quilted red housecoat worn above everything else, with an apron on top of that again, a scarf on her head and short, cream-coloured wellington boots on her feet. She usually carried a bucket over her arm like a zinc or green or blue plastic handbag, for she had an array of these accessories, in which she would carry eggs from her hens, windfalls of fruit she gathered, vegetables from her gardens, and, once, a dead rabbit curled in the bottom as if asleep. She had killed it with one blow of her stick, she told us, and demonstrated how. If you have to hit them twice their blood turns and spoils in them, she said. She was going to skin it and cook it with wild mushrooms she had foraged in the woods, a dish '*para chuparse los dedos*', to have you licking your fingers. She always talked to us in Castilian, as if it were more correct to be talking to foreigners in this foreign tongue she had learned at the village school and spoke with a primped-up politeness, not at all the way she scolded her touched brother, Juanito – who was always getting in the way as he darted and dodged round the byre – in sharp, shrewish Catalan.

As Conchita hand-milked her cows one by one she talked

to them, telling them and us in her singsong praisevoice
how beautiful they were, calling each one 'reina maca', lovely
queen. She would say the milk was very rich – all the good
grass and fresh air, she claimed, though there was hardly a
breath in the closeness of the byre – so we had to be careful
how much of it we drank, because being city people we
wouldn't be used to it, as if it was a potent elixir that might
go to our heads.

Juanito was simple and whimsical, forever going off at
tangents. Many times a day we would hear Conchita calling
'Juaaanitooo, Juaaanitooo', as she tried to get him to come and
help her with something. He was never much help, for he
could stick at nothing for very long before dodging off to do
whatever came into his head – cut sticks for the besoms he
made, or go visiting in Burg, or take a step of the road with a
passer-by, or bring in firewood with the donkey he kept in a
byre beside Casa Felip, where Mary one day talked to him
over the half-door, all the while wondering why he did
not get up from squatting on the ground. She only realized
afterwards what he had been doing.

Almost every day Juanito would come to visit us in Casa
Felip, always with something in his hand: a few leaves of
Hepatica nobilis (like a small wood anemone), which he said
was good for the kidneys (on account of the kidney shape of
its tri-lobed leaves, we supposed), or *Pulmonaria*, for the lungs
(from its spottedness), or other herbs that were meant to be
efficacious against whatever might ail various parts of you. His
mother, La Pobladora, an old, bent lady dressed head to foot
in black who tottered all day on her stick in Conchita's wake,
was reputed to know about natural cures, and was even said
to be a witch. On other days Juanito would be carrying a
branch of elder, which he said was good to smoke, though he
did not smoke himself, or one of his sturdy, well-made twig

brooms, or a piece of ash, the hard wood used for making *esclops de fusta*, the clogs with risers on the soles that were worn to keep feet out of the muck in the byres. He never came empty-handed.

Juanito repeated everything over and over, especially his running reports on the weather: *'Nevarà, nevarà, nevarà'*, it'll snow, it'll snow, it'll snow; *'Plourà, plourà, plourà'*, it'll rain, it'll rain, it'll rain; *'Farà vent, farà vent, farà vent'*, it'll be windy, it'll be windy, it'll be windy.

— *He tocat la noia, he tocat la noia, he tocat la noia.*

I touched the girl, I touched the girl, I touched the girl, he would rhyme, grinning wickedly out of his puckered eyes as if he had broken some childish taboo and now wanted to see the reaction of the big people.

— *Quina noia has tocat, Juanito?*

What girl did you touch, Juanito?

— *La noia ignorada de Portugal, la noia ignorada de Portugal.*

The unknown girl from Portugal, the unknown girl from Portugal: the refrain of some old song of which that was the only fragment he had left.

Someone had given him a harmonica that he always carried with him in an inside pocket. In lulls in the conversation he would get it out and run it up and down his mouth, squalling a jumble of notes that never became a tune.

Juanito would sit and talk and play his harmonica in the kitchen of Casa Felip for hours sometimes, being spoiled by Mary and Barbara with cake or biscuits or plates of food, until Conchita's calls of *'Juaanitooo, Juaanitooo'* rose to a certain irrefutable pitch we learned to recognize, and we would have to send Juanito off, laggard and reluctant, giving a last few defiant blasts on the mouth organ as he went down the path. Then we would hear a shouting and barging match when brother and sister met, a close-fought sibling squabble that turned the air blue and purple and bruised all around their gingerbread house in the lower part of the village.

That first summer we were there Conchita hired a man with a tractor and a cutting bar to mow the grass in a big meadow she was renting. Afterwards Tony and I turned it for her with pointy-pronged metal graips for which Juanito had made the wooden handles. When it was dry, we raked the hay into rows ready for the baling machine Conchita had also bespoken. This arrived up the mountain in a clatter of self-importance and then broke down in the middle of the field after spitting out a few bales from the first line of hay it had gobbled up, which seemed to have choked it. While it sat slumped and shame-faced in the middle of the field, Juanito approached it from the side with a handful of straw he tried to push up into its maw, as if it were a hungry animal only needing to be fed to get its strength back.

Another day we were digging a patch of garden for her to sow potatoes when Conchita called us. Esquirolet had not been able to rise after having twin calves in her first parturition. She was lying sprawled on the ground in the barn of Casa Felip, her legs awkward under her, her tongue protruding, lowing softly. Conchita's mother was trying to get her to drink a broth of herbs she had boiled up in a three-legged black pot. Juanito was shaking grain in a basket under her nose. Esquirolet was having none of it. She lowed again and looked sad. Somebody said the thing to do was turn her. We got a limb each and pulled her through three hundred and sixty degrees, the gyration lubricated by the wet skitter in which she lay. To no avail.

Toni de Burg came with his livestock lorry. As we slid Little Squirrel up a ramp into the back of it, Conchita drew her shawl up over her head and wailed about what might become of them now, and she on her own with her sick

mother and her daft brother, and nobody in the world to look
after them but herself.

Juanito kept repeating,

— *Morirà, morirà, morirà.*

She'll die, she'll die, she'll die.

Esquirolet was bumped in the back of the lorry to the
abattoir in La Seu d'Urgell, two hours away. She arrived
sufficiently alive to be classified as meat. Conchita at least got
the price of the carcass, and still had the two calves, which
survived their mother.

A short while later I read that young cows calving after a
winter indoors feeding only on hay often suffer from a calcium
deficiency, especially if they have twins. All they need is an
injection of calcium in liquid form and they will be back on
their feet within hours.

The Parting Glass

In the September of that first summer we spent in Farrera we
went to do the wine harvest with Monsieur Aupy at Le Puy
Notre Dame near Angers in the valley of the Loire, where
Mary and I had worked two years before. The Aupys, with
whom we had become very friendly during that previous stay,
gave Mary and me a room of our own in a stable near the
Nissen hut where the other grape-pickers slept. It was in that
stable that Mary told me she was pregnant, something we had
not exactly planned, but that seemed right and timely and
cumulative, somehow, after all the passion we had shared in
Barcelona and then the idyllic months in Farrera.

We decided we would get married in Farrera when we
returned there after the wine harvest.

We had to engage the priest, a reserved, rotund fellow who wore dark glasses and ate his lunch on his own every day in the Hostal Rey in Llavorsí; write off for waivers, or whatever they're called, from parish priests at home in Belfast to confirm that we weren't married there; have the banns read in the church in Llavorsí, since normally there was no Mass in the church in Farrera; and get a *libro de familia*, a book of the family, such as all Spanish married couples have, with its pages for first nuptials, second nuptials, third nuptials, births and deaths: a family's whole life between waxy blue covers engraved with the armorial shield of Spain.

In late November Tony Dumphy and I walked across the mountains to Andorra to buy cheap drink for the wedding feast. We started out late one day, slept very badly that night on planks in an abandoned bothy where there was no hay, and reached Andorra La Vella, the capital of Andorra, on the evening of the next day. There we ended up stretching out in our sleeping bags on the tiled landing of the third *pensión* that had no room, from which the woman had shouted out through the locked door for us to go away, after we had been overlong at a feed of Cointreau we had talked ourselves into during the long descent to the Andorran border through Ars and Civis.

We decided we would go back by a different and, we hoped, shorter route than we had come. After we had bought the fill of our rucksacks of drink in a brightly lit supermarket where 'I'm Dreaming of a White Christmas' kept repeating on the loudspeakers, we took a taxi to a *hostal* below the Pass of the Eagle. From there we would cross the upper reaches of the Tor river to get into the valley of Santa Magdalena on the far side and from there to the Pass of Sound.

On the grounds that as shepherds on a spree we might as well be hung for sheep as lambs, we had an early lunch in the *hostal*, three courses and a bottle of wine, followed by a glass of brandy and two black coffees each. Afterwards we death-marched up to the pass, puffing, blowing, cursing and sweating. At the top we lay down for a siesta. Just as I was falling asleep, Tony roused me, whispering,

— Look, man, buzzards!

A pair of them were soaring above the valley in front of us, at more or less the altitude where we were, so we had a perfect view of them as they sparred and feinted at one another with talons spread, tumbling and screeching through the misty air. We got out our binoculars to watch them. As we did, one of the buzzards excreted a long, ragged gout of whitish shit that the two of them chased downwards as if it were prey.

— Maybe they thought we were dead and were coming to peck our eyes out, Tony hazarded, and laughed.

The monkish Cointreau of the night before accompanied us as the Spirit of Remorse as we tramped round the head of the valley beyond the pass, a laden grey sky seeming to be pouring down the mountain after us. We had a map but had found it unreliable on the outer journey, or our map-reading skills not up to making much sense of it. With the cloud around us we could see no obvious landmarks. The clump of bothies we were seeking did not appear. There were no signposts along the path we followed, which soon petered off into a narrow, little-trodden track.

We had not consulted any weather forecast, so we were surprised when it started to snow: a few flakes at first, then shrouds of it falling, silently and stubbornly, without a break. I could see Tony was worried. I wondered if we had made a serious mistake in starting out at all. Going back seemed as far and as hard as going forward. We would see the bothies or some sign of where we were soon. I thought we should continue along the track. It was sure to lead back to a bigger path. There was nothing for it but to keep going.

Within an hour the snowstorm had blanketed the little we could see of the landscape. The snow on the ground was only a couple of inches thick as yet but it made the going heavy. We lost the track altogether.

— We should just head straight up and see if that takes us over into Santa Magdalena. It has to be that way, I insisted.

I could see Tony's faith in me was wavering, and might blow out at any minute.

— All right, he said. But I'm not so sure.

It took us a seeming age to climb straight up through the forest, tripping on fallen branches hidden by the snow, our rucksacks catching on the trees, as we tried to find the least obstructed path. We had no watch and no compass, so we neither knew how long our trek was taking us nor what direction it was taking us in.

I remember consciously deciding that I would keep talking. I had read somewhere, probably in *The Commander's Annual for Boys*, the first book I had ever owned, that that was what you had to do, to keep your spirits up. Anyway I have always had an overweening belief in my ability to get out of any scrape, a cockiness got from a boyhood spent roaming the bandit-infested hills and treacherous bogs around Belfast. When I wasn't talking, I whistled.

As darkness fell we got very lost, not able to see more than a few yards in front of us. A wind was now howling through the tops of the trees, shaking snow from the branches. In clearings it was beginning to drift. For a while we seemed to be going round in circles, feet freezing in our wet boots, weary enough to understand how exhausted Arctic explorers make holes in the snow and crawl into them to die.

I kept talking. Tony talked back, and whistled a bit too,

though every time I looked at him he avoided my eye, as if afraid of what he might see there.

We crossed the exposed ridge of the watershed and came down on to a wide path through the woods, but could not decide if we should turn right or left. We looked at the map, using our coats to shelter the matches we lit. It had to be to the right, if we were where we thought we were, but we still had not seen any of the landmarks that might have confirmed this.

Just then horses with bells round their necks came plunging and rearing down from the forest and trotted off to the right. We decided to follow them. It turned out to be the road to the hermitage church of Santa Magdalena we were looking for. We had been there in the autumn with people from Burg collecting mushrooms in the woods and cooking them with oil, salt and garlic on pieces of slate over open fires. We sat in the Romanesque doorway of the church eating the last of the sausage, bread and chocolate we had, reminiscing about the heat of that long-ago day and the taste of the slate-fried ceps.

Somewhere in the swirling heavens above us the moon came out. It lit our trudge along the winding forestry road through snow that was now a foot or more deep. We did not take any more shortcuts, though I suggested a few. Tony said we should just stick to the road. It took us up to the crossroads of Bedet, where twisted metal tickets of shot-peppered signs on a red and white striped pole were like prayer flags welcoming us back into familiar territory. The snow stopped for long enough for us to make out the Pass of Sound in the distance. We opened a bottle of Bushmills whiskey and had a capful each to celebrate.

We arrived back in Casa Felip after midnight with ice on our hair and eyebrows and my beard, the bottles of booze bulging in our smugglers' packs like penitential stones. Mary and Barbara were sitting at a blazing fire, reading and knitting, and probably worrying too, though they did not betray it as they hugged and kissed us a welcome home from the snowy wastes.

Tony had always been jovial, adaptable, ready for anything, a great smiler, but now he was uncharacteristically silent and pensive, as if he had just looked into a scary, unsuspected corner of his life. He went to lie down for half an hour. When he came back into the kitchen to sit at the fire he said the one moment he had been really afraid and thought we were goners was when we were walking across the ridge of the watershed where the snow had already formed a crust we broke through at every step and sank in to our knees, the wind was whipping our faces with sharp ice crystals, and I had stopped talking.

The next day, when we went to get milk, Conchita told us about a woman from Farrera who had set out one winter to walk the same route we had taken and was not found until the following spring, curled up dead in the corner of the bothy where she had taken shelter.

On the tenth of December all the native inhabitants of Farrera came to the wedding, along with Oppen and Carles Carbó, and friends who came up from Barcelona, about forty people in all, though no one from either of our families, for whom it was all too far and all too sudden. We forgot to ask the morose cavemen from El Castell, an omission we have always regretted, as if we had neglected to invite the bad fairies.

Mary wore a green corduroy dress she had sewn on Generosa de Casa Marsal's sewing machine. I wore a collarless white shirt Mary had embroidered with a breastplate of flowers and a multi-coloured happy jacket she had knitted. In this regalia we led the tatterdemalion wedding march up the mucky main street to the 1629 church of Saint Roch.

The church was cold and damp, but Colm had brought armfuls of chrysanthemums from Barcelona and their heady perfume took some of the chill from the air. During the ceremony he moved around photographing us and the congregation with a Kodak Brownie, whose grainy images were to be all the wedding album we would ever have, now reduced by the attrition of the years to one curled, cracked, black-and-white snap.

Mary and I had been rehearsing the Catalan troth-plighting for weeks beforehand, so when the priest prompted us, we were able to say, without looking at the responses sheet he held out before us:

— *Rep aquest anell, senyal del meu amor i de la meva fidelitat.*

Take this ring, sign of my love and of my fidelity.

We were the first couple to be married in the church for more than forty years. Colm was a witness to the fact in the *Liber Almarum*, the Book of Souls, which we signed in the vestry, after we had discovered that Barbara, our bridesmaid, could not sign because she was a woman (not, as Colm claimed, because she was a Protestant: for years afterwards he would boast of having said to her at the consecration, in a loud stage whisper we had heard from where we sat in front of the altar, 'Kneel down, you Protestant bitch!'). It was overcast all day and snowed a little that night, like Christmas. My uncle, Brian Cooley, manufacturer of Coolie Ice Lollies, had sent us £100 for a wedding present, out of which we paid the priest and lived for another few months.

The long day's celebration in the *menjador* of Casa Felip, which Mary and Barbara had transformed into a hall of rich array with a festive board of good things to eat laid out on the big deal table, ended with songs, for in those days we all

sang. Tony Dumphy had a beautiful voice and an extensive
repertoire made up of Irish songs (to which he would add by
taking *Sodlum's Book of Irish Ballads* up the mountain with him
when he was minding the sheep), and Frank Sinatra numbers
and bar-room ballads he had learned in the Vauxhall, the pub
his mother – whom he called the Old Queen – had kept in
Manchester. As Mary and I were preparing to go to our room
upstairs, he sang 'The Parting Glass', his head thrown back, a
finger in his one good ear – being entirely deaf in the other
from a boyhood accident – eyes closed, ardent:

> Oh, of all the money that e'er I had, I spent it in good
>   company,
> And of all the harm that ever I done, alas it was to none
>   but me.
> And all I've done for want of wit to mem'ry now I
>   can't recall,
> So fill to me the parting glass, good night and joy be
>   with you all.

> If I had money enough to spend and leisure time to sit a
>   while,
> There is a fair maid in this town that sorely has my
>   heart beguiled.
> Her rosy cheeks and ruby lips, I own she has my heart
>   enthralled,
> Then fill to me the parting glass, goodnight and joy be
>   with you all.

A Crib in a Manger

Mary and I read a book by Frederick Leboyer about natural childbirth. There was a photograph in it of a new-born infant, umbilicus still attached, being held up by the heels by a triumphant, smiling doctor, with everyone in the fluorescent-lit hospital operating theatre laughing their heads off, except the child himself, who is bawling off his.

We wanted our child to be born at home, into calm and love and candlelight.

Anyway the nearest hospital was in Tremp or La Seu d'Urgell, three or four hours away by the time we could get a taxi to come up from the main valley. We didn't have a car and there was no car in the village. We found a midwife called Maria Ángeles Gasia in Sort who was willing to come to Farrera when the time came. Mary saw her regularly in the months coming up to the birth. She also went a few times to the doctor who held a surgery once a week in Tírvia, a town in the valley that Farrera overlooks. They both reassured her that everything was perfectly normal.

In the middle of the afternoon of the fifteenth of April 1977 Mary phoned me in Sort, where I was teaching my English classes, to say that her waters had broken and I should get back to Farrera as quickly as I could with the midwife.

As we were driving in the taxi up the rough road to this remote place where Mary and I had cast our lot, in a lull in the conversation with Juanito the taxi man – who was also postman, messenger and milk collector, and would have to be our ambulance man, if the worst happened – I looked out across the vastness of the mountains that had seen so much birth and death since their own birth millions of years before, and felt very small and very frightened, as if I had connived at the one risk too far, where our foolish idealism would end in stillbirth, septicaemia, blood and tears.

I said none of this to Mary, who was smiling and confident when she met us at the door of Casa Felip. Sitting up side by side on the horsehair mattress on the floor of our room, she and Maria Ángeles talked like mother and daughter in the complicity of the moment of truth that had arrived. Mary rested, may even have slept a bit, after Maria Ángeles examined her and told her it was going to take a good few more hours. Downstairs in the *carabiner*'s kitchen we made tea for Mary and a meal for ourselves and Maria Ángeles. As we ate it she told us about other births she had assisted in mountain villages. Most of her work was now done in hospital. She hadn't been at a home birth for at least ten years.

As darkness fell we lit candles all over the house. On the long table in the *menjador* Tony set up the wooden cradle on rockers he had made over weeks of patient work out of planks pillaged from an abandoned house. He had used a sharpened, flattened nail to chase the profile of a dipper on its headboard: the tubby, tortoiseshell-backed, cream-breasted, cold- and wet-defying, overgrown wren of a bird that had become a mascot of the mountains for us.

Our daughter was born at five o'clock in the morning, tiny, slick-skinned, dark-haired, perfect, and completely silent, not a cry – years later Maria Ángeles would say she was the only baby she had ever seen born with a smile. Mary asked for the child to be put in her arms, with the umbilicus still attached: my damp-haired, smiling madonna, babe in arms, lit by the honeyed light of beeswax candles in our wood-walled Bethlehem.

While Maria Ángeles cleaned up the baby, I carried the

basin with the afterbirth down the steep stairs from our room. In the light of a candle in the kitchen I counted the star-like points on the liverish membrane of the placenta, as Maria Ángeles had instructed, and Maeve's name came to me. Of all the names we had considered, this one seemed just right for our warrior queen. When I came back from throwing out the afterbirth for the foxes and suggested the name to Mary, she immediately agreed.

When we knew all was safe, Tony Dumphy and I stood at the bird table outside the front door and drank the last two glasses of a bottle of Jameson's fifteen-year-old whiskey we had been keeping for just this moment. In the dawn stillness a scops owl called its tireless *droot-droot-droot* from the far side of the village. There are no scops in Ireland. In the woods a tawny owl cried its *tuwhit-tuwhoo* that is never heard in Ireland either. A nightingale carolled from a brake of bushes on the hill behind us. The nightingale does not exist in Ireland.

We also thought we heard the chirrup of a dipper flying up the river, but that may have been wishful thinking.

After Maria Ángeles had gone back down the mountain in Juanito's jeep, along with the churns of milk he collected from Farrera and the other villages in the valley, I got into bed beside Mary, who was cradling the sweet-smelling, peaceful, still silent Maeve on her other side. As I looked over Mary's shoulder, Maeve made a little mewling noise, her first sound, as if she were glad to be there with us and wanted to tell us so.

Maeve was the first child born in Farrera for over thirty years. The next day, and over subsequent days, the locals congratulated us, as they had when we were married, with the customary Catalan blessing on any happy life-event of

'*Que sigui per molts anys*', that it might be for many years. Even now, more than twenty-five years later, people still ask after Maeve as '*la nena que va neixer a Farrera*', the girl who was born in Farrera.

A month later Maeve was baptized in the kitchen of Casa Felip, in a blue plastic baby's bath with yellow ducks on the bottom of it, by Father Joan Giralt, a priest to whom I had taught English on my days in Sort, with Toni Strubell as her godfather and Barbara Gamble as her godmother. We gave her Eulàlia as a second name because we had discovered that the tenth of December, the date of our wedding, chosen for no other reason than that it had been the first date on which the priest was available, was the day of the winter *festa major* of the hamlet of Alendo, just across the valley from Farrera, whose patron is Saint Eulàlia, to whom its hermitage church is dedicated. The Hill of Saint Eulàlia in Barcelona is just round the corner from Straw Street, where we had convinced ourselves Maeve had been conceived on the one visit we had made there out of our mountain fastness.

We decided that we wanted Maeve and any other children we might have to grow up knowing they were Irish first and foremost, rather than floating in the nebulous nowhere some of the children of expatriates we knew seemed to inhabit. We would move back to Ireland. I was going to look for a job as a fisherman so that we could live by the sea.

During our last days in Farrera we had the same conversation over and over with Juanito:

— *Ja tornareu, ja tornareu.*

You'll come back, you'll come back.

— *Però quan, Juanito?*

But when, Juanito?

— *Un altre capdesetmana. Un altre capdesetmana.*

Some other weekend. Some other weekend.

— *I com, Juanito? Irlanda és molt lluny.*

And how, Juanito? Ireland is very far away.

— *Amb l'àliga de ferro. Amb l'àliga de ferro. Amb l'àliga de ferro.*

With the iron eagle. With the iron eagle. With the iron eagle.

We left at the end of May, carrying all we owned in a small suitcase and two rucksacks, and Maeve Eulàlia in a wicker basket.

We went first to Barcelona and stayed there for a few days to retrace our old map of the city so that Maeve could feel it was her city too, always contriving to return to Toni Strubell's flat in Carrer de la Palla by way of the Plaça Sant Felip Neri and the Baixada de Santa Eulàlia, our sacred places.

Saint Eulàlia had been patron of Barcelona until she was displaced by La Nostra Senyora de la Mercè. She had been martyred in AD 304 by soldiers under the command of the centurion Dacian for having disobeyed the edict of the Emperor Diocletian ordering all his subjects to offer sacrifices to the Roman gods. On her and now also our daughter's eponymous hill, a narrow, curved street between the cloister of the cathedral and Carrer dels Banys Nous, where El Portalón was, we stopped to read these verses by Father Jacint Verdaguer on a tiled plaque underneath her glassy shrine where there were always fresh flowers:

> *Veyent acostar les flames*
> *també recula Dacià;*
> *la tanca dins una tina*
> *que té sagetes per claus,*
> *tota encerclada de glavis*
> *i ganivets de dos talls.*

Baixada de Santa Eulàlia,
tu la veres rodolar
d'un abisme a l'altre abisme
per aquells rostos avall,
deixant per rastre en les herbes
un bell rosari de sanch.

Seeing the flames get closer,
Dacian also stepped back;
he had her shut into a barrel
which had daggers for nails,
and was encircled with swords
and two sizes of knives.

Down the hill of Saint Eulàlia,
you will see her roll
from one abyss to another abyss
down those steep slopes,
leaving for track in the grass
a beautiful rosary of blood.

As Juanito's iron eagle climbed out of the airport and banked across the night face of Barcelona, then turned inland and headed north over Montserrat, with Maeve Eulàlia sleeping peacefully in her Moses basket on the seat between us, I peered out the window to see if I could pick out the lights of Farrera as we crossed the Pyrenees.

It was too dark.

II

The Solid-place-in-the-bog of the Son of the Red-haired Man

I have lived in important places, times
When great events were decided: who owned
That half a rood of rock, a no-man's land
Surrounded by our pitchfork-armed claims.
I heard the Duffys shouting 'Damn your soul'
And old McCabe stripped to the waist, seen
Step the plot defying blue cast-steel –
'Here is the march along these iron stones'.

Patrick Kavanagh, 'Epic'

A Kind of Commune

Shortly after we got back to Ireland, I went to Killybegs in County Donegal and hung around the harbour asking on every boat that came in if they had a berth, as I discovered a fishing job was called. I eventually got one on the *Sea Bridger*, a 65-foot trawler with a crew of seven.

A few weeks after I became a fisherman, Mary and Maeve came to join me. We rented a once-thatched, now slated cottage at a place called Towney near the village of Kilcar, within sound if not sight of the sea. One Sunday almost a year later, I misheard the midnight shipping forecast from the BBC and thought the boat would not be going out the next day – perhaps wanted to believe that it would not go out, so much did I enjoy being at home and away from the boat's confinement, putrid smells from the scuppers, pitchings and tossings, long, cold watches, and bloody hard work in a waterproof with holes in it that meant I was always soaked to the skin as we shot and hauled nets, gutted and boxed fish on the heaving deck, and lay down to sleep in our clothes. When I did go into Killybegs on the Tuesday I found the *Sea Bridger* had gone out, short-handed, which boat crews do not like.

I went out once more, under a cloud, slung my hook, and became a lapsed fisherman, with all my maritime ambitions well and truly requited.

We moved to Dublin.

On the tenth of April 1979 our son Eoin was born in our bed in the front room of the flat we were renting on the top floor of 8 Palmerston Park, with Mrs Payne as midwife in attendance and Doctor Walshe as doctor on call.

Dr Walshe had dropped in a few times to see how the labour was going, leaving his leather bag of birthing instruments sitting in the corner in case they would be needed. I had looked into it while he was away. The jumble of clamps, scissors, forceps and other surgical tools that lay in the bottom of it had given me pause, as the sight of the mountains had at the time of Maeve's birth, but Mary was happily hopped up in bed with Mrs Payne, the two of them being brought draughts of midwife's tea by Bríd Brennan, the actress, an old friend from Belfast who was our house-guest and birth-guest, so I said nothing.

Eoin was born at 8 o'clock in the evening. An hour later, as I went down through the rest of the house to tell our neighbours, I still had a clutch in my throat and tears in my eyes. The people from the other three flats came up to see the boy child now wrapped in his swaddling clothes, already suckling on Mary's breast. They looked at him in the bemused and slightly embarrassed way that people who do not have children themselves look at other people's newborns.

I became restless with my job teaching English as a foreign language to Saudi Arabian and Libyan airline clerks, and so I scrutinized the jobs section of the *Irish Times* every day. One morning in mid 1980 I spotted a small, plain, boxed ad looking for a Resident Director of the Tyrone Guthrie Centre, an artists' retreat being set up at Annaghmakerrig, Newbliss, County Monaghan. I bought an ordnance survey map and located Annaghmakerrig House amidst the lakes and drumlins near Shercock, County Cavan, where my father had once kept his caravan at McSwigan's caravan park on the shores of Lough Sillan and we had spent many weekends and holidays.

.The first time Mary and I went to see Annaghmakerrig, after I had applied for the job of running the Tyrone Guthrie Centre, we approached it along drumlin roads awash under an autumn downpour that made them switchback waves in a heaving green sea of hedges and fields. After missing the unmarked turn, and stopping to ask directions at a desolate shed of a pub called the Black Kesh, we found the estate up a winding, pot-holed boreen, through the white gates the woman in the bar had told us to look out for that were in fact just two iron pillars, with one side of the gate missing altogether and the other lying twisted in the ditch. Where the rhododendron-congested entrance avenue emerged from an overgrown woodland – at the other side of which we caught a glimpse of a yard of derelict stone buildings – we stopped to look at the house without getting out of the car, leaving the windscreen wipers flapping back and forth. There were slates missing from part of the roof. Window openings gaped without frames or glass. Many of the chimney pots on the tall stacks were either broken or missing altogether, giving the roofline a snaggled, gap-toothed look. A dirty yellow tarpaulin was stretched over a pile of something on a raised lawn. There were cars and vans parked on muddy verges. A few men in overalls moved around as if they had been summoned for an emergency. In the streaming rain stains of damp hung like tongues of seawrack down the house's grey plastered walls, as if it were a vessel that had been wrecked by the storm and cast up there from the vast-seeming lake at the foot of the fields in front of it.

That day we did not go any closer, fearful of intruding.

Shortly afterwards, when I knew I was going to be interviewed for the job, I spent a couple of days in the National Library in Dublin reading James Forsyth's biography of Tyrone Guthrie and Guthrie's autobiography, *A Life in the*

Theatre. In the oak-wood quiet of the reading room these books were hand-cranked film projectors throwing out flickering black-and-white images of the antic life of an Anglo-Irish Protestant family full of the *amour propre* of its own history: medical doctors, clerics, soldiers, actors, ladies of learning and leisure, long-livers, solid achievers. This was a world new to me – heretofore only intimated from books, imagined from plays and films, guessed at from the woods of estates where I had trespassed – but at the same time strangely familiar, as if it had always been there waiting for me. After I finished reading on the second evening, and set out to walk home through a darkening Dublin of double-decker buses lurching with their cargoes of souls towards the netherlands of commuterdom, I knew I wanted this job more than I had ever wanted any job in my life.

In 1804 a Dr John Moorhead had bought Leysborough Demesne, as it was then called, from patients of his who had got into debt. In 1849 Tyrone Guthrie's maternal grandfather, William Tyrone Power, then a young army officer, was sent to supervise a famine-relief scheme to deepen the ditch that drains Annaghmakerrig Lake into Kilmore Bog. He met Dr Moorhead's daughter, Martha, at the Big House, married her, and eventually retired there. One of the portraits in the biography shows General Sir William Tyrone Power, as he was titled when he was made Commissary-General-in-Chief of the British Army, in all his bemedalled, barrel-chested splendour: a benign- and busy-looking man with long sideburns, bushy whiskers and an imperial storekeeper's air of confidence that all was and always would be right with his well-stocked world.

He it was who had the plain, square-fronted Leysborough House extended, adding Dutch gables to the western façade;

the drawing room, dining room and master bedrooms at the front; a kitchen, dairy and laundry wing at the side; and the stone-built farmyard at the back. He also had the lawns banked, the greenhouse built, the well dug, and the oak walk, orchards, vegetable gardens, shrubberies and flower gardens laid out, in a mighty work of earth-moving done by manpower, spade-power, pickpower, and horse and cart.

It was during his time that the house and its estate reverted to their original name, Annagh-ma-Kerrig, as they spelled it, from the Irish *Annagh Mhic Dheirg*, meaning 'the solid-place-in-the-bog of the son of the red-haired man'.

Tyrone Guthrie, born in 1900 in Tunbridge Wells, would always acknowledge that he had inherited at least some of his passion for the theatre from his grandfather's father, Tyrone Power. A portrait by Lawrence Crowley RHA shows Power, an actor-manager of great renown on both sides of the Atlantic in his nineteenth-century heyday, in three different roles in a play called *The Groves of Blarney*. In those poses – leaning against a table with his waistcoat buttons undone, sitting on a chair with his breeched legs stretched before him, and standing beside a dresser with his hat cocked back on his head – he bears a close resemblance to the young Tyrone Guthrie.

Guthrie would later say that his own physique (six foot four, or five, or even six, depending on who was telling you) and his voice (booming, ironic, precise and fruity) were all rather too big for the tiny stages of student drama, but at Oxford he found that he had the bug, as much from the clerical side of the family – his paternal grandfather had been Moderator-General of the Church of Scotland – as from the theatrical branch. Once he recognized his limitations as an actor, Guthrie became assistant stage manager to the Oxford University Dramatic Society, what he called being 'handed a brush and told to brush up'. His talent would be for organizing the acting of others as producer and director, in the days when these roles still overlapped. After a stint with the BBC in Belfast he was appointed artistic director of the Scottish National Players, a short-lived attempt to do an Abbey Theatre in Scotland. He then worked for ten years at the Old Vic in London, first of all as assistant to its founder, Lilian Baylis, then as her successor, in what had originally been called the People's Theatre, 'to be used primarily for the performance of high-class drama, especially of the plays of Shakespeare, and of high-class opera, or the holding therein of public lectures and musical or other entertainments and exhibitions suited for the recreation and instruction of the poorer classes'.

At the Old Vic Tyrone Guthrie directed Alec Guinness, Flora Robson, Laurence Olivier, John Gielgud and other rising stars of the era. During rehearsals he would place himself in different parts of the theatre, listening for dead spots or lack of projection, clapping his hands to get the cast's attention, bustling and bullying the production along. His favourite expressions were 'Rise above!', when things were going badly; 'Come back, dear, and astonish us in the morning!', if an actor were not getting it right; or just 'Onward!', when badgering actors to put more pace into it. Throughout his mercurial career he would use his imperious Anglo-Irishness as a double-edged sword with which to cut his way through the theatrical jungle.

By the time Guthrie left the Old Vic in 1947, when he was himself forty-seven years old, his reputation was stellar. He was invited to direct plays in theatres all over the world. He founded the Shakespeare Festival Theatre in Stratford, Ontario, and the Guthrie Theater in Minneapolis, Minnesota, both built around thrust stages on the model of ancient amphi-theatres and Shakespeare's 'round O'. Guthrie went to Strat-ford and Minneapolis because he was an instinctive regionalist

– before the term was even invented – who believed in the energy and integrity of small places that are not provincial, do not ape the metropolis, but simply are themselves as best they can be.

In the same spirit, in the 1960s, already troubled by his 'dicky ticker' and on doctor's orders to take it easy, he set up a factory to make jam in the old Great Northern Railways station in Newbliss, disused since the closure of the railway in 1956. The Guthries had always been jam-makers themselves from the fruits of the gardens at Annaghmakerrig, so why not do it on an industrial scale? By the example of taking most of the shares himself, Tyrone Guthrie persuaded local farmers to become shareholders in the company and to set aside land to grow the soft fruit that was to be the raw material, so that their children could be employed in its processing and not have to emigrate, as so many did then.

The jam was called Irish Farmhouse Preserves – 'Made according to the recipe of Sir Tyrone Guthrie', as it said on the label. The manager was Joe Martin, son of a man who had once owned half of Newbliss and then, like King Lear, had divided his kingdom between his three children. One got the pub, another got the shop, and Joe got enough land and money to be a bit of a businessman, though his father seems not to have passed on to him his gombeen acumen. The jam factory went bankrupt from production and storage problems, orders not filled, harvests delayed or destroyed by the weather, gluts of fruit in the good years fermenting in the sun in bins in the yard and the imperfectly sterilized pots popping their lids on the shelves of classy shops where Guthrie got it introduced by having the likes of Alec Guinness bring samples on their travels.

A lot of Tyrone Guthrie's own money went into The Jam, as it was known, including fees of a thousand dollars a time earned for lectures in America in the last years of his life. It is not true, though, as the local myth would have had it, that he died in his armchair in the morning room at Annaghmakerrig on the fifteenth of May 1971 with a final bankruptcy notice in his hand. The missive he was holding was a rebate on the rates.

Since Guthrie and his wife, Judith, had had no children, Sir Tyrone – the first theatre director ever to be knighted – had pondered long and hard as to what was to be done with the house and land when he died. In what he obviously saw as an act of restitution to the Catholic Irishry expropriated by his Protestant ancestors, he bequeathed to his steward, James McStravick, the house adjacent to and contiguous with the Big House in which McStravick and his family lived, the farmyard and its buildings, the gardens, 50 acres of freehold farmland, woodlands and scrub, 300 acres that were on 150-year leases to the Forestry Department of the Irish government and would revert to McStravick's descendants in 2086, the hundred acres of lake, and three cottages: in effect, all of the Annaghmakerrig estate up to the walls of the Big House. He had considered leaving him the house too, until he was dissuaded by his sister, Peggy, and her husband, Hubert Butler, who had lived in Ireland all their lives and were under no illusions about the papish peasantry and what it was capable of. They would always say that there was an element of pique in Guthrie's last testament, a certain crossness even, as he insisted that his idealistic whim would prevail, despite their doubts.

As it was, Tyrone Guthrie left the Big House to be an artists' retreat, but not a rood or square perch of land beyond its walls. This was the 'Tolstoyan will' that would come to bear so much on our lives.

★

After I learned that I would become director of the Tyrone Guthrie Centre on the first of January 1981, Mary and I went to visit Annaghmakerrig for a second time a few days after Christmas, with Maeve, who was now almost four years old, and Eoin, who was almost two.

We met James McStravick's wife, Lizzie, the custodian of the keys. She showed us round a bit, gave us our bearings, and sized us up too, I felt. Something in her wariness and her proprietorial air made this first meeting seem like the beginning of Act 2, Scene 1 – Enter Usurping Strangers. When she demurred at leaving us on our own, saying she had had no instructions from anyone, I had to insist she give us the keys, surprising myself with the bossiness of my tone.

Left to ourselves, we ate sandwiches and drank tea from a flask in the bare drawing room, looking out at the lake, the wintry gardens and the dark pine forest in the distance. After our picnic we climbed up the main stairs, helping Eoin up step by step, our voices and our footsteps echoing in the empty hall. We looked into all the rooms. Maeve ran from end to end of them, pointing out things, lifting up tools that were scattered among the sawdust and ends of wood and other materials the workmen had left when they had gone on their Christmas holidays. We went up one of the metal staircases into the maze of attic spaces that were being converted to bathrooms. Underneath a window set into the apex of one of the roofs a lightwell looked down into the sub-aqueous depths of the hall. Another set of stairs led down to the back corridor. At the far end of this L-shaped passage we opened a door into the big room at the back of the house where the furniture was being stored while the building work was going on. It smelt overpoweringly of old books, the thousands of them we could see piled on shelves that bent under their weight, among heaps, rows and stacks of other stuff. While I examined the books and Mary held up pieces of material to the light from the tall windows at the back of the room, Maeve delved through this Santa's cave like a diving duck, bobbing up with the head of a porcelain doll, then a box of clay-brick puzzles, a fur collar, black and white boa feathers, a tasselled shawl.

— Are we really going to live here, Daddy? she asked me, her red-cheeked face aglow.

— We are, I replied, just as all-our-Christmases-at-once excited as she was, as we all were, even Eoin, who seemed to understand that something important was in the offing.

I'm not sure when it occurred to us that there might be a job for Mary, too, for that idea took a while to incubate and crack its egg, but I think Mary and I both knew, that day, that this was something we would do together.

Animalkerrig

In the last years of his life Tyrone Guthrie had been patron of an attempt to set up a commune on a nearby estate in County Cavan. It did not prosper. Whether influenced by this or not, he had set out his vision for Annaghmakerrig in five simple phrases in his will, ordaining the creation of 'a place of retreat for artists and other like persons . . . so as to enable them to do or facilitate them in doing creative work . . . who shall have the right to use my dwelling house and all its contents . . . to walk over the land, boat or fish on the lake . . . provided they do not pluck the flowers or interfere with standing crops'.

Mary and I are both practical people, from practical stock, so we poured our practical hearts and souls into making this aspiration a reality. It became our shared vocation: the calling for which we had been listening and readying ourselves all our lives.

Beyond the practical necessity of making the house a home again, there was a business side to Annaghmakerrig that I also enjoyed. I discovered that I had an aptitude and an appetite for what up until then I would have scorned as 'being a bureaucrat' – writing letters, filling out forms, keeping accounts, applying for grants, dealing with applications, answering the phone – in the one-man office I set up in the butler's pantry.

Every couple of months in the first year we had a meeting of the board that was appointed by the arts councils of the Republic of Ireland and of Northern Ireland. There were five members from each side of the border and a chairman. The centre was vaunted as a flagship project of cross-border cultural collaboration, a rhetoric I very quickly absorbed and put to work to get money from the funds that were popping up along the border like mushrooms after autumn rain.

At the start of the meetings, in the library we made in the one-time dining room, the chairman would set his watch to go off with a bleep after exactly two hours. For the most part, whatever we had to decide would be decided by that time, and I would be left to get on with it until the next time. After one early meeting at which we had spent an hour and a half discussing two proposals for wallpaper for the drawing room, eventually deciding on a blue Laura Ashley print, one of the board members took me aside and told me I should 'never let a committee decide the colour of the wallpaper'. After that, Mary and I made all such decisions on our own.

As I went up and down to Monaghan from Dublin in those first months, trying all the different routes to Annaghmakerrig through the drumlin countryside of lakes and little hills, I was on the look-out for somewhere we might live in the locality. After viewing all kinds of bungalows, shacks at ends of lanes, mansions beyond compare and price, and flats in some of the nearby towns, I eventually discovered we could rent a ramshackle house owned by the McStravicks that stood cheek-by-jowl with theirs in the one-time dairy and laundry wing that adjoined the Big House at Annaghmakerrig itself.

We would be able to live over the shop, as it were. Mary and I also thought this would be a perfect place to bring up our children.

From the day in March 1981 when we moved there to live, Maeve and Eoin began to explore their new surroundings with all the eagerness of their nearly four years and nearly two. Maeve's first attempt at the name was Animalkerrig, for all the animals there were around it, especially the half-wild cats that roamed the farmyard and outbuildings. Within days of our installing ourselves in the house next door to the McStravicks, squads of these cats started to gather at our door to be fed by Mary, who attracts stray animals wherever she goes. At feeding time Maeve would wade out into the scrum of them milling over and through and round one another to get to the dishes; a bossy little missy who sternly insisted that all cats, no matter how stupid, were entitled to their fair share. A few weeks after we arrived she brought me up to the hay barn in the farmyard to show me a litter of kittens she had found. She burrowed into the hay like a ferret and emerged with a tiny kitten in each hand. We tamed those and they became the first domestications of these feral felines, to whose genes we added other adoptions of our own: Ginger McCabe from Drumard; Big Tom, who just appeared one day, yarming, and never left until the day he died, eight years later, keeled over by a stroke at our door, yarming to the last; Tomasina, who had one litter of kittens and never another, though she came on heat twice a year and trawled and trolloped about the yard and the Big House; Pacheco, in memory of a Farrera cat; then Black

Person, Mama Puss, and various White Persons from a strain of albinos that predominated for a while.

Later, Maeve and Eoin would keep a pair of rabbits called Ronnie and Pandora in a red and white Pop Art hutch made by one of the artists. There would be an injured rook called Crusty Christopher, whom we nursed until he was able to fly again; a battery chicken we liberated after it had fallen on to the street in Newbliss out of its cage on the back of a lorry taking it to the chicken factory in Cootehill, which we gave away as a layer and which turned out to be a cock; a few ducks which joined the cats at the door for a while; a hamster Maeve kept in a cage in her room; and Jeff the dog, who was cowering under the wheels of a car one time when we came home from a trip and was adopted immediately. Years afterwards he would be succeeded by Molly, a recent mother whose pups must have been taken from her, for her teats were still hard with milk. She had got lost when she set out to look for them. Instead she found us.

As the builders continued their overhaul of the house, the first members of our staff, Doreen Burns, Ann McGuirk and Ingrid Adams, each of whom had her own history of involvement with the place, started to clean and clothe it once more. These Trojan women polished floors, shined banisters, hoovered books, washed, wiped, scoured, rubbed and scrubbed. Mary worked with them, making and repairing cushions, curtains, seat covers and other soft furnishings. Every morning they would take an unhurried coffee break together in the kitchen, where they would discuss the jobs to be done and, over the years, a million other things.

With a local man, Benny McKenna, son of a second-hand furniture dealer, I set to work on sorting, restoring and moving the old furniture from the big room at the back of the house, which would become the music room. Wearing dust masks like two aqualunged archaeologists, Benny and I dived through this fabulous biblium-aquarium and brought to the surface chipped toothmugs, a bronchial inhaler, broken combs, nibs for ink pens, embroidery sets, rusted paper clips of antique design, parts for a sewing machine long since seized. There were inlaid glass cabinets, long-seated armchairs for the long-legged people the Guthries had been, linen tablecloths with browned edges, fittings for oil lamps, a dinner gong, all the bits of a big brass bed, ewers, basins and washstands, picnic sets, pots and pans, carpets, clothes, faded curtains, stale blankets and musty sheets. In leather and tin trunks stuck with steamer labels from journeys Tyrone and Judith Guthrie had made, we found packets and envelopes full of much-stamped passports, stubs of tickets, used chequebooks, and invoices rolled in batches tied with elastic bands that snapped when you touched them.

I loved handling the books, especially once I had saved them from a scheme the board of the centre had almost agreed to, just before I arrived, to give three-quarters of them to the Monaghan County Library. The county librarian had wanted to use the collection as a bargaining counter to get grant money for a Tyrone Guthrie Memorial Thingamagig that was also to be a teachers' resource centre and a God knows what else. My first of many unilateral acts as director was to kill that idea stone dead, and tell the board about its demise afterwards.

The books belonged in the house. They were its memory: books on gardening, plants, birds, animal husbandry and agriculture, many theological tomes, enough family bibles so that every room could have one beside its bed, Victorian novels, collections of the poems of Tennyson, Byron, Wordsworth, travel books, military memoirs, a 1932 edition of the *Encyclo-*

pædia Britannica, and plays, of course, in hundreds, many of them with dedications by their authors to Tyrone Guthrie or to 'Dear Tony and Judy', the diminutives by which the Guthries were known to their friends and family. There was a first edition of *Poems* by W. B. Yeats with a handwritten note on the first page saying it had been 'read alternately by Rudyard Kipling and Hugh Macnaghton on Rottingdean Beach to Eva Macnaghton and Amelia Scott on September 12, 1900'. In a blue-cloth-covered book of pressed algae made in 1859 for the Reverend David Guthrie by Miss P. Kaven of The Thwaite, Coniston, Westmoreland, the colours of the seaweeds – each page of specimens being protected by a leaf of fine tissue paper – were pristine: coral, amethyst, amber, rose, shades of brown, with their Linnaean names written out in tiny copperplate beneath them.

As walls were painted and carpets laid, Benny and I distributed furniture, pictures, books, bibelots and knick-knacks throughout the house, under the aegis of Mary, who with Our Girls, as we already knew them, not patronizingly, but affectionately, would breathe a soft, balmy femininity into every corner of Annaghmakerrig.

I made Fred McKenna (no relation to Benny) the permanent handyman. He would be the ship's carpenter who checked and repaired and tightened every spar and board of the relaunched *Anna McGarrigle* (one of the pet names we came to have for the place), kept her pumps and engines working, and her crew happy, too, for he was ever genial, and a lesson in persistence. He never gave up on a problem until he had found the solution, which he would recount to me in detail, for he had the countryman's sense of the day as something to be filled with the jobs to be done, not with a certain number of hours to be put in. He took a pride in his work that filled me with pride, and love even, for should one not love beautiful people with whom one has had the privilege to work, and want, even now, to take the cap from his decent, honest, loyal head and bestow fond kisses upon his patient, balding pate?

Many times the *Anna McGarrigle* would have sunk without Fred.

For those first ten months, as we worked to make this gaunt house a home again, until it gleamed with the cleanliness next to godliness that made it so Protestant-looking and -smelling, Our Girls told us stories about the people who had lived there and the names of some of the rooms; how the decor had been in the old days; where different pieces of furniture had stood; who had lived where on the estate; where they all were now; the things they had done and said – as if we were resettling the old ghosts to make room for the new ones we were about to conjure up.

The playwright Brian Friel, for whom Tyrone Guthrie had been a mentor in the early years of his career, performed the opening ceremony in October. When he went to the microphone on the front steps, looking leonine and magisterial, with his *capo di tutti capi* face, Mr Friel said,

— There is a language for occasions like this and there is a private language for friendship and love, so today I won't speak of my own affection and admiration for Tyrone Guthrie, nor of my great debt to him. I know his spirit is here with us today.

He put on his glasses and read an extract from a letter he had received from Guthrie a few months before he died:

The days slip by and hour by hour seems full of occupation but you look back a week and nothing seems to have been accomplished but flim-flam. We shall all come to the end of our lives and, looking back, there'll be nothing but flim-flam. Michelangelo will have thought the ceiling of the Sistine Chapel flim-flam, and so maybe does God. The important thing, of course, is not achievement but effort. And it seems to me that the hardest effort consists in doing terribly boring, repetitious things which pay no dividend except that, if they weren't done, there'd be chaos. Really all that any of us, even the great geniuses, do, is keep the brush from encroaching into the yard.

Friel folded up the letter and stowed it in his inside pocket, took off his glasses, and continued:

— Keeping the brush from encroaching into the yard is a good enough definition of a life devoted to art, and a good enough working description of what may happen in the various rooms of this house. Guthrie himself kept many a yard clear in his day – in Belfast, in Edinburgh, at the Old Vic, in New York, in Dublin, in Israel, in Denmark, in Stratford, Ontario, in Minneapolis, Minnesota. We haven't even begun to calculate how much we owe him.

Once the first artists came to stay, we made it up as we went along. There had never been an artists' retreat as such in Ireland, though I did think about Coole Park, where Lady Gregory had ensured that house was kept for W. B. Yeats and others ('Don't you think you should go up to your room, now, Willie, and write?'), and of other kinds of community, like Findhorn in Scotland, Taos in New Mexico, kibbutzim in Israel, and of the similar communities of artists I began to discover all over the world, with which we would organize exchanges: sending playwrights to New Dramatists in New York, poets to the Frost Place in New Hampshire, and all kinds of artists to Banff in the Canadian Rockies, the Åland

Islands in Finland, Santorini in Greece, Ravenna in Italy, La Rectoria near Barcelona, and many other places.

In creating the ambience that would draw artists from all over Ireland and all over the world to this retreat nestled among the sometimes bitter and sectarian little hills of south Ulster, Mary and I made sure there were no formal rules and regulations, no notices, no interference with the artists' right to be and work there. Annaghmakerrig imposed its own civility. Everyone who was a guest there was made to feel free to do as he or she wished within the constraints of that civility.

In the tours of the house I came to give I always liked doing the 'he or she' bit, because of the more than 2,000 individuals who stayed during the eighteen years we were there, somewhat more than half were women. Many of these were among the rising bevvy of young Irish women artists who have evened the artistic gender balance in one fell generation. Others were older women writers, painters and composers who had had to sideline their careers to rear families, and now came to Annaghmakerrig as part of reimmersing themselves in their art; to have days or weeks of only doing their art, instead of art *and* a job, *and* a family, *and* a husband, indeed.

Over those years, in exhibitions, book dedications, catalogues, collaborations and other acknowledgements, we would see the fruits of these sojourns being printed, sung, hung, performed and otherwise disseminated in ports from Reykjavik to Brisbane, Belfast to Berlin, Omagh to Yokahama. For Mary and myself, harbourmistress and harbourmaster of the *Anna McGarrigle*'s home port – and, in other ways, for Maeve and Eoin, who attended many of the recitals, try-outs of plays, readings, *vernissages*, open days and other events – the privilege would be that through knowing them, we would hear writers' voices in our heads as we read their books; see a painter's frailty in charcoal drawings of the human skeleton; understand the temerity of an artist dedicating his entire life to an abstract, intellectual, chess-master exploration of black and red; catch a phrase in a play that its writer had picked up from one of the locals.

Artists left pieces to the collection that grew around the original artworks in the house: a print on hand-made paper of blobmorphs by Mary Farl Powers alongside framed posters from the Guthrie Theater in Minneapolis; a twelve by twenty foot version of Velazquez's *Las Meninas* painted by Mick Cullen on a canvas that covers one wall of the music room, facing a mirror – ironies reflecting ironies; a brooding portrait of a mother and son by Eithne Jordan at the head of the main stairs cheek by jowl with a marshland winter scene in hues of brown in a roughly gilded wooden frame; a carpet with the twelve stars of the European Union, each inset with an image of one of the coins from the original constituent countries, by Antonio Muntadas; *Big, Red, Dead Sheep* by Catherine Harper in the drawing room.

These and other pieces were the museum within, while in the gardens around the house I imagined a museum without, a place of dialogues between earth and sky, lake and forest, past and present, the cultivated and the wild. Walking on the estate in those early days, and looking from every direction at the house standing on its flattened motte, in the growing delirium of my ambition I saw it sometimes as the squaring of the circle of its rath predecessors, the ring-forts that stand on the hills around it, and sometimes even as a kind of spaceship of creativity whose energy could transform the run-down estate – if only the aliens we were could wrest some measure of control from the earthling to whom the departed lord had left it.

In the early years, though, I had to content myself with reclaiming the first bits of garden that were bought from James

McStravick – the pond garden at the back of the house, the lawn to the west, an area below the sundial in the knot garden, a shrubbery above the car park – and learn to be patient and tactical in the opening engagements of the land war that would be waged to win this landscape for the extra-terrestrials.

As I cleared a bed here, scythed a patch there, dug out diseased shrubs by their roots and trailed out banks of nettles until my hands were stung to claws, I often recalled old Mrs Guthrie's companion Bunty's bon mot, 'Ireland will never be without scutch grass and ignorance', and bethought me how in Ireland it was the Protestants who had gardened, while the Catholics had merely subsisted. Ornamental gardening in Ireland has always been a Protestant preserve. In the Monaghan poet Patrick Kavanagh's peasant universe there are no Protestants, and hardly any cultivated flowers or ornamental plants either, other than a solitary lilac bush at the door of his family home. The plots on to which the characters of his poems and novels 'drove the dung' grew potatoes, turnips, swedes and cabbage: 'swinish food'.

From all those days of working in the gardens, I have the memory of the sound of Maeve and Eoin's voices, the sense of their presence everywhere, as they appeared and disappeared about their childish pursuits in this place where there was so much space, so many people to look out for them, the safest place imaginable, I thought – not smugly, but gratefully.

When Maeve and Eoin's cousins came to visit from Belfast, they played football on the east lawn, or spent hours with their dolls and toys in the tree house I had built for them in the big oak at the car park, or went with me down to the lake to swim. On other days Maeve and Eoin and I went there first thing in the morning to shock ourselves awake with a plunge into the always cold, sometimes bone-shivering water.

Maeve and Eoin's closest friends in the locality were the Toman children, who lived in a house on the eastern boundaries of the estate. Olga Toman was a mettlesome, flame-haired girl who was obsessed with horses. She wanted to have a horse, and may even have wanted to be a horse. She had a false ponytail that she tied on to the back of her hair and a toy horse's bridle that she put round her head while Maeve mushed her along, whinnying as she high-trotted, head lowered, snorting and pawing the ground.

Olga's brother Karl, who was Eoin's age, had a growth deficiency, and was tiny, pale, air-boned, with a most intelligent and watchful face. As Karl joined in football matches as best he could, Eoin always watched over him and made sure he was never hurt by any rough stuff.

When Karl had to stay at home to rest after his hormone injections, Olga, and latterly their younger brother Ralph, would come on their own to Annaghmakerrig to play with Eoin and Maeve. All four of them would sometimes walk back to Tomans' together to see Karl: down the northern avenue, past May Richardson's gate lodge with its latticed windows and roses growing on an arch over the door, where May would always have a sweet or some other treat to give them; out the White Gates and down the Crappagh Road past Kevin and Kitty and Sonny Smith's house, where Sonny, who was in his seventies then, would be out in the garden among his drills of vegetables, his pipe bobbing in the gap it had worn in his teeth as he greeted them; past the old Crappagh schoolhouse where Bob and Martha Kirk lived; and finally past Archie and Willie Norris's homestead on the site of an old rath near Crappagh Cross, where they would often meet Archie out on the road on his crutches after he got the two hips done, or might see Willie on his old-fashioned red Massey-Ferguson tractor with his terrier on his knee looking out through the windscreen as if it were doing the driving.

Olga and Maeve always went this way because Bob Kirk, Willie and Archie Norris and Patsy Toman, Olga's uncle, were all horse-dealers who bought and sold animals at fairs and marts. In the rushy, bachelor-farmer fields that stretched along the road from Crappagh Cross to the Tomans' house at the edge of the Annaghmakerrig forest there were always ponies, stallions, mares with their foals, donkeys and mules, to which the children offered the sugar cubes or bits of bread they brought with them.

Karl, meanwhile, would be patiently waiting for them in the old house tucked into the edge of the wood.

The Tomans moved to County Cavan in 1988. Karl died on the thirtieth of March 1995, aged sixteen. Mary, Maeve, Eoin and I went to his funeral. The light-drenched modern church was full of young people, fresh flowers, music, songs, and gratitude for a life that we discovered had touched hundreds more people after he had left our little orbit. In the tributes that were paid, his classmates read from things Karl had written. Everyone talked of his bravery and intelligence, his sensitivity and humour, his pluck and his puckishness.

On the way home in the car we agreed that none of us had ever seen Karl show self-pity.

A Black Box

One night in May 1990 Mary came into the office in the Big House that had once been the butler's pantry, where I was working late. She said I should come down home with her immediately. She would tell me why when we were outside.

We went out together through the quiet kitchen. The long

curtains of Barcelona Flamestitch were drawn over the French windows that look out on to the gardens, a clean white table-cloth was on the round table, the big table had been cleared, the dishwasher was humming and slushing through its cycles, and a smell of tobacco lingered from after the dinner that Mary had cooked earlier that evening for the artists.

When we had gone out through the door into the entry at the back and she was sure we would not be overheard, Mary whispered to me, looking terrified, as I had never seen her before, speaking the words as if she could not believe that she was speaking them,

— Eoin says he has been sexually abused by Fintan McStravick.

Fintan McStravick, then in his early twenties, was the son of James and Lizzie McStravick. They had been our next-door neighbours for all the years we had lived at Annaghmakerrig.

Eoin was sitting on the church pew at the table in our kitchen. He was ten years old, dressed in blue-striped pyjamas, a checked dressing gown and slippers, such a beautiful child, always – curly-haired, fine-featured, bright and energetic, and now calm, as if he had decided something and this was it and he was going to see it through.

After I sat down beside him on the pew and put my arm round him, with Mary on his other side, Eoin told us everything, in his own childish way.

When we asked him why he had not told us before, he said,

— He told me not to tell you, not to tell anybody, ever. He said he would get me if I told. He said he would find me and he would get me. I told Natan about it. Natan told me I should tell you.

Natan Megged was Eoin's Israeli friend who had lived for a year with his parents and his sister in Maggie's Cottage on the Crappagh Road, which we had bought a few years before so that artists could stay there with their families. Eoin said Fintan McStravick had left him alone while Natan was there. He was afraid it might start again now that Natan had gone back to Israel.

We told him we were glad Natan had told him to do that. He had done the right thing in telling us. He did not have to be afraid any more. He had been very brave. We would make sure it never happened again.

— Daddy, will I get Aids? Eoin asked.

— No, son, you won't.

We both kissed him, and held him, and told him how right he had been to tell us, reassuring him, first of all, and trying not to betray our own panic, and just keep breathing in the vacuum of the aftershock.

Mary took Eoin up to bed, as she always did, and stayed with him until he fell asleep. When she came back down again, we hugged one another. Mary cried, who has always cried easily, as if her heart had swollen and burst in her chest. I cried too, who never cried, because I had cried so much in my own childhood, cried until I was a man, and would never let anybody make me cry like that again, would never show weakness, until now, when that was all I could show.

Natan Megged is a year older than Eoin, and therefore a bit younger than Maeve, so when he came to live with his parents – Eyal, a poet, and Nona, a potter – in Maggie's Cottage in 1989, the children had all gone together to Latnamard National School. The school stands beside the Catholic chapel at one end of the long boomerang wedge of a parish that is Aghabog, with the Church of Ireland church weighting it at the other end. When Natan started being bullied, not just for being a Jew, though there was that in their jeering, but for being a foreigner, for not speaking like the rest of them, he stopped wanting to go to school at all, as we discovered after he missed a few days, then a whole week. We told Maeve and Eoin they had to look out for Natan and make the bullies leave him alone. So they did, and the bullies backed off.

Natan and Eoin were inseparable for that year. They went to school together, played football together, went on jaunts with Eyal and Nona or with us, for Natan's ambition was to visit every Irish county before he left. He succeeded.

Now that Natan had gone back to Israel, Eoin was frightened that Fintan McStravick might get him again.

Eoin also told us that he and Maeve had watched a programme on television about how Esther Rantzen had set up Childline. Eoin had asked Maeve if she would tell us if something like that was happening to her. Maeve had said she would.

So Eoin told us.

Maeve would not tell us what had happened to her for another six years.

The next morning, I confronted Fintan McStravick. I told him he could never come back to Annaghmakerrig again. We did not know what we were going to do, but that was the one thing we were sure of: that he could never go near Annaghmakerrig while we were there.

As Mary and I talked on the first night of our knowing, and then on subsequent days and nights, we found memories that were like signs that had been hidden by the branches of overhanging trees, which we only recognized now that we were out in the middle of the crossroads surrounded by the wreckage of the crash.

We began to stumble towards finding the truth among all the lies Fintan McStravick told, shameless liar that he was. In trying to find ways to recount this story, for I cannot tell the details of what this monster did, all I can say is that for a decade and more, as we discovered the extent and the enormity of what he had done, and some of the why he had done it, it was as though we were wandering in a dark wood with no way out, only glimpses of deeper, darker, ranker places, where no light shone, or would ever shine.

It is hard now to know when exactly Mary and I learned what, or thought what, or said what. In those first years, the two of us – in a quiet corner of Bannon's lounge in Coote-hill, or on a journey somewhere, or at night on our own in our own house – would go over what we knew, what we had heard, what we had read, what we had imagined, what we had seen, trying to steady one another and to find ways to show our children we loved them without suffocating them with our apprehensions. In all those years of knowing, and sometimes seeming to know nothing else, the knowledge was a virus tirelessly reproducing and attaching itself to every corpuscle of our waking and sleeping thoughts.

We had been so grateful to get our jobs at Annaghmakerrig. With the friends we had found there, all the people who had joined our cargo cult, we had spent years unwrapping this gift from the gods of the travellers we had been. But this last box, a black box with black ribbons, had stayed in its wrappings until the very end.

It contained a bomb. We knew, now, how the bomb had been made.

We knew too who had carried it into our family and buried it there, hidden for years, fizzling and spluttering in the darkness, until the night Eoin told us it was there, and our world shattered.

For years afterwards it was as though the bomb was still exploding slowly. Its septic shrapnel embedded itself in every part of our lives: shards of anger, loathing, disgust and shock that could catch you at any time, while you tried to use your own body to shield those you loved most, who had been violated in their innocence by this man whom we still had to pass on the road, or see in the local pub, the Black Kesh, leering and laughing with his mates, acting as if nothing had happened.

As we came to dread going out in case we met him, and began to be prisoners in our own home, we felt this secret hemming us in on all sides. Stories were told in the locality to make it seem that Fintan McStravick had left Annaghmakerrig because he and I had had a row about land, and we were drawn into a conspiracy of silence it would take us years to understand and unmask.

And always the if: if we had stayed in Farrera; if Tyrone Guthrie had not made his 'cross will'; if we had caught Fintan McStravick just once; if we had only taught our children to be more suspicious; if we had only told them more forcefully to tell us if anybody ever tried to do anything like that; if we had not been so been so trusting and neighbourly ourselves; if we had even once imagined such viciousness to be possible; if, if, if . . .

Most of all, if we had not returned to live in Ireland, where so much of the institutionalized and personalized abuse the Catholic system had fostered was being revealed simultaneously with the discoveries we were making.

There was a Saturday night, within weeks of Eoin telling us, when we had dinner in our own house for the writer Michael Harding, the writer Leland Bardwell, and the painter Dermot Seymour, who had become our close friends. As we told them what we had learned, I became extremely emotional about how Catholicism had poisoned Ireland, and now it had poisoned our lives. The diffident Mr Seymour, the Prod from the Shankill Road who had grown up, he always said, as a kind of orphan – his mother dead and his father a 'bus-kicker', shell-shocked in the war – had tears in his eyes. Leland, Big House Protestant by birth, bohemian by choice, hugged us. Michael Harding, still then a Catholic priest, who had seen the worst cruelties of the religious war when he had been a curate in Derrylin in south Fermanagh, took us both in his arms in a big, comforting embrace.

The next morning Father Harding said a Mass in our kitchen, with Eoin and Maeve, Dermot and Leland, Mary and me. As other people passed outside on their way to and from other kinds of religious services, and artists went about their business, life going on outside our kitchen window as usual, the sun shone through it and bathed the room in a refulgent, redemptive light. Michael said we were taking this symbolic meal together for the special intentions of everyone there, especially the Loughlins. We only had curranty bread, so he blessed and broke that. He blessed a bottle of Spanish *cava*, the only wine we had, and we all had a sip of that.

During those first years of knowing, I believe Mary and I, each in our own way, suffered a paralysis, a numbness, an arrested development of all the parts of our life at Annagh-makerrig we had most enjoyed and most cultivated: knowing our neighbours in the easy way that our years of living in country places, learning country ways, country talk, country forbearance, should have allowed. Now, everywhere we went, with everyone we met, we wondered what they had heard.

Maeve and Eoin would both say later that Fintan McStravick had stolen their childhoods. From Mary and me he stole our peace of mind, for ever. To have peace of mind you have to be complacent, as I knew I had been complacent, and arrogant even in my pride at having followed our starlit destiny to a place where our love story, our idyll, our charmed life together had found, I thought, its perfect playground.

I would never be complacent again.

We found a photograph of Maeve and Eoin and their friends at one of the Hallowe'en parties we had always had at Annaghmakerrig for them and the children of the staff and neighbours. They all had their faces painted and were dressed up in witches' hats, old coats and plastic bags. They were looking startled by a Roman candle, which could be seen flaring in the foreground. We now knew that beyond the flash-lit huddle of Hallowe'en fear caught in that photo-moment a truly terrifying beast had been prowling the shadows. We had that photograph framed and hung it on the wall above the table in our own kitchen as a talisman to ward off the banshees crying at the windows.

We remembered how easily upset Eoin had sometimes been when he was younger, like the time when we were on our way to Farrera through France and he had lost his purse with his holiday pocket money. He had been inconsolable, his desolation out of all proportion to what had happened, just one of all kinds of little and big things that seemed to go wrong in his life, as if everything were out to thwart him. We remembered how Maeve had started to bite her nails when she was six or seven, how she had been afraid to stay with her friend Lorraine Hamill in her family house, and how she had got fat in early adolescence, as was not her physiological type.

The more we knew all this in helpless retrospect, the more we knew anger – Mary, who had never in her life felt real anger until now, and I, who before this believed that I had learned to understand and control my own anger.

Perhaps Mary and I were bad for one another in that way. She hates confrontation or bad feeling of any sort. We both of us, in our different ways, were compromisers, palliators, peacemakers, who hated the tension that hung over Annagh-makerrig, for all that we made sure, discreet to a fault, that the artists-in-residence were not aware of it. This place we had loved so much, perhaps even loved too much, became a private hell.

At the beginning, the life of the farm at Annaghmakerrig had been of a piece with the peasant life we had known in Farrera and with the rangy cattle- and sheep-rearing in the hills of Donegal. I had felt that the farm helped to anchor the Tyrone Guthrie Centre in the agricultural sea that surrounded it, and had even hoped that, with time, we might find ways to help in the farm's improvement.

It did not take me very long to see that this particular farm was beyond improvement, degenerating as it was in direct proportion to how much James McStravick worked at it: from dawn to dusk, up and down, ceaselessly busy, usually with a Senior Service in his mouth from the packets of ten that Lizzie McStravick bought for him, from which he ripped the top part of the cellophane to open them, and then, when he had finished with them, threw away the packet, still with the rest of the cellophane on it, as a mean-spirited, pig-headed, thick-witted entropy propagated all around him.

He hardly ever came into the Big House or the office in the butler's pantry, a residue of habits of deference perhaps, so it was generally outdoors that I met him, in the gardens, in the yard or in the fields. He was quite deaf, but never wore a hearing aid. He had a grunting way with him, a cross between a 'Hoomph' and an 'Aaahh?' to show that he hadn't heard, which also served to give him intervals in which to scheme for ways to earn a bit of extra money for himself that his wife, who controlled the purse strings, would not know about. He was Fine Gael in his politics, because his family all were, though I never heard him say a good word about any politician (or anyone else, for that matter). As far as he was concerned they were all on the make, or cute hoors, or haverils, a local word he once defined as 'casterated he-goats that feed upon noxious weeds'. His blathering, humourless conversation mostly consisted of gleanings from the *Northern Standard*, the local paper, which he read from cover to cover every Thursday evening, when it appeared, to know who had been fined for drunk driving, or had lost their farm, or had had their herd condemned for tuberculosis, or had gone bankrupt, or been killed in a car accident. He was always telling me about nasty things that happened in the locality, like the time a man drowned in his own dungstead and was discovered to have a fortune of money hidden all over the house, or the time a neighbourman who had lost a couple of fingers in a silage harvester asked his sworn enemy in the pub one night had he heard about his trouble? and what did he think of the state of his hand now that they had sewn it up for him at the hospital? holding it out for him to see, and the enemy said,

— Sure isn' it a lot n'ater on ye now?

Within living memory, Jimmy Daly, the head gardener, with a team of under-gardeners, had supplied most of the vegetables, fruit and flowers for the Big House. In the annual cycle of work on the estate, they would have tended shrubberies and herbaceous borders, mown lawns, kept roads, paths and drains open, planted trees, cut hedges, sown and saved harvests, sometimes assisted by hearty forays of the Guthries themselves, who often invited their guests to join them for briar-slashing parties, or firewood-cutting bees, or, once, a voyage by boat to drop water-lily roots in wooden chests of compost in the sheltered north-west corner of the lake, where they have since formed a wide-spreading colony.

After the Guthries died and James McStravick was left everything, the knot garden disappeared under a welter of weeds; the orchards, vegetable gardens and Oak Walk were ripped out to make pasture; the wooden frame of the greenhouse rotted; the straw-roofed summerhouse collapsed with a soggy sigh under the weight of tangled rose stems; the lawns turned to mossy meadows.

McStravick was the bogman from the back hills who now owned the demesne. He made fences out of sticks scavenged from the woods that rotted within a few years, sagging and buckling and eventually collapsing under the weight of scutch grass growing over them. He had only to touch a gate for it to fall off its hinges, never to be put back again. He hacked trees out of hedgerows to cut logs to sell for drink and fag money, and then left the lopped branches lying in heaps that would rot and subside as the grass grew up through them and the cows grazed round them, until his fields were obstacle courses for his own machinery. His tractor ailed under him like a maltreated mule, belching protests of black smoke. His car spluttered and wheezed with mechanical bronchitis. His silage rotted. His hay grew mould. His lazy beds were full of club root, canker and weeds.

Since he had inherited the property, McStravick had made a stab at a bit of this and a bit of that in the stone-built farmyard at the back of the Big House, in the out-offices that had once been grainstore, fruit loft, dairy, carpentry shop, hay barn, byre and stables, each section with its own name and function in the self-reliant economy of the Big House. Now the yard buildings had no gutters, so that rain ran down their walls to sap the foundations. The roofs sagged. In places they had collapsed altogether. The sheds were full of redundant household objects, for the McStravicks never threw anything away, just moved it down to the yard: an old freezer in which Lizzie

McStravick fattened turkey chicks for Christmas, banjaxed washing machines, a sofa retired from sheer exhaustion, a bockety dresser, broken bedsteads, old mattresses, rubbish in heaps and scatters. Dead cars rusted in weed-choked corners. Cows were milked in the byre twice a day by a milking machine that stood in a hut James McStravick had built of concrete blocks with a corrugated iron roof. The blocked sump behind the stable made a dung-swamp that oozed under the building and eventually into the lake itself. Hens were kept in cages in a shed just outside the back door of our house. The droppings that were cranked out from under them on a felt roller were left standing in piles that bred swarms of flies. One of the first purchases we made for the Big House was an Insect-O-Cuter with a murderous blue light. We also put flyswats in all the rooms.

As they got to driving age, the young McStravicks and their cousins began to use Annaghmakerrig as a place to race their jalopies round and round the farmyard in clouds of dust, roaring and rallying along the avenues of the estate and then sliding to a halt in front of the Big House with the engines revving hard and the country and western blaring. For a period they rode a motorbike up and down Sir William Tyrone Power's banked lawns and over a jump of straw bales and planks they erected on the Half Moon meadow in front of the house.

Visiting artists, wondering at all the commotion in this supposed haven of peace and tranquillity, would ask me who these young fellows were.

— They're just the McStravicks. They own the place.

Finally, a year before Eoin told us what had happened to him, after protracted negotiations in which James McStravick used every weapon in his armoury of lying, humbug, hypocrisy, wheedling and whingeing, we managed to buy the farmyard from him, along with a cordon sanitaire of twelve acres of gardens and lawns surrounding the house.

We found the money with which to restore the Victorian farmyard roof by roof, stone by stone, beam by beam, door by door, window by window, to make five houses around the courtyard in what had been barns and byres. The Long Building (so-named by me in a fit of the South Seas) became three studios, with a rehearsal and performance room upstairs. Murnaghan Brothers of Ballybay, whom Fred called the Murnyahans, were the contractors, tradesmen as skilful and patient as Fred himself. We would hear them arriving at eight o'clock every morning, and then, minutes later, the first kick of the cement mixer or the dumper coughing into life as they set to work, whistling as they went.

The yard was finished and gravelled for Sunday the twenty-eighth of July 1991, when it was to be opened by President Mary Robinson. She came in her Rolls-Royce, with the Irish flag and the presidential flag flying from miniature masts at the end of the long bonnet, preceded by two police outriders, to be met and welcomed at the front door by the then chairman of the board, Máirtín McCullough, our good and constant friend, who would retire soon afterwards, his wife, Mary, and my Mary and me. As we showed President Robinson and her husband round the house, she looked at everything, listened attentively to our explanations, and asked interested, intelligent questions. The tour ended with her meeting Doreen, Ann, Ingrid and the other workers, all radiant at receiving the President's compliments on how well the place looked.

Macnas Theatre Company of Galway were to be the spectacle later in the day, so their band of merry players, on cymbals, drums and *trompettes volontaires*, led the procession the long way round through the crowds who had been waiting: out the back door, through the pond garden, President Robinson and Máirtín in front, then my Mary and Mary McCullough and Mr Robinson and me, moving at a stately pace, the President giving all the onlookers the beck and nod, a lovely sunny day, flowers out everywhere, and friends of the place everywhere too, like human blooms, all smiling.

We had rigged a red ribbon across the entrance to the farmyard. President Robinson stood at the lectern and microphone we had set up in front of it and spoke warmly, without a script, from the briefing I had sent her, about the great man Sir Tyrone had been and of the generous, visionary legacy he had left; about Peggy Butler, his sister, and her husband, Hubert, and how they had fought for ten years for the legacy to be acted upon; the history of Annaghmakerrig itself; its place in the local community; the cross-borderness of it all; and the wonderful job of restoration and conservation that had been done on the farmyard.

The President cut the tape. Everybody followed her down the steps to look at the new houses and studios and then have the lunch that Mary and Our Girls had been preparing for a week.

Mary and I felt we had invited everyone we should have. We had pored over the guest list for weeks beforehand, making sure to omit none of the people we had come to know, all our friends from the overlapping parishes of Aghabog, Monaghan, Ulster, Ireland and the world, and all the McStravicks, except one, all celebrating with us the spirit of renewal that Mary and I hoped would someday shine again on us and on our children.

This was only a year after the discovery for us. Throughout the day of the President's visit Mary and I carried that knowledge with us, as we now carried it everywhere: a stone that would not stop growing in our hearts.

As we were accompanying Mrs Robinson back to her car, I wanted to take her aside and tell her the real story of this place.

In 1995 we bought the rest of the estate from James McStravick, lock, stock and barrel. He and his family finally left on a day when we had made it our business not to be there.

In the peace that followed McStravick's quittance, marking as it did the end of the land war, I walked the estate with Molly the dog and learned, all over again, like a man making a map on a tabula rasa, every march ditch, stream, copse, hedge, fence and gate. In my own quest for transcendence, I believed I discerned a wholeness to the 450 acres, where the lake was a third eye of enlightenment gazing out of the *Anna McGarrigle*'s mystical body.

I saw Annaghmakerrig as allied with the Ark Centre for Permaculture at Drumard near Clones, where Marcus McCabe and Kate Mullarney were creating an eco-village that would be part of a UNESCO-sponsored global network, and with the Camphill Community at Robb's Farm on the Ballybay Road near Swann's Cross, where people with disabilities look after gardens, greenhouses and farm animals, and practise crafts like basketwork, weaving, knitting and preserves-making, in a community based on anthroposophical principles, as Annaghmakerrig was a community founded on ART, with a capital A, a big R and a mordant T.

I commissioned the forest planners MosArt to prepare a scheme for the renewal of the landscape to go with the strategic development plan I had written for the new era I believed was now dawning, when Annaghmakerrig would, at last, come into its own, and my own transmogrification into Capability Brown from Andersonstown, the Fenian improver, would be complete. They took as their text these lines by St Bernard of Clairvaux: 'Believe one who knows: you will find something greater in woods than in books. Trees and stones will teach you that which you can never learn from masters.'

Expulsion from the Garden of Eden

In February 1996, when I came back from a week's fund-raising, Mary met me at Dublin airport, as she often did. We had come to value the time these journeys to Monaghan gave us to talk. It was late when we got home. There was a letter waiting for me from the writer and painter Brigid Murray, a good friend and a confidante from the first, who happened to be staying in one of the new houses in the farmyard. Mary had not known the letter was there, and she did not see me opening and reading it. In the first paragraph Brigid talked about how sorry she felt for us now that we knew the full extent of what had happened.

I stopped reading and went in to Mary in the kitchen. She told me that Maeve had told her a few days before that she too had been abused when she was very young and over years by Fintan McStravick, who had denied it when I had asked him, five or six times, practised, cowardly, snivelling liar as he was.

Maeve had been resolved to tell us by going to see a counsellor at St Patrick's College, Maynooth, where she was now a student. Mary said she had wanted to tell me as soon as we got in the door, because she had wanted to tell me in our own house, after the journey home: protecting me, as we were all protecting one another, because any opportunity for things to be normal, even for a couple of hours, was like a holiday.

After Mary told me I cried, more helpless, choking, galling tears. I cried for Maeve, most of all. Ever since we had found out what had happened to Eoin, we had suspected that she had been abused too. Now she had confirmed it. On her visit home she had talked to Mary at length and told her many of the details, including that the first time she remembered that Fintan McStravick had masturbated himself in front of her had been on a dirty mattress in the hay barn where I had seen her dig out the two kittens from their nest in the straw in the first year we had lived at Annaghmakerrig. She had been only five or six at the time. Every time Mary had asked, Maeve had told her that nothing had happened. She did not want to cause us any more trauma after seeing how devastated we were when we found out what happened to Eoin: another of the layers upon layers of protectiveness we were spinning like a cocoon to protect our love for one another from the winter that had closed in around us.

I cried for Eoin, for everything that Maeve had told Mary had only shown more graphically and more hauntingly what a depraved predator Fintan McStravick had been, and thus added more frames to the loop of film in the big bad projector that had installed itself in our minds. And I cried for Mary, too.

Now that there was nothing more we had to know, it was our children who began to lead us out of the labyrinth of lies. Bit by bit, painfully, with many backward steps, they came to be in charge of their own and our recovery, another of the words we learned that I had never thought would apply to my own life, or Mary's life, or our children's lives.

We rebuilt our palace of fond and foolish dreams on pillars of talk, counselling, and love, above all, a love Mary and I constantly, tortuously, tearfully affirmed and reaffirmed to our children and to one another. It has been a long, toilsome, painful reconstruction.

As far as we know, Fintan McStravick went once, in the first panic of being found out, to see a psychiatrist in Monaghan, and once to see the local priest.

His father never went to see anybody.

It was Maeve who determined us to take legal action.

It would be more than two years from the day in 1996 when we first informed the police until the case was actually heard. In this time we learned a lot about the Irish justice system, its caution, its checks and balances, and the number of people who, willy-nilly, come to know about a case as it wends its way from desk to desk, session to session, court to court, becoming more public all the time, in spite of being heard in camera. We knew, from the first appearance of a short paragraph in the *Northern Standard* about an Aghabog man having been charged with the sexual abuse of neighbour children, that everyone in Monaghan knew.

On the twenty-sixth of October 1998 Maeve came back from Scotland, where she was now studying, for what we had been told would be the trial itself the next day at the Central Criminal Court in Dublin. We went for dinner to Catriona Crowe's house in Nottingham Street with Colm Tóibín. As Maeve herself said, Colm and Catriona had known her and Eoin all their lives and had been like surrogate parents to them, named years earlier by Mary and me in our wills as their guardians should we die. Colm had been the first person we'd phoned on the night Eoin told us. Maeve's gangly, funny friend Laura Cotter from Monaghan, who had just returned from six months of travelling in India, was also there. All of us were tense and apprehensive.

Maeve began to talk about how little she knew about what

was happening. Why did nobody tell her things? We told her she knew as much as we did. We could not decide anything. It was the Director of Public Prosecutions versus Fintan McStravick. We were merely victims and witnesses who might be called to testify or might not. It was out of our hands.

Maeve became very emotional, indignant and righteous. Why were other people deciding how this case would be conducted? How could it even be conceivable that he might get off? What did they mean by dropping some of the charges without asking us? What right did they have?

After much argument, it was Catriona, always wise, who said that from now on Maeve and Eoin had to be completely in charge and know everything that was going on. They should make all the decisions. Nobody should address them through us.

After dinner, when we went back out into the cul-de-sac of Nottingham Street, we found that the back window of our car had been broken. The thieves had rifled through bits and pieces we had foolishly left there. A bag belonging to Laura had been stolen. Then Laura remembered that her constant bedtime companion, Genie, a pointy-faced stuffed animal, had been in her bag – her beloved Genie whom she had deliberately not taken to India with her for fear she might lose him – along with some money, her student card and other personal things. She didn't care about any of those. She only cared about Genie, whom she had had since she was a small girl.

We phoned the police. A squad car appeared within minutes. As we were describing to the two guards what had happened, what had been stolen, their faces lit up. Was there a small blue rucksack with girl's clothes in it? Someone had phoned them to say they had seen such a bag being tossed over a wall. They had gone to the place and climbed over the wall to retrieve it. Perhaps it was the one we were looking for.

From the boot of the squad car they took out the bag. It was Laura's. The purse with the money was gone, but Genie was there. Laura hugged Genie close to her, then threw her arms round the two young guards and kissed them effusively, and embraced the rest of us one by one, holding Genie's grubby face against our cheeks.

The next morning we met at the Four Courts, Maeve, Eoin, Laura, Colm, Mary and I. Under Gandon's airy rotunda it was like the set for a play directed by Tyrone Guthrie, with bewigged barristers standing about, tipstaffs clearing paths for judges, prisoners being marched in chained to uniformed guards, a sense of important business in the offing. Yet for all the bustle, and the grandeur of the building, there was withal an intimacy that seemed to say: in this place everything will be known and nothing will be kept secret any more.

The official from the State Solicitor's office and the prosecuting barrister talked to us about what was likely to happen. We made sure all their remarks were addressed to Maeve and Eoin.

Across the hall we could see Fintan McStravick talking with two men in gowns and wigs. Over the next hour or so the barristers and the solicitors went back and forth. He was willing to plead guilty to a shorter list of the sample charges, but not to indecent assault of Maeve, as it was called, which we had been told was rape by another name, since it had been listed as rape on the charge sheet up until this point. Would we agree to the dropping of that charge if he pleaded guilty to the rest?

The prosecuting barrister explained all the implications of this. McStravick was trying to get out of the indecent assault charge because it carried a penalty of up to four years. If we pressed for that charge to be put, he might contest it. The case would then have to go before a jury. The hearing was likely to be postponed again. We should think about it and let them know our thoughts. Once again they told us it was not we who would decide but the Director of Public Prosecutions. He would take our views into account, then act in whatever way he thought was necessary to get the best judgment possible.

The case was postponed that day. Maeve remained determined that the charge of indecent assault be pressed. Her rationale was simple: it was what he had done. When we communicated her insistence to the office of the Director of Public Prosecutions, they assured us that this charge would be included on the indictment.

On the eleventh of January 1999 we returned to the Four Courts. The case was on the list for that day, the first day of the legal term.

There were even more people milling about than the last time. We were told that juries were going to be sworn in for different trials that were beginning. An usher summoned everyone into Court No. 1, a couple of hundred or more, to learn if they would be called for jury duty. We had to push in from the back to see and hear what was going on.

The judge enjoined everyone in the crowded court that anything they heard there was not to be repeated outside. A few accuseds were called and had charges read out to them. Most of them pleaded guilty and were told their hearings would be scheduled at the court's convenience. One man pleaded not guilty to rape and a jury was appointed there and then.

Fintan McStravick was then summoned to the front of the

court. It was the first time we had seen him that morning. The charges were read out to him one by one.

As each one was read out he was asked how did he plead, guilty or not guilty.

He pleaded guilty, one by one, to all the charges.

Mary and I held hands as we stood beside Maeve and Eoin, astonished by the public nature of the arraignment and by hearing Maeve and Eoin's names and the name of Annaghmakerrig repeated all those times in front of this mob of potential jurors.

The case was postponed for a month for lack of a judge to hear it.

On the morning of the seventeenth of February we returned to the Four Courts and went to a small court upstairs for the hearing. The judge ordered anyone not directly connected with the case to leave the room. No one did, so there were guards, court reporters, including one we recognized from the *Northern Standard*, a stenographer, solicitors, barristers, and a few others whose function I could not determine, perhaps forty people in all. Fintan McStravick had his girlfriend with him. Neither of the McStravick parents had appeared at any of the court sessions we had attended.

The judge made it clear that he had read the book of evidence, including a statement that Fintan McStravick had given to a probation officer in which he had said that he had not done any of the things he was accused of. In a sarcastic tone of voice, the judge said there was too much of that kind of thing going on, completely innocent people being brought before the courts. The accused had pleaded guilty to all the charges. This was not a trial of the facts. It was a hearing about the effects his crimes had had on his victims.

The barrister acting for McStravick took Sergeant Denise

Flynn through her evidence – how she had taken the state-
ments, who had been present, what the accused had said. The
barrister tried to trip her up and catch her out. Denise, whose
steady professionalism we had come to trust and respect, stuck
to her policewoman's facts.

I was called next. The barrister struck a pose with one leg
up on the bench behind him, a hand holding one lapel of his
gown, his wig skew-whiff. He suggested that I had used these
incidents – or some such word, for he did not say abuse – as a
means of getting rid of the McStravicks from Annaghmakerrig.
I said I had not signed any of the documents to buy them out.
The contract had been signed in the name of the board of the
Tyrone Guthrie Centre (even though I well knew that I had
done all the dealing to strike the price, my face an adamantine
mask and my mind set to flint). He said I had tried to entrap
his client by making a recording of an interview with him (as
I had, at an early stage, using a private detective agency to set
it up). I told him I was not sorry for anything I had done to
defend and protect our children.

Maeve gave me a big squeeze of the hand as I went to sit
down again.

Her own evidence was matter-of-fact, determined, passion-
ate and articulate. She confirmed all that had happened. She
described the effects the abuse had had on her. She said that
she had come to the court to see justice done. She believed
Fintan McStravick deserved to go to jail. She said a large part
of her motivation was that he would not be able to do to other
children what he had done to her and Eoin.

When it came to his turn, Eoin, who had been at first
reluctant to begin the legal process, spoke in a clear, strong
voice. When he was asked why he had come to the court, he
said it was because he too wanted to see justice done.

Fintan McStravick's girlfriend was called. His barrister asked her leading questions. Even though she had been going out with Fintan McStravick for some years, he had not told her what he had done until one night, she said, when Maeve and Eoin had smashed a glass door at his house. The barrister did not ask her to explain further, but we knew that had been the night a year before when Maeve and Eoin had had the taxi they were taking home from Monaghan stop at the house where McStravick was living. Maeve had gone in through the back door and surprised him in bed. He had struggled into his trousers. Maeve had spoken her anger in one sweep of invective. She had said everything she had to say to him, she told us afterwards, and was not sorry for one word of it. Eoin had been outside the window, and then outside the glass door, unable to trust himself to go in, for many, many times he had said that he would have loved to kill Fintan McStravick, and he might well have done so that night, as he raged and kicked the wall, and then kicked the glass door and smashed it. Fintan McStravick had not told his girlfriend what he had done until she saw the broken glass and wanted to know why.

There was a break for lunch. As we came back up the stairs to the court Fintan McStravick was facing in towards the wall of the landing, leaning his head on his arm, sobbing the way he had when I'd confronted him, as if there were buried in him an ugly child that had never grown up.

In her summing-up the prosecuting barrister asked for the maximum sentence to be imposed because of the gravity of the crimes that had been committed.

The defending barrister stood up. I could see McStravick's solicitor, with whom I had had so many dealings about property over the years, slipping notes across the table to him.

The barrister talked again about how I had used these events, as he called them, as a pretext to clear the McStravicks out of Annaghmakerrig, and about all of the difficulties there had been over property. He said that Fintan McStravick had been given the impression that if his family left Annaghmakerrig there would be no more about it. It had taken years for the case to be brought. The incidents had happened a long time ago. He had moved away from Annaghmakerrig as soon as what he had done was discovered. He had been going steady with his girlfriend for three years. He was a hardworking young man who had built up his own business as a panel-beater. They were saving up to be married. He lived in a small community where the facts were already known. He had already suffered a lot. It would affect the rest of his life if he was sent to jail.

When the barrister sat down, the judge summed up. He said he was going to ignore a lot of the pleading of the accused's barrister. Those matters were not relevant. The facts were that the accused had done these things. He had pleaded guilty to the charges. They were very serious charges. He went over them all again, one by one, saying the names of the acts, stark and plain.

Fintan McStravick was given the maximum sentence of four years for indecent assault on a minor, and three years for all the other charges, to run consecutively.

As we went past him on our way out, where he was sobbing into his hands while prison guards stood by with handcuffs at the ready, Maeve leaned down and said,

— I hope you burn in hell.

On the tenth of December 1998, a month before the case came to hearing in the Central Criminal Court, the board of the Tyrone Guthrie Centre met in closed session, meaning without me. They had been doing a lot of that in recent years, as my relationship with them had deteriorated almost to vanishing point.

All the members of the original board and the first wave of their successors, with whom I had raised the more than £1 million of capital that had been used to buy out James McStravick and restore the estate, had resigned or been let go by the arts councils. Out of a turnover that was now more than £500,000 per annum, the arts councils contributed £160,000, and we, the staff, found the rest. There was also an accumulated deficit of £160,000 – more or less the amount that had been used to buy the property from McStravick. This debt never seemed to go down. In my zeal (which must have seemed hysterical to any outsider who did not know the whole story, as indeed it sometimes seemed even to Mary) to right all the wrongs, shrive my own sense of guilt over not having known what was happening to our children, and make the battlefield of Annaghmakerrig an earthly paradise once more, I spent every penny we got as soon as we got it on some improvement, project, scheme, or another, as well as on just keeping the flying saucer of creativity busy and full all year round.

Now I had spent £12,000 on a new fire-alarm system, without the board's explicit say-so under the new rules to which they were trying to get me to adhere, and it was going to be showdown time: no matter how hectic and driven I may have been, I could still read writing on walls as they whirled past me. I was summoned to meet the chairman, Seamus Hunt, an accountant from Belfast, in the library. As soon as I came through the door and heard his peremptory, head-masterly 'Sit down there', I said I wanted Mary to hear whatever it was he had to say.

Mary came back in with me. The screed Hunt had scribbled to say that they had no further confidence in me and that I was to leave my post and the premises of the Tyrone Guthrie Centre by the thirty-first of January 1999, which all of the board had signed, was read out to us.

As soon as we had heard the diktat, Mary said, with tears starting to her eyes,

— I just wish we had never come here.

We said we would go off for a walk and would have an answer for them when we got back.

We went down through the kitchen, where Our Girls were preparing lunch; out through the back entry and past the shell of the McStravicks' house – the Steward's House, as I had insisted it would be called henceforward – which had remained empty, smelly and haunted since they had left; past our own house, the Resident Directors' House (with plural apostrophe, please note), which we had so much loved, in which we had loved so much; up through the farmyard, Baltic-bright with fresh woodstain on the doors and windows of the houses and studios we had made out of James McStravick's Augean stables; and out on to the northern avenue, whose arrival vista I had contrived so that the lake, lawns, gardens and Big House appeared like Shangri-La at the end of an arboretum where once there had been only rampant rhododendron.

Mary and I stood there, on the same spot from which we had seen Annaghmakerrig for the first time almost twenty years before, and talked.

We made our decision as we walked back towards the house. We had had enough of the curse o' God things that had happened, the curse o' God arts councils, and now the curse o' God board.

It was time to reach down our rucksacks.

Leaving Annaghmakerrig was hard. Very hard.

Eoin came home from Belfast to help us pack and to be there for the farewell party we gave for our friends from Monaghan and elsewhere, including the Mexican ambassador, *nuestro buen amigo* Daniel Dultzín, whose cook, Maria Purificación de los Santos, he had sent up from Dublin to prepare the funeral meats for this *noche de los muertos*.

Eoin told us that friends of his and friends of ours, like Monica Frawley, theatre designer, shape-shifter, tower of fun, dear, dear friend and comely counsellor, had said to him that he should try to support us in this time of change in our lives, and so he said he would like to come with us, as we had not dared to hope he might.

The three of us left, our Okies' car packed to the gunwales, on the evening of the seventh of March 1999, just after dusk. Our beloved Molly the dog, whom Eoin had always called Maeileog, reigning Queen of Animalkerrig, looked at us one last time, as if she knew it was the last time. She did not make to climb into the back of the car as we had spoiled her to do. We thought then we were only leaving her for a few weeks until her vaccinations had taken and she could get a visa on her doggy passport, but in fact she would be adopted by an Italian writer, Gogo della Luna, who kept her for a while in Guthrie's study in the Big House, and then took her home to her shoebox of a flat in Dublin, which Molly fills to over-flowing with the special love strays bring to those who rescue them.

As we drove off, from the corner of the lawn Yvonne Cullen played the slow movement of a Bach suite on her cello, while the other artists-then-in-residence stood in the dark with candles burning in their hands. The tears we shed would be the last we would ever cry at Annaghmakerrig.

After visiting our families in Belfast, we took the night crossing from Belfast to Liverpool and drove through England to catch the high-sided Brittany Ferries boat from Plymouth to Santander. As we sailed through the Bay of Biscay, dolphins schooled around its prow like harbingers of oceanic freedoms.

Driving across northern Spain we bought a *Best of Dire*

Straits tape and one called *Sombras de la China* by Joan Manuel Serrat off a whirligig in a petrol station. We played them loud as we motored through the semi-desert of Aragon into our adopted, nearly native, fruitful province of Lleida, and then into the Pyrenees by the familiar route along the valley of the Noguera Pallaresa through Tremp, La Pobla de Segur, Sort and Llavorsí, and finally to Farrera.

III

From the Wreckage

O Earth O Earth return!
Arise from out the dewy grass;
Night is worn,
And the morn
Rises from the slumberous mass.

Turn away no more:
Why wilt thou turn away?
The starry floor
The wat'ry shore
Is giv'n thee till the break of day.

William Blake,
Songs of Experience, 'Introduction'

No Mercy

So, you see, we have returned to Farrera not just to rebuild a house but to rebuild our lives.

In our first week back in Spain we paid off a mortgage on Casa Felip (the same Casa Felip we had rented twenty-five years before and then bought in 1989) with Solbank in Barcelona. This mortgage had been drinking our life's blood for years. We had taken it out in the depths of the Spanish economic recession of the late 1980s, when we were entering our forties. It was our first ever mortgage. It was at an interest rate of 18 per cent for the first couple of years, and then 14 per cent. After some renegotiation it was down to 11 per cent, but by that time we had missed so many payments that I endeavoured not to have to walk past the sunless Solbank on Casp Street when I was in Barcelona. I tried not to think about it too much in Ireland, either, until I would get phone calls from a woman called Mercedes dunning me to pay the missed instalments. She must have been employed for her grating voice – the Rasp from Casp. Rather than the Catalan I knew she spoke, into which I was always trying to lure her, she would insist on talking to me in a Castilian that was raw and smarting as sun through smog, grating and tetchy-making, and none of yer oul' Irish *plomás* now, which sometimes works on the Catalans, but not on the Castilians, who have still enough memory of empires won and empires lost to show no quarter to Irish *índios* withholding the gold. The greatest relief of having paid off what we still owed, which was more or less the same amount it had always been, is never having to hear Mercedes's merciless voice again.

Almost as soon as we had put a stake through the heart of the Solbank mortgage, we had to start looking for another one. We had some money of our own from the threads of the flakily gilded parachute with which we had jumped from the burning zeppelin of our previous lives, but we knew it would not be nearly enough to renovate Casa Felip for ourselves, let alone to convert the barn into another couple of houses that we planned to rent out to artists and all-comers. This would be a source of income, and maybe a pension scheme too, for we had cashed in our pensions when we left Annaghmakerrig and were now living on them.

We needed to get plans drawn up by an architect so that we could secure a building permit from the municipality of Farrera. Without such a permit we could not even apply for a mortgage.

An architect called Joan Albert Adell was doing plans for another building in the village. Doctor Adell is an expert on Romanesque architecture. He has done restorations all over Catalonia, which is as scattered with Romanesque ruins as Rome is with Roman ones. We asked him to do our job too, since Casa Felip, while not Romanesque, was certainly a ruin. Half of the barn roof had collapsed two years before with a loud crash like an explosion, according to my brother Michael, who had heard it go. What remained was a cadaver dessicated in the Spanish sun to bones of stone and mud walls under a punctured skin of wormy wood and mossy slates.

We told Adell we wanted to have the old house made over as our own home. The two houses in the barn would have their own separate entrances. We gave him the scale drawings done by an Irish architect friend ten years before in the first flush of our optimism about fixing the place up. This optimism had somehow survived the many summer visits we had made to Casa Felip, with Mary fashioning paper shades for bulbs and applying the odd lick of paint to cheer herself and the rest of us up, and me cleaning the pig shit, cow shit, dog shit and rat shit from the barn, in hopes that one day we would have more than just the price of the fare to get there.

Six weeks later Adell brought us four copies of the plans and a specification as thick as a PhD thesis, each set handsomely presented in a yellow folder with red ribbons at the corners. The house itself would be simply restored, keeping all the existing openings, enlarging a few of them and adding two new windows to give light at the back. He had slated for demolition and removal the jerrybuilt cabin where the *carabiner* and his family had once lived, where we had lived ourselves, where many of our friends had also lived. The house's roof could be patched and repaired, then made wind-proof and waterproof by spraying insulating foam on the underside. He wanted to leave the ground floor of the barn as it was. On its upper floors he had divided the spaces as we had asked, with big south-facing windows where now there were only holes half-filled with stone.

All this, he calculated, could be done for 15,365,000 pesetas (€92,000) – his fees, taxes, builder's profit, everything included. Even then I wondered if he had maybe spent too much time in the Middle Ages.

I brought a set of the plans to sweet Roser Bardina, the municipal secretary, in her office in the old schoolhouse of Burg, beside where Joe had jiggled his juggernaut. She put our project down for approval at the next plenary meeting of the *ajuntament*. No one looked at it, we were told afterwards, and it was approved without demur. We paid a 1.5 per cent municipal tax on the declared cost of the works and got an official receipt with the Ajuntament de Farrera rubber stamp: an oval medallion of a spotted-coated, bearded, jauntily hatted, dogsnout-faced man with a staff over his shoulder and a gourd dangling from the end of it, who looked like an ancestor of all us erstwhile hippies. Roser told me this was Saint Roch, patron of the Farrera church.

In Sort, the capital of the Pallars Sobirà, I went to the land registry on the dark ground floor of a block of flats, through a door between a notary's and a hairdresser's. The open-plan office within was presided over by the formidable-looking registrar sitting at a slanted desk on a platform that raised her a couple of feet above the rest of the women there. This had to be the Maria Propasseït whose signature I had seen on papers pinned up on the village noticeboard declaring properties known from time immemorial to belong to this one or that one to be now truly theirs unless an objection was lodged to her office within three months.

A petite girl took my particulars. She brought the register, a folio-sized book she strained to heave up on to the counter. She opened it and showed me where our mortgage with the vampire Solbank had been inscribed, now overscored with thick red biro lines of cancellation that were like ligatures tying it down lest it escape and start sucking our blood again.

The entry showed the house was unencumbered by any other mortgage or lien. The girl made me a copy of it and had it signed by the registrar, who looked over and gave me a distant, dignified, Dickensian nod before she did so.

Armed with this documentation, Mary and I went to see the manager of La Caixa in Llavorsí. We told him we had attended the classical music concerts he used to organize in the Romanesque abbey church of Santa Maria in his hometown of Gerri de la Sal. The concerts had been a lot of work for one man, he said. Now that he was the manager here he was too busy to think of starting them again. There was nobody in the office. His only colleague had just gone out for breakfast. Maybe this was the quiet time: eleven o'clock in the morning. I could hear the big clock on the wall ticking.

He said he was sure La Caixa would look at our proposal with interest. However as a *caixa*, a savings bank – its full name being La Caixa de Pensions i Estalvis, The Strongbox of Pensions and Savings – the interest rate would be a point or two higher than with an ordinary bank, for reasons to do with the peculiar legislation under which a *caixa* operates in Catalonia, the special trust it enjoys and the social and cultural work it does, as far as I could understand.

We also made a tour of the seven banks and *caixes* in Sort. They were all offering more or less the same rate, somewhere around the 5 per cent mark, or a bit more if we wanted a fixed-interest mortgage. We thought this might be the best kind of dead wage for us, at our age, if the rates started to rise again from the historical rock bottom where they now were.

After looking over the leaflets given to us by the various managers, who had all been polite, if circumspect, we plumped for the Banca Catalana as the one which seemed to be offering marginally the best deal. We also thought its Catalan dullness and discipline would be good for us.

Early one morning we went to Sort to open an account there. We had to fill out four different forms in quadruplicate and show our passports. The manager, who had been cautious and costive on our previous visit, looked ropey and unsteady this morning, as if he had not slept too well.

We told him we wanted a mortgage from his bank. We gave him a set of Adell's plans, a page on which I had written out our likely incomes for the foreseeable future, the business plan I had cobbled up, a list of our assets, including a cottage we owned near Annaghmakerrig, a copy of the building permit with dog-faced Saint Roch's seal, and the certificate of unencumberedness from Senyora Propasseït.

We asked him to set the application process in train.

— *Caldrà estudiar-ho,* he said.

It will have to be studied.

As he said it, a nervous tic pursed his mouth like the neck of a drawstring moneybag puckering shut.

He said the project would have to be assessed by a firm of architects which specialized in doing valuations. We would have to pay the cost of this, about 50,000 pesetas (€300), whether the application was successful or not.

I was so sure it would be successful this seemed merely a detail.

About a week later Eva Petrarch, the assessor for the Banca Catalana, came from Barcelona. Her name seemed a good omen for a place which might one day house artists. With a Sony digital camera she took a few snaps of the parlous house and the ruinous barn. She had other jobs to see. She did not dally.

Two weeks after that we got a report from La Petrarch which valued the property at 49 million pesetas (€294,495) once the renovations were completed. If we got 80 per cent of that, 39 million pesetas (€234,294), we would be away on a hack.

The manager said he would now send away the project and proposal, with Senyoreta Petrarch's valuation, to the committee in head office which would decide.

For six weeks I had the Banca Catalana tower on Diagonal in Barcelona constantly before my mind, from all the times I had seen it on my way into the city, its twenty storeys with cascading plants a vertical botanic garden, as somewhere up there the sober-suited Catalan bankers looked over the documentation I had so carefully prepared: saying, well, maybe their prospects are a bit precarious, they don't seem to have much in the way of assured income, but look at all they have done, all the money they raised for that place they used to run in Ireland, the business plan they have prepared, and see how well Senyor Loughlin writes Catalan, all the accents, grave, acute, cedilla and umlaut, in the right places (over which I had laboured for days); sure we'll take a punt on them, it's only 39 million pesetas.

Then one day Mary, blanched with shock as if she had just witnessed a fatal accident, told me the manager had phoned. They were not going to give us a mortgage. We would not have the income to pay the monthly quotas. We were nearly in our fifties. It would be over too many years. The property in Ireland was as if it were on the moon as far as security was concerned.

As I listened to Mary, I felt my own colour drain away and a shiver run through me: as chilled by this rebuff as if I had dived naked into an ice-blue tarn at the foot of a glacier and swum out so far I might not be able to get back before my balls froze off and my heart gave out.

An Amphitheatre

I began to write a memoir: a messy autopsy I performed upon myself with a blunt scalpel and little skill, trying to find the tumour that had made me blind to what was happening to our children. Therapy, I suppose you could call it, though I did not think of it like that. I thought of it as writing the book I had always thought I might write one day, even if I had never imagined it would be this book. It made me nauseous

some days just to think about it. I kept writing it anyway, like
an alcoholic drinking his way through the Antabuse.

We were renting a house called John's Haggard – 'haggard'
being Monaghan for 'rick yard' or 'hay yard' – while we
limbered up to tackle our own. I mulled over my life upstairs,
at a cherrywood-veneered desk I had bought in Andorra and
set up in front of the big windows that overlook the valley,
while Mary worked at a correspondence course in interior
design in the kitchen below me, from which I could hear every
smallest sound through the wooden floor. As she measured and
drew, absorbed in the acquisition of technique to complement
the talent for judging colour, texture and form she has always
had, finding her way to being a designer as I was groping
towards being a writer, I found the regular slap of her metal
slide-ruler on the boards of the long deal table we had brought
down from the *menjador* of Casa Felip oddly comforting: every
slap the ring of a steel-tipped pilgrim's staff on the iron stones
of the hard road it had become our lot to travel.

She and I would have lunch together then, laved in the
spring sunlight that poured through the tall windows of the
kitchen, and talk, all the time in the world on our hands,
semi-retired (*mig jubilats*, in Catalan, half-jubilated) as we
were, in this haven where the phone did not ring and the
postman brought only friendly letters.

In the afternoons, determined to have a garden even if it
looked as if it would be a while before we had a house, I
would go up to work in the long coffin-shaped wedge of
ground under the south-facing cliff behind Casa Felip. This
garden surveys Farrera across the slatescape of the house's roof.
From there the village was a play in the near-vertical, an
everyday drama of exits and entrances whose characters and
sound effects I was learning all over again: human voices I

recognized and could put names to; the barks of dogs, bleats of sheep, moos of cows, whinnies of horses; the engines of jeeps, cars and tractors passing through the main street; the roar of a chainsaw in the wood where Tony Dumphy and I had cut our winter fuel a quarter of a century before with a bowsaw; the plaintive threnody of a nightingale in the wood-land at the garden's end; the leaf-rustle of a lizard darting for cover; and inaudible, conjectured mole song, for there were signs of them everywhere in the garden (how do they get up this high and how do you get rid of them?) – all amplified by the resonant acoustics of the amphitheatre of the valley.

On one of those spring days I weeded and readied the garden for turning over with the municipal rotavator Cisco Solé was to bring up to me in the evening, once he had oiled and greased and tightened it after its long hibernation on the ground floor of l'Estudi, the one-time village school, and then used it on his own plot.

Cisco is burly, Tolstoy-bearded, bald down to his earlobes. When he is in Farrera he usually wears blue dungarees, and is shod in summer with *espardenyes*, the natty, rope-soled sandals that are tied at the ankles like ballet pumps, or felt-sided, rubber-soled Chirrucas, the work shoes whose trade name has been genericized among the country people to simply mean 'the shoes we always buy'. He is always carrying a tool or a bunch of tools when you meet him: a scythe and gloves, a basket with secateurs and trowel crossed in the bottom of it, or the complete armoury of axe, pruning saw, digging fork and mattock with which he goes to garden, as to war.

He works for a living at a washing-machine factory in Barcelona and lives in Sant Feliu de Llobregat in its western suburbs. He often drives the three hours it now takes from there – for in the last twenty-five years the roads have improved out of all recognition – late on Friday evening. He spends all day Saturday and Sunday at whichever is the most pressing of his myriad works on the House of the Barracks that he and his wife, Lala Ricarda from the Dominican Republic, bought fifteen years ago from the Bigarrets, who own the big house beside it. He leaves again late on Sunday night or in the early hours of Monday to be at his post on the production line for the morning shift.

From afar, as occasional revenants from Ireland, and now from near, we have watched Cisco's renovations of the House of the Barracks as they have unfolded phase by phase, slowly, meticulously, and often marvellously: a roof of hand-quarried local slate it took him a summer of weekends and all his holidays to lay; a set of polished wooden steps built into an interior wall we count out like a decade of the rosary as they are finished one by one, with only three to go now to reach the hole in the ceiling; a fireplace he took a year to research, studying, measuring and discussing every old fireplace in the village, then another year to build. When he is here with Lala, who is a tropical treasure island in our mountainy sea, they camp out in the temporary builder's yard the House of the Barracks has become; sleeping under mosquito nets among stacks of flooring, piles of doors, leans of windows, and a cement-mixer that stands in the middle of the room like an outsize family pet waiting to be taken for a walk. Yet they manage to make the House of the Barracks – where the un-married *carabiners* were once quartered – one of the warmest and most hospitable houses in this most hospitable of villages, with its pot-bellied stove, conversational sofa, cornucopian sideboard, cellar-larder provisioned as for a siege, and a table for ten that takes pride of place in front of the red and white curtain that shrouds their sleeping place.

Cisco is from the fruit- and cereal-growing plains of La Segarra. In a terraced field near the Farrera river he has planted

an orchard where he grafts varieties from his frost-free homeland on to the local stock of apples, pears, cherries, quinces,
in search of a balance between fruitfulness and resistance to
cold and disease. One year in three late frosts kill the fruit
blossom. Cisco is nothing if not dogged.

After lunch, when I go to l'Estudi to see how the rotavator
works, Cisco shows me how to yank the motor into life with
the starter cord. I follow him as he steers it phuttering on its
two high wheels along the main street, a lunar exploration
vehicle sniffing for rocks and Cisco a baldy spaceman in blue
trews. Marsal hears us coming down the hill beside his house
and comes blinking out of the cellar where he has been having
his siesta on an old sofa among sprouting spuds and hanks of
last year's garlic. He smiles at us, for Marsal loves to see work
being done, and can't understand, if there are so many people
unemployed, why they are not up here digging gardens,
herding cows, building barns and clearing the forest back from
the fields. I stop to talk to him. We discuss the work a rotavator
can do in a day, not like the old days, he tells me, when they
dug their gardens by hand or ploughed them with mule or
horse or ox. In some years, his family alone produced as many
as 5,000 kilos of potatoes for themselves, to feed their pigs and
for sale.

Still trying to imagine what 5,000 kilos of spuds would look
like in a pile, I catch up with Cisco on the Path of the Mother
of God of the Ridge. I help him to lift the rotavator down the
long flight of stone steps into his garden. He shows me how
to take off the wheels and put on the digging spindle. From
the top of the steps, as I am leaving, I watch as he begins to
work it, a mechanical wild pig held by its hind legs, snuffling
and grubbing through the deep, dark soil Cisco and Lala have
made there over years of digging and dunging.

Late that evening Cisco brings the rotavator up to me in

the garden of Casa Felip. Black storm clouds are gathering above the mountains to the south-west so I wrap it in a sheet of plastic. I have never used a rotavator before. I think I may be a little afraid of it.

For days after the storm ceases I postpone starting up the rotavator, which peers out reproachfully at me from under its plastic cover. The wind that blows from the east has a raw edge to it. The dust it carries makes my eyes stream. I tell myself it's not really spring yet anyway. Day by day, though, the snow is melting off the high mountains to the west, leaving streaks of dirty white running down the giants' cheeks (you *can* see profiles of recumbent giants there in certain lights, if you let yourself), as if they have been crying icy tears. Still cold as it is, with heavy frosts at night, I imagine I can feel the effort it is for the trees at this altitude to put on leaves. As yet only the precocious wild cherries erupt in plumes of white flower out of the black and brown bruisings of the winter-blasted landscape.

To avoid the rotavator's accusing eye, I go for a walk up into the Burg valley. On the hillside above Burg I mistake a whinchat for a red-backed shrike. In the old days on these stony slopes we had often seen these latter hooked-beaked hunters perched on bushes from which they would swoop on the small birds and big insects they spike on thorns as larders for later. I see it's not a shrike when the whinchat takes off, its flight undulating its mockery of my error. A few minutes later I spot a lammergeier with its unmistakable orange-yellow belly and boxplane shape rising above Farrera. It is called *quebrantahuesos* in Castilian, *trencalòs* in Catalan, bone-smasher in both languages, from its habit of dropping bones on to rocks to crack out the rich marrow on which it lives. Through my binoculars I see the black wattle hanging over its beak – by virtue of which it is also called bearded vulture in English

– as it soars back and forth a few times to gain height, then glides, with hardly a flap, its arrow-flight-shaped tail twitching back and forth to control its gyrings, until it is just a speck against the pine forest.

Twenty-five years ago there were no lammergeiers left here. Now they are making a comeback. Just like us.

Coming down through Burg I see the people there have their gardens ready, for almost every garden in Burg is still used. The walled plots have broad beans well up and staked, cabbage and lettuce plants in, garlic planted from the autumn of last year, overwintered chard in bushy clumps, tall cabbages plucked to a punk shock of leaves: all to make a pussyfooting paddy green with envy.

Thus shamed and inspired, the next morning I get the rotavator going. It bucks and wallows and gets stuck in a hole of its own digging, then frees itself again as I adjust gear settings with one hand and steer it with the other, heaving it back and forth to stop it burying itself. I push in barrowloads of sheepdung I have brought with the dumper from one of Oppen's piles and scatter it all over the surface. As I dig it in with the rotavator particles of dry, dusty sheepshit fly in a cloud around me, getting in my mouth, all over my sweaty face, into my hair and down my boots. I wonder if it wouldn't be easier and cleaner just to dig with a spade or a fork, in the old-fashioned way, like Marsal, who remains happily unmechanized in all respects.

But by late evening, when I have raked the soil over, there is a fine tilth throughout, just like they have in the gardens of Babylonian Burg, whose ancestral example I am proud to follow.

First Homes and Second Homes

As we contemplate how we will renovate Casa Felip, I look with a keener eye at the other buildings in the village, most of them relatively unchanged from how I remember them always to have been, bar some cracks, bursts and leaks, the odd capsizing and a few sinkings.

Of the forty-four named houses there were in Farrera in the early 1900s only twenty or so are now extant, among barns and byres and an ambiguity of ruins. Many of the existing edifices are rebuildings of earlier structures. Some of them have stones set into them with the dates of their construction or reconstruction, usually in the first decade of the twentieth century: 1907, 1903, 1905. A few have earlier ones: 1832 on Casa Coté, 1780 on Casa Victória, and 1611 on the only remaining original wall of John's Haggard. On Casa Joan, the House of John, the house of the haggard of the same name, there is a stone from the rectory that was demolished, along with other buildings, to make the main street − after a couple of bombs in the Civil War helped to clear the way. This stone has Monsegnor Pesaci Ramó 1632 carved on it, the name of the priest at the time, above a Maltese cross and, underneath it, a square divided into four boxes incised with the papal keys and Masonic-looking stars and ladders; the whole looking like a small boat in full rig of sail. On the southern wall of the church of Saint Roch, the one that runs along the main street, there is a stone that states, simply, S. Roch ✝ 1629. Farrera is listed as a parish in the document commemorating the consecration of the cathedral in La Seu d'Urgell in 869, which is about as old as it gets round here.

By the beginning of the twentieth century, Farrera had

reached its point of maximum expansion. Every potential house, barn and garden site was owned and named. Some of the houses were no more than cabins squeezed between other houses.

The few hundred people living in Farrera then worked the land right up the valley sides, taking advantage of every declivity to trap earth behind walls made from rocks cleared from the fields, creating the patchworks of interlocking plots that can be seen in the black-and-white aerial survey photographs of the 1950s that are kept in the municipal archives. In its own valley, which almost all Farrera's buildings overlook, the resurgent forest is absorbing these fields that once peeled the mountainside to soil and rock, as if the forest had never really left but had hovered over the humanized landscape as a ghost waiting to take arboreal flesh again. The larger meadows that remain, the ones that can be worked with machinery, are fringed by hedges, copses and collapsed stone walls that blur boundaries which would once have been defended 'with blue cast-steel'; a tired old land war that the renascent forest is now winning, hands down.

As we would discover once the novelty of our return had worn off and we became part of the human drama – a soap opera is called a *culebrón* in Spanish, meaning a snakelike story that unfolds episode by episode – Farrera is a living community that continues to evolve, with some seven or eight houses lived in all the year round: enough to supply a full and varied cast of characters for all the twists and turns of its serpentine plot.

Alex Crombie lives in Casa Martina on El Castell, the Upper Farrera where Richard Betts had set up his ill-fated beehives. Alex is willowy in an Anglo-Saxon sort of way, and brash and sure of herself in what an Irish person can't help thinking is a very English way. She has tried a bit of everything in Farrera, and is as tenacious as it takes to have lived here for nearly twenty years. She had two children, Kedu and Marina, called Mimi, by her first man, Robin Lee. He died when he was in his thirties. She has three other children by her second man, Enric: twins called Tina and Poma, who are lanky, like their mother, and of recent years have blossomed into coltish mannequins, and the elfin, curly-blond-haired Merlin, a little sorcerer of charm and politeness. Kedu grew up in his own make-believe world when for many years he was the only child in the village, peeping round corners at us when we were there on our holidays, building himself huts in the woods, sleeping sometimes in his tree house where he dreamed his savage dreams of being a sky pilot. He now works as a roofer and recently got married to a conventional Catalan girl very unlike his mother. Mimi, who was always knowledgeable about insects, animals, flowers and plants, is doing a degree in agriculture in Barcelona between bouts of living on Ibiza. For the last few years the twins and Merlin have been living with their father in El Maresme (The Marsh), north of Barcelona, at sea level, whence Enric travels all over Catalonia as a blacksmith in a big van with a forge in the back of it, shoeing horses, doing ironwork and growing muscles like internalized Pyrenees.

In a ruined haggard beside her house Alex keeps Samoyed dogs for breeding and occasional sale, along with a sentry-go of mutts and mastiffs which guard El Castell like canine crusaders.

To the left of her house is the squat, one-storey, glass-fronted, cross-eyed, lopsided shack the German carpenter Udo Klipell built, and then sold to other Germans called Eni and Ingo. They lived there for ten years with their son, Paul. Shortly after Udo sold them the bunker he built a three-storey red-brick house beside it, which overshadows it most of the day. Here he and his wife, Pili Sarroca, lived with their daughter Sita. Now Pili and Udo are getting separated and are arguing about who gets to keep the monstrosity: the house, not the child, who is a dear. Subsequently Eni left Ingo and moved in with Udo at the Mill Forge in the valley below Tírvia, where he has his workshop. There is also a man called Edu, an ex of Alex's, who lives off and on in a white snail of a caravan which skulks shyly in the corner of a field at the entrance to the village. In the same field, but more prominently placed, and altogether more outgoing, is La Caravana, a wooden wagon sitting up on blocks off its wheels, with a yellow tarpaulin neatly pinned and tucked round its roof. It was brought here years ago by German hippies who arrived in a cavalcade of vans, lorries and buses, stayed for months, then departed, like a fairground upping sticks, taking their hamburger stall and day-long dopers' PA system with them. They left the chrysalis of La Caravana to pupate into a crashpad for the youth of the village, their friends, friends of their friends, and friends of the friends of their friends, much as Casa Maria had been for us in our day.

Claudi Cortés and Tere Segura, who lived for four years in Casa Felip after we left the first time, now own Casa Llucio at the western end of El Castell. Originally a dwelling house with barns and stores, it is a cliff-hugging, medieval-looking terrace of stone and half-timbering. Claudi and Tere ran a restaurant in the walled Roman town of Guissona in their native province of La Segarra for roughly the same twenty years that we were running Annaghmakerrig. They are our best friends here, partly on account of the parallel trajectories of our lives, but also because of the instinctive sympathy they have always shown for the trouble that befell us; their lives have not always been easy either. Mary thinks Claudi is a steadying influence on me, while, conversely, I like the effect Tere has on her. Tere has a girlish, generous, infectious laugh, and loves to discuss all the mysteries, joyful, sorrowful, glorious and luminous, of Farrera's *culebrón*, in which, of course, we all take the most intense interest, hating to miss an instalment.

When Claudi and Tere lived in Casa Felip, where we visited them a couple of times, they had the *carabiner*'s cabin so warm and welcoming that in winter it was known as Casa Felip Tropical. They used the old black range in the corner to boil vats of jams, juices and jellies from fruit they collected from hedgerows and abandoned orchards. They stored the pots of conserves in a rock-walled larder downstairs, where the ancestors (in the sense of all those who had lived there before us) had kept their grain in big wooden bins and hung their cured meat from hooks under a wooden canopy out of reach of the rats and dogs and cats. Claudi and Tere did the same with the sausages and hams they made from the pigs they kept, which Claudi butchered, butchering having been his first trade. Now that they are back in Farrera, living in their own house, they are recapitulating some of this self-sufficiency. Last September Claudi killed and dressed one of Oppen's lambs when it was fat and succulent from the summer grazing. In the autumn they collect mushrooms that they dry, preserve in vinegar or make into pâtés. They have one of the rooms of the unrenovated part of Casa Llucio stacked with shelves of produce they have made, like a stand at a country fair. They are both of them canny and saving, recyclers to the manner born. They are proud of their principled, vegetarian children: Acarona, who has come to live with them in Farrera while cogitating her future, and Joel, who lives in a squat in Barcelona. He sustains himself with out-of-date food he collects from shops and restaurants. He went to be a squatter when he was sixteen with 10,000 pesetas (€60) in his pocket. That was three years ago. He has not asked his parents for any money since.

Jordi Viñas, he of the little boxes, and his companion, Carme Albert, now own Casa Marquet, just down the main street from the square under the belfry of the church. It was renovated twenty years ago by Alex's first man, Robin Lee. Robin was good with his hands, could do anything in fact, bricklaying, carpentry, plumbing, electrics, stonework; he could also handle horses, farm and garden, even managing to grow melons one year, a small miracle at this altitude. Jordi and Carme, though, have never lived in Casa Marquet. They prefer to live in the apartment that goes with Jordi's job as town clerk in Llavorsí (he having shed his hippie garb but not his hippie ideals, for he is associated with every ecological and environmental lobby in the region), where there are all the amenities of a rubber-river-rafting boomtown: two bars, four hotels, a supermarket, bakery, medical centre, newsagent, school, kindergarten, swimming pool.

Jordi and I came up with the idea of El Centre d'Art i Natura de Farrera (for the name would take a while to come and there were no buildings in the beginning) during a long discussion in August 1989. I am nearly certain it was the night I was bickering with Mary in Carles Carbó's room in Casa Maria and the scops owl landed on the clothesline and looked at me with its soothsayer eyes. I was all for coming back to live in Farrera if the idea grew wings. Mary was not so sure.

In order to promote the notional centre, we met the Minister for Culture of the Catalan government, Joan Guitart (aka, Jordi said, Johnny Guitar), who was sympathetic and encouraging, and a host of other local, provincial, regional, national and international entities and nonentities. As we travelled the hundreds of kilometres in Jordi's car we talked about what might be done to rescue Farrera from the depopulation and despair into which it was falling fast, for at that nadir there were only Oppen and his companion Anna Salvat, Alex and her kids, Marsal and Conchita, as the *quatre gats* – four cats, Catalan for nearly nobody – living there all the year round.

On one of those journeys Jordi told me about the co-operative that had been formed in the mid 1980s, the last attempt there had been to create the much mooted commune. Four or five couples pooled their capital to buy or rent what land they could, add more sheep to Oppen's herd, have a few cows, work gardens together, and purchase machinery with which to make hay while the sun shone. Some were sleeping partners who only put in money, a few were working partners who laboured on the land, and others were a bit of both. The cooperative lasted only a couple of years. Jordi is always careful and tactful in his speech, but he could not gainsay that the cooperative's overheating and the subsequent conflagration of friendships had been acrimonious, leaving a pall of disappointment whose dark shadow we would sometimes feel passing over our own proselytizings.

El Centre d'Art i Natura – as Jordi and I eventually christened it with an eye to the main funding chance – is based in l'Estudi, the school that succeeded the school that is now Marsal's chicken coop, and in Casa Ramón beside it, both in the shadow and lee of the back wall of the church, overlooking the main square. Its directors, Lluís Llobet and Cesca Gelavert, feed their guests in Casa Vinovis above it, the three-storey house they built themselves on the walls of the low, dark cabin in which the village schoolteacher had once lived without benefit of sun at any time of the year. I am glad to say, in case you are wondering, that I have nothing whatsoever to do with the day-to-day running of the centre, being merely, with Jordi and other worthies, a member of its board. Mary and I enjoy meeting the artists and naturalists who stay at El Centre, attending their exhibitions, hearing their music as we pass by, meeting some of them as old friends – and equally enjoy not being responsible for them. We're on sabbatical from all that until we start hosting our own protégés at El Refugi Irlandès – which is what we shall call the houses in our barn, if we ever have houses in the barn.

Overlooking the middle section of the village, at the head of a flight of stone steps up from the main street, sit the two square-fronted blocks of Casa Maria, mother-house to so many of us. Carles Carbó, looking now like Jesus might have if he had lived into his forties, recently sold the house half of Casa Maria to Oppen and Anna, keeping the barn to make a house for himself one day. Now Casa Maria is having another childhood, filled with Anna and Oppen's son Roger's toys, a Wendy house in the corner, videos of the Teletubbies in Spanish stacked beside the TV, and mobiles twisting and turning in the wind from the balcony door every time the sheepdogs blunder in or out, as they do dozens of times a day.

Oppen and Anna now have more than 200 sheep. In the winter they keep them in the stalls on the ground floor of Casa Maria and in a bigger byre close by. In the barn which will one day be Carles's house, where Oppen once kept rabbits, they breed odd Catalan sheepdogs and even odder border collies. All the collies have a louche ancestral look to them, a cock-eyed, crook-necked stare that takes all moving objects in the world, including humans, for bold sheep needing watching, at least, if not a little chivvying too, and a snap at the heels now and then, just to show who's boss. The long-haired Catalan sheepdogs are so matted and dusty it is hard sometimes to tell their fronts from their backs. All the dogs spend the day lying in strict hierarchy on the wooden steps up to the front door, which is on the first floor. The pack howls when another dog passes. Every house in the village has at least one dog. Some houses have two or three. Alex has at least a dozen. That makes for a lot of barking.

Many times a day, Anna, who is patient and forbearing, never known to say a bad word about or to anybody, goes out on to the balcony of Casa Maria to shout at the dogs. She remonstrates with them in long sentences that appeal to their better natures and threaten terrible punishments. The dogs bark back. Another dog passes. All the dogs set to yammering, yowling and yapping once again.

For nearly twenty years Barbara Taanmann has lived in Tressó, beyond the Pass of Sound, but within the municipal jurisdiction of Farrera, which extends over square miles of mountain to the east to meet those of the villages of Civis, Ars and Asnurri, on the border with Andorra. She therefore counts as a Farreran for the purposes of this informal census.

The village of barns at Tressó was built by Farrera families who brought their herds up there in summer transhumance. Barbara rents a couple of these bothies, part of her philosophy being, she says, not to own property. She has four children by two different fathers. Neither of the fathers now lives there.

Barbara is smallish, lank-haired, taut-muscled. In her youth she was a pole-vault champion and competed in an Olympic Games. You feel her energy as a small, close sun when you meet her: five feet four inches of impatient, sub-atomic whirling and colliding. She is a tireless talker, her Catalan rife with local idioms she has learned from consorting with the peasants. She makes a virtue of being one of them and not one of us. She despaired of us completely when she lived in Farrera for a while when she first arrived and was briefly a member of the hippie cooperative.

Barbara is a go-it-aloner, a formidable, semi-mythological personage who astounds and intrigues our valleys and neighbouring valleys with her pertinacity, very much in the manner and mould of the peasants themselves, who admire her, I think, as much as I do, for she is the only one of all the aspirants to the authentic, self-sufficient, back-to-the-land life we have known here to have actually achieved it, on her own terms. She milks her own cows, makes cheese and butter, and also has horses, sheep, goats, hens, chickens, ducks, geese, rabbits, a couple of incongruous-looking toy dogs with erect, hairy ears, and guinea pigs in a cage in the kitchen. Marsal says she once found a young pine marten and took it in to rear in the house, where she gave it her own milk out of a feeding bottle. It didn't thrive, but not for want of trying on her part.

Of recent years she has been surrogate mother to a number of children with life difficulties who are sponsored by a German government scheme to go abroad to safe but challenging situations where they can grow up away from bad influences. The rough road to Tressó, which is also the road to Andorra, is often cut off by snow and ice in winter. When it is impassable Barbara parks her white jeep in Farrera and they go up the mountain on snowshoes. In her first years there, before she had a jeep, her children skied down from the Pass of Sound on snowy days to catch the school bus from Farrera, and walked back up again in the afternoons, carrying their skis.

My brother, Michael, who is a robotics engineer, was living in Barcelona and came up with me to look at Casa Felip after Mary and I bought it. He was very shocked. We are from a semi-detached house in Andersonstown in Belfast, what the hell are you going to do with this monstrous liability? he seemed to be asking me with his worried eyes – which actually had tears in them at one point.

Subsequently, Michael, then working on an industrial estate on the banks of the smelly Llobregat river under the flight path of the airport, went up from Barcelona to spend occasional weekends in Casa Felip. He came the first summer we were there as home-owners, along with Colm Tóibín, who has remained a firm friend of us and of Farrera. One day, when the three of us were standing out on the balcony of the *carabiner*'s cabin, I suggested they should buy the barn we could see next door, just down the path. Colm laughed. What was it called? El Paller d'Andreu, Andrew's Hay Barn, I said. More like Casa Cagada, the House of Shite, he rejoined, for it was full of the leavings of Alex's many aborted enterprises – she had been renting it for a while – and the dung of several generations of animals that had been housed there, back to Juanito's donkey. But they did buy it, almost as a jape, after the usual complex negotiations that attend any deal here. Over the next couple of years they had it fixed up, so that it is now a comfortable, spacious, open-plan, glass-fronted house which has kept a lot of the charm it had as a barn. In the summer swallows – possibly descendants of those displaced from the barn when it was gentrified – nest under the eaves of their terrace, two pairs every year, 'the same ones, or others like them', Colm says, quoting Elizabeth Bishop. He says that one night, while he was sitting on the sofa quietly reading, a scops owl landed on the high ledge of the glass panel that divides the terrace from the living room and looked in at him for ages, wide-eyed with malevolence.

It seems we all eventually get our familiars here, even if we are running a bit short of scops.

After they had bought Andrew's Hay Barn, Michael, the youngest of our family, red-haired and sweet-natured, met Verónica Rapalino, dark-haired, also sweet-natured, and the youngest of her family, from Argentina. She is the daughter of cattle farmers on the pampa. She suffered no vertigo at the 1,365 metres of altitude in Farrera, in fact was enchanted by it. As soon as the house was habitable, Michael and Verónica moved here to live. Michael has set up his own business, telecommuting from Farrera to factories in Toledo, La Coruña, Madrid and Zaragoza for which he designs storage and stock-control programmes. Their two sons, Eloi and Dani, would be born in the hospital in La Seu d'Urgell, trebling the village's population of children under ten.

The other habitable houses of Farrera are second homes of native families who emigrated in the desperate years after the Civil War, of a few astute outsiders who bought places for antedeluvian sums in the 1960s and 1970s, and of later runners-in, like ourselves, who were second-homers for a long decade.

Most of the second-homers see themselves as sublunaries of Farrera's dark star, and get very involved in its doings, both when they are here and in absentia: a film-maker, a professor of painting, two teachers of art history, a professor of botany, a music teacher, a member of the Catalan parliament, a painter, a medievalist, a designer of modular furniture, a history teacher, a man who repairs one-armed bandits, a kindergarten monitor, a nurse, a graphic designer, a librarian, and a couple of others about whose avocations I am not so sure.

Paco Lloret, the botanist, has the most petite, delicate and expressive hands, with which he is always examining flowers and plants as if to find their souls without hurting a petal of their pretty heads. His wife, Teresa Quirante, is a music teacher. She is shy and good-natured, and often looks bemused by the post-hippie miasma in which she finds herself, having certainly never been a hippie herself. The two of them have formed El Club Excursionista i Esportiu de Farrera, whose members are mostly second-homers, excursionism being a long tradition the Catalans share with other European bourgeoisies that have mountains at their backs. Paco and Teresa, known collectively as Los Pacos, organize outings three or four times a year and send us maps and a few pages that describe the botanical, biological, topographical, geological and historical points of interest on the proposed route. On the first of these excursions we attended we tramped through the Defile of the Dead Bullock in the Pre-Pyrenees. Part of the path was a tunnel through the rock with one wall missing, three or four hundred metres above a dammed river. We stuck close to the inside wall. When you did look down there were monster carp in the deep, still, blue water below, like sharks waiting for feeding time.

We had arrived at the meeting point in eighteen different cars. I counted them. Afterwards only Michael and Verónica's and ours went back to Farrera. The rest dispersed to first homes in Barcelona, Sabadell, Terrassa, Sant Cugat and Llavorsí.

Twisted Mountains

Facing Farrera, on the patchily wooded mountainside beyond the Alendo torrent that cleaves its way through conifer forests from the heights of Juverri, is the village of Mallolís. It faces north, and in December and January gets hardly any sun at all. It is lightless now through most of the winter, ever since a young couple called Vicenç and Mercé, who had managed to survive there for seven years, keeping cows, making cheese, baking bread, collecting fruit from the abandoned orchards, digging gardens and fighting off wild pigs, became Jehovah's Witnesses and moved to Valencia, where they have settled among orange groves and olive trees.

At the end of the dirt road west from Mallolís, the village of Montesclado, lying out on its headland like an iguana drinking the heat from the sun of the wide valley to the south into the pores of its cold-blooded stone, has three or four houses open all year round. At the main turn of the road which descends in lariat loops from there, down where the Alendo, Farrera and Burg rivers meet among wet meadows and tangled woodlands, cluster the barns and houses of Glorieta. It gets little sun in winter, being at the bottom of things. Its last year-round inhabitant, Isidre of Casa Valentí, moved some years ago to the solarium of Montesclado when he married a woman from there. He brought the congenital gloom of the bottom-dweller with him, which no amount of sun can burn away. He says himself he always imagines the worst will happen. He is the municipal treasurer, as well as being farmer, forester, fire-watcher and shepherd.

To the west of Glorieta sits the hill town of Tírvia on the tawny, pillared hill over which its mostly abandoned terraced gardens are spread like tattered ra-ra skirts in shades of ivy green. It is called Tírvia as a derivation of Tri Via, meaning the three ways, because it stands where the valleys of Farrera, Vall Ferrera and Cardós meet. Being high and defensible on its buttress of rock, approachable by vehicle only from the northern side, in the closing months of the Civil War Tírvia was held by Republicans covering the retreat of their broken armies up those valleys north into France. The Nationalists bombarded it from Montesclado, which overlooks it. Their shells, which must have made perfect dropping trajectories, flattened its close-packed stone and half-timbered houses, tumbled the medieval arcades, destroyed the twelfth-century Romanesque church, and drove the Republicans out.

Tírvia was rebuilt after the war by one of Franco's reconstruction brigades. A retired taxi driver who is always walking the roads round there told me one day, when I met him on the road above Glorieta, that he had been a member of that brigade. From our vantage he showed me how they had put this little Dresden back together again: the main street rebuilt as a long terrace of one-storeyed cottages, the new town hall surmounted by a square campanile with a steep-tiled roof, and the church reassembled from the jigsaw puzzle of its rubble, with touches of the original Romanesque on the belfry above an unRomanesque clock that marks the slow hours and days and months and years of the town's decline.

In spite of the new heliport manned by the local emergency service, whose yellow helicopter is emblazoned underneath with what reads, every time they fly over, as 'BOMBERS' to my English-speaking eye and mind (*bomber* being the word for fireman in Catalan); despite the swimming pool and bar called El Complex Musical that opens for a couple of desultory months in the summer; and notwithstanding the Alpine-style *xalets* built on what once were gardens as second homes for middle-class Catalans who like their mountains with all mod cons, the year-round population of Tírvia is small, and mostly elderly.

Some of them are known by their trades. The retired baker El Pastisser (whose woodfire-baked bread is a Proustian constant of our remembrances here) is tall, frail and hesitant, skin transparent with age, veins blue and prominent on his face and hands, nose and cheeks pinched, but still rakish in the black beret he has affected from the time he did his apprenticeship in four different *forns*, as he calls them – ovens – in Béziers, Besançon, Carcassonne and Montpellier, whose guttural, twanging langue d'oc French is a perfect fit for his mountain accent. The retired blacksmith, El Ferrer, is muscled and portly, with an air of fearing no man, woman or horse, and is always ready to give his views on local events, his voice scorched hoarse by all those years of conversing over forge fires. The semi-retired builder and entrepreneur, El Nadalet, whose name translates as Little Christmas, owner of the Little Christmas hotel, still tends the bar there and has his walkabout every day to see what's stirring, who's passing by and what the news might be, for there is always news for those who are on the qui vive for it. You often see the three of them sitting on the bench with the grapevine shading it, watching the workmen going into the Little Christmas for their lunch, tourists bracing themselves for the rocky road to Andorra, and, at almost any hour of the day or night, the chief *bomber* driving up and down from the heliport in the fire-red BOMBERS truck.

As El Ferrer says, melancholy sometimes as his extinct forge, this place is finished. The last few old ones will die, and then there will be nobody left, just the odd builder fixing up houses for the tourists, but none of the old trades, nobody like him or the other artisans who would have made and repaired things for the hundreds of people who once lived in Tírvia and in the villages higher up.

Alendo, Mallolís, Montesclado, Tírvia and Burg are the villages you can see from Farrera if you walk round the Head of the Ridge. To the west, beyond these, is the valley of the Noguera Palleresa into which all our rivers run, which in turn, many miles to the south, joins the Ebro. Further west again is the great dividing range of mountains that marks the border of this province of Lleida with the neighbouring province of Huesca. Some of the peaks of these Twisted Mountains (the whole range does not seem to have a single name, so Mary and I have taken to calling them that, with a special emphasis on the *twisted*) rise to almost 3,000 metres. They are a monumental foreclosure of the west, an ever-changing arras that fills the horizon. Their higher slopes are treeless, snow-covered all through the winter, barely greening in the summer. There are no villages there and no ski stations, just craggy wilderness, for it is part of the outer zone of protection of the National Park of Saint Maurice and the Twisted Waters, the only national park in Catalonia, whose enchanted peaks (els Encantats) we see to the north of the cleft the valley of Espot rips in this rocky curtain.

This view is awesome, *collonut*, as the Catalans say, with its root in *collons*, balls, and a suggestion of their shrinkage at the contemplation of whatever the prospect might be. Which testicle-withering gigantism of scale is perhaps why modern (male) painters and sculptors have never sacralized chains of mountains but only isolated, odd peaks that stand up out of more humanized landscapes: Miró at Montroig, Cézanne and Matisse at Mont Ste-Victoire, Dalí at the Cape of Crosses at the Mediterranean end of the Pyrenees, Chillida at the Basque end where he mounted his fierce, ferrous interrogations of the Atlantic Ocean, and Soutine, Picasso, Chagall & Co. at Céret at the foot of the Canigou in France, an outlier of the Pyrenees distinct enough to be a mountain in its own right. I cannot think of a modern artistic movement that celebrated entire *cordilleras*, not since Caspar David Friedrich and the Romantics anyway, and that's a while ago. There is just too much of them. In this vastness, the human note diffuses and gets lost, like a failed echo.

Mountain art is architectonic rather than painterly. Here in the Catalan Pyrenees, the Romanesque churches, monasteries and hermitages enclose volumes of dark, cool air as a refuge from the immensity beyond. The art they contain, or once contained, is of the human face and the human body close up, with little background and no scenery, since scenery had not yet been invented when these images were made. The thirteenth-century altar frontal from the church of Saint Roch in Farrera, now in the Museu Nacional d'Art de Catalunya in Barcelona, shows the Creator of All – *El Pantocràtor* – sitting on two cushions on a bench surrounded by the man, lion, ox and eagle of the evangelists Matthew, Mark, Luke and John, and the rest of the apostles. It was looted in the name of conservation in 1911 when frescoes from all over the Catalan Pyrenees were being systematically and scientifically transferred into osier frames like the upended hulls of currachs and sailed to safe keeping in Barcelona. After further voyages in search of a permanent home, they were eventually housed in the National Palace that was built for the International Exhibition in 1929. In that baroque bombast on Montjuïc, above the Plaça Espanya with its *son et lumière* of floodlights shining through triumphal pillars on to erupting fountains for car shows, tourism conventions and ideal-home exhibitions, these exiles brood in their wooden cages of fantastic light and colour in rooms that hum with air-conditioning, rather than fading and flaking in the churches with glassless windows of their origins.

Without these frescoes and altarpieces the stripped churches can seem austere chapels of hard sects which scorn adornment, when in fact their interiors once pulsed with the hallucinating pigments used by the roving master-painters of a thousand years ago to depict an idealized, sanctified humanity, and the possibility of salvation at the end of a hard life.

A Buddha of Beatitude

Every day as I go up or down from the garden I shout to Conchita de Poblador in her house, or have a talk with her where she sits sewing on her balcony in the sun.

Conchita spends only the summers in Farrera now. She passes the worst of the winter with relatives in the lowlands near the city of Lleida, in some comfort, for they are well-to-do, with all the commodities, she keeps telling you, partly to let you know how well looked after she is, and partly to boast, for she is proud of their prosperity, descendants as they are of a family of five who emigrated from Burg in the 1950s. Such celebrations as they have for christenings and weddings and saints' days and birthdays! They keep their own pigs, and chickens, and rabbits! They have over five hundred sheep! Such fields and gardens and orchards as they have! Such a house! It is like a luxury hotel! It has two wings with five rooms on each wing, and two bathrooms, such as you would not believe! Everything Conchita tells you about them has a marvelling exclamation mark attached.

Conchita calls her house the Convent of the Poor Pobla-dora, Poblador being the name of the house, not her family name, which is Català i Ambatlle. Everyone calls her Conchita de Poblador. The wooden lintel over the door has 1872 carved into it, the year the house was built. Above the door is a small window with a wooden shutter and no glass, for none of Conchita's windows have glass. The shutter is usually open during the day as a sign that Conchita is home to visitors. When you knock on the door and call out her name, she puts her head through this aperture, smiling, voluble in her welcome, pouring out a horn of talk, saying how pleased she is to see you, she will be down immediately, as she is, though always more slowly than you imagine, for a house so small, as if she were making final adjustments to the stage within before appearing at last at the proscenium of her door.

— Come in, come in, she says.

She is wreathed in smiles, roly-poly, dressed in a much-patched red nylon housecoat over a blouse and skirt, with tight-fitting trousers under the skirt and a glimpse of lace-fringed petticoat over the trousers, a pink, moth-eaten cardigan thrown over her shoulders. Her dyed auburn hair – which has helped to keep her age as indeterminate now, when she is in her seventies, as it was when we first knew her – is tied and secured with a comb at the back under the scarf she always wears. Now that I think about it, I have never seen Conchita's hair down except in photographs of her when she was younger, when it shows long and black and wavy around a dark, high-cheekboned, long-eyed, heavy-browed face, the kind of face you see framed and hung on museum and restaurant walls hereabouts among the flails and scythes and wooden hayforks, a face that is of these mountains, where the Basques, who were the first Iberians, have left echoes and vestiges of themselves in the names of places and in the faces which still inhabit those places.

Now that her mother and her brother are dead, and she has her peasant's pension and the savings from her thrifty life, it is as if Conchita has not just retired but has retreated into her own little world, for these days she almost never leaves her house and its immediate environs. Her body is as compact as that circumscribed world, the maximum possible amount of flesh compressed into the minimum of space, so that not another ounce could be contained within it. Yet for all her portliness, and her seventy-five years, about which she is not at all coy, Conchita moves nimbly, with an erect bearing, in plimsolls with the heels tramped down, as she precedes me into the main room of the house, turning round to tell me, again and again, that I am welcome.

As we stand and talk under the low wooden ceiling of the main room she puts on an apron she takes from the back of one of the chairs at the table against the far wall, then ushers me into the kitchen. This is divided off from the main room by a wooden wall with a low door you have to stoop to pass through. The floor inside is made of big, flat, whitish, yellow, blue and grey-green flagstones rubbed to a marble smoothness and graininess with years of use. Running along the length of the wooden wall is a bench made from half a hollowed-out elm tree that has been lyed and scrubbed to a white that is all the more white for the blackness of everything else from the smoke that has kippered Conchita's house for a century and a half. The half-tree bench is so smooth and shiny you feel you could lift your legs, give yourself a good push with one foot and slide from one end to the other, and that is more or less how you do sit down, as Conchita hooshes you up towards the corner so that she can drop down the single leaf of the small rectangular table on its two hinged legs that is normally secured upright against the back wall with a wooden catch, and trap you there until you have run the full gamut of her hospitality.

The only window in the kitchen is a tiny opening on the street wall. It is covered with a piece of plastic that has browned with age and sun, or perhaps was always brown. On the sill in front of it are bottles and rusty tins containing dessicated marigolds, daisies, hollyhocks and grasses: a May altar gone past its pray-by date. The one bare bulb dangling from a wire in the middle of the wooden wall is always on when there is a visit, and in the daytime gives a greyish, underwater light.

When Mary is in Belfast and I go to visit Conchita on my own, she always asks me first about her. Have I heard from her? How are things? How is her mother? When I tell her that Mary's mother is much the same, between the bed and her wheelchair, paralysed since she had a stroke three years ago, Conchita says,

— *Aiiy mother!* What can we do? Life is hard, but we all

have to bear it. I nursed my mother for all those years, until the very end. It wasn't easy. I washed her and dressed her and fed her and did everything for her. Up to the very night she died I slept with her in the same bed. I never complained. These are duties that have to be done, no matter how hard they might be. It wasn't easy. But what other remedy was there? Faith of God, what else could I do?

She asks about my father. His memory is worse, I tell her. Sometimes he does not recognize his own children. He has a bad heart. His spirits are very low. He would like to die, he says sometimes.

— *Aiiy mother!* she says, in a drawn-out, sighing singsong. Thanks be to God I have all my faculties, except my teeth. I've never been to a doctor or a hospital in my life.

— Not once?

— Never, she says, with sharp pride. Not one time. And I have never had a headache. I have never been bored. I always have something to do. I can always entertain myself. I never find the time heavy or the day too long.

As Conchita bustles in and out from the other room, the two of us talking back and forth, I lean forward under the chimney opening that is the breadth and depth of the kitchen and look up its mineshaft dark at the daylight oozing under the big piece of slate that covers it at the top. Like everyone else here, Conchita used to keep a couple of pigs every year to fatten for slaughter. Hers lived their brief span in a cellar under the kitchen. When we used to visit her in the old days the sausages and hams she made from the pigs were strung to be smoked on wires that are still there across the inside of the chimney, where a last withered, wrinkled intestine, like a mummified squeak, still hangs. A set of fire-irons with hooks and chains swings on a spindle between pivots embedded in the back wall. Under the psoriasis of soot encrusting the iron there are spirals and traceries engraved by a long-dead farrier, who also wrought barley-sugar twists down each side and two Persian-looking birds with open beaks on top of them: a Vedic altar to the Indo-European fire gods the peasants carried out of the Fertile Crescent of long, long ago.

Conchita almost never lights a fire now, preferring to put on more layers of clothes when it gets cold. One day, when she did light a fire for us, it smoked so much we were driven out of the kitchen into the main room, with Conchita encouraging, almost herding us to go back in, saying that when it got going it would stop smoking. When we went in and sat down again, crouched low on the elm bench, trying to keep our heads below the choking swirls of smoke, Conchita said it was always like this when the wind was from the Pass of Sound. She kept poking the fire, which made it worse, telling us it would be fine in a minute. We could have our little chat then. It was impossible. We had to go and sit in the other room, watching wraiths of smoke lick out of the low door of the kitchen as if in search of us.

She does all her cooking on a two-ringed gas burner in the corner of the main room beside a stone sink whose plughole lets the run-off straight on to the street outside. She does not have mains water but fetches what she needs from either the village trough outside Casa Marsal or the new trough under the east window of John's Haggard. We sometimes see her there washing her clothes in a bucket, swirling them round with a stick, rinsing them in the trough among the tadpoles and pondweed, and then wringing them out ready to dry on the bushes in front of her door. She does have electricity, strung through the house on brittle wires with porcelain connectors and old-fashioned black switches, from the first installations that were done in the 1960s, though she is frugal with the electricity too, and never turns on the fridge someone gave her years ago, for all that she did tell me one day she was a *gormanda* of lightbulbs and never stinted on them.

Since we have been back here she gets us to do errands for her when we go to the valley. There are always the same few items on the note she gives us, written in pencil on a scrap of paper she holds up close to her face and reads out to you like a schoolgirl conning her lessons: four yoghurts, three bits of frozen cod (to be kept in our freezer until she needs them), a big loaf of bread, a five-litre carafe of white wine, sometimes a bottle of sweet muscatel (if she is expecting visitors), and three tins of sardines in olive oil, 'This sort,' she says, giving you the cardboard box from the last ones you got her. Cisco Pubill of Alendo, who keeps the best garden in the valley, from which he produces hundreds of lettuces for sale in Andorra, often brings Conchita potatoes, or a cabbage, or clusters of carrots with their green tops still on them. I bring her down some of whatever is in season from our garden, too, and on my next visit she reports to me how good whatever it was had been, telling me how she cooked it, how it tasted, how much she had left, in an incantation punctuated with exhalations of the *'Aiiy mother!'* that is her chief ejaculation.

Conchita has left the village only once this year, to go with Mary to Sort to get money out of the bank. We were weeks persuading her to go, hoping that she might buy herself an oil-filled heater so that she would have something she could plug in rather than have to light the smoky fire, but in the end she showed no interest in going to the *electrodomèstics* shop, and just came home after she got her pesetas out of the bank. Now she is telling me she will give me a cheque to cash for her, to pay the few thousand pesetas she owes me for things I have brought her. I tell her not to worry, there's no hurry, we will sort it out another day. But debts prey on her mind and she likes to get them settled as soon as she can, counting the money out to you from where she keeps it in cups and jars on the dresser that occupies one wall of the main room.

She comes back into the kitchen with a white-frill-fringed, neatly folded, much washed, pinkish napkin that she flicks open, showing me where she sewed it the other day, where it had ripped on a nail, a whore of a nail, she calls it. She lays the napkin across my knee, with all the solicitude of a maître d'.

— Will you have a glass of wine and a bit of cheese? It's lovely cheese. It's grown a bit of a mould, but it's still very tasty.

— Really, Conchita, nothing much. I only came in for the chat.

— But you have to have something.

— A bit of cheese and a glass of wine, then. That would be very kind.

She goes to a plastic bag hanging among other plastic bags in the far corner and brings out a blue-checked tablecloth that she spreads over the end of the table, smoothing it down at the edges.

— You shouldn't go to such bother, Conchita. You don't need to for me.

— Ah, but I do.

She goes out to the main room and brings back a *porró* of white wine, a Pyrex glass on a yellow saucer, and a thin sausage she extrudes from its plastic packet as she lays it on the table in front of me along with a short-handled sharp knife, saying,

— Eat, eat. It's very good that sausage. My visitors from Andorra brought it the other day.

I cut off a couple of rounds. It is good, though bits of it stick in the snags of my teeth and I am already sorry I don't have a toothpick with me.

She tells me about the visitors from Andorra.

— They are really lovely people. They come to see me

every year. He is a cousin of my mother. He is from Ars too. He moved to Andorra when he was young. They have a shop there. Now his son and daughter-in-law run it. I'll show you a photograph they brought me.

She reaches down a shoebox of photographs from a shelf above the table. She digs into it, peering closely like she peers at her sewing.

The family looking out from the photo she hands me — the father small, dark, mustachioed, the mother taller, with permed fair hair, wearing a knitted jacket over her shoulders, the son and daughter-in-law casually but expensively dressed — are all smiling broadly under a plastic sign which says HOUSE OF ARS — CAMERAS CAMCORDERS TOBACCOS ALCOHOLS PRESENTS SOUVENIRS.

— Lovely, I say.

— So they are. Lovely people, she concurs.

Conchita has boxes and envelopes full of photos. People like to get their photograph taken with her, and send her copies. Artists staying in Farrera have done series of images of her. Ten years ago an American photographer, Rachel Brown, took a black-and-white photograph of Conchita's dresser with its cups and plates and glasses in neat rows, the lace-cut newspaper border along the top, spoons and knives and forks hung neatly and symmetrically on nails all along the front: a dresser dressed to the nines. Pinned to the wooden wall beside the dresser are out-of-date commercial calendars, invoices for feed for the long-dead cows, electricity bills, a voting card for the municipal elections and arrested eddies of other papers. If you look closely at the photograph, just to the left of the calendars, you see a blurred after-image of Conchita herself coming down the stairs: an ectoplasmic apparition in her own grotto.

She hoards her boxes and packets of letters, cards and photos in Juanito's bedroom as was and in the room beside it, and upstairs in the three tiny, wooden-walled rooms that are packed floor to ceiling with shelves and more boxes. One day she invited me upstairs to sit on the balcony at the round table with the red cloth where she passes the sunny days. On our way to it, she opened the doors of a tall press to show me her larder: tins of sardines, jars of preserved fruit and pots of pickled vegetables from her relatives' place in the lowlands, bags of rice and pasta the mice had nibbled, a stack of tins of La Riojana asparagus, plastic bottles of oil, and a neat stack of packets of paper tissues, one of which she gave me for the snuffle I had. She lifted the lids of wooden coffers to show me sheets, pillowcases, woollen blankets, tablecloths, doilies and pieces of material neatly folded: the trousseau she had never got to use. She took out a piece of the lacework she used to do when she was minding the cows and spread it out over her hand so that I could look at it. The contemplation of that intricate stitchery up close, with my glasses on, brought back to me from all those years ago a vivid image of Conchita on a misty day saturated with the green of spring, sitting on a stone wall, a big, black umbrella over her, leaning forward, intently concentrating on the lacework in her hands, as her big, beige cow-children pastured in the field around her.

Conchita puts the box of photos aside. She lifts the *porró* and pours me a glass of wine out of the thick spout at the top.

— Drink, drink, she says.

She goes over to the corner where the plastic bags are and takes out a half round of cheese from one of them. After inspecting it closely, she pronounces,

— It's a bit mouldy, but it's very good.

She sits down at the table and carves at the cheese with the sharp knife. It is a soft Manchego with a waxy skin. She cuts off a not-so-mouldy wedge, gouges out the last few blue bits, peels the wax skin from it, and thrusts it on to the plate in front of me.

— Eat, eat, she says, pushing the plate towards me.

The cheese is good, if rather bland. It knocks the rough edges off the wine.

She goes out again and comes back with an unopened packet of Marieta biscuits. She struggles to get it open, eventually takes the knife to it, and then shakes a scatter of them on to my plate.

— Eat, eat.

I don't particularly like Marieta biscuits with cheese, so I take one and nibble a corner of it, then set it down on the saucer beside the glass so that I can slip it into the top pocket of my shirt as soon as she goes out again.

— Eat, eat, she insists, pushing the biscuits towards me again.

— It's fine, Conchita, one's enough. Why don't you have something yourself, to keep me company?

— I will, I will.

She doesn't. She rarely eats or drinks herself when there are visitors, so intent is she on seeing to their needs.

Conchita sits down on the elm-tree bench on the other side of the table, wiping her hands on her apron and sighing a long, heartfelt *'Aiiy mother!'* Through the opaque plastic of the window there is an inkling of dusk as seen from the end of a burrow. The single bulb on the wooden wall has warmed to remembered candlelight. For a moment of contemplative silence Conchita and I are two voyagers in a stone time capsule whose only clock is the Caixa de Montserrat calendar on the far wall with its red block letters telling us it is 1976.

She tells me about other visitors she has had. The forestry manager, Jaume Hidalgo, had come the other day with his fiancée, Cristina, 'really beautiful, and smart too, she has her own career, she has studies', briefly lost to him a year ago and now found again. They are going out foreign together, to a country very far away.

— Vietnam, is it? I ask.

Conchita thinks that might be it, but she's not sure. She tries to pronounce it, as if she has never heard the word before. Beetnum, she calls it.

Pili Sarroca had been to visit her yesterday. Those were her cigarettes over there beside the pile of old packets, most of them empty, some with a few still left in them, that Conchita keeps. She does not smoke now, though years ago she might have had a cigarette or two at the *festa major* in a long black holder that went with the shawl, mantilla and fan she dons for special occasions. Pili has become Conchita's chief friend and main visitor. She is from the rail- and road-head of Fraga on the border between Catalonia and Aragon, which is like being from Dodge City, and she has something of the sassy cowgirl in her manner. Conchita tells me Pili is smarter than you would think, *molt espavilada*, very capable, and very *decidida*. Conchita does not pry, but hints that she knows Pili is going through a hard time in her divorce from Udo, her German husband, and says she shouldn't be annoyed like she is, she is '*molt bona persona. Una santa.*' A very good person. A saint.

— Pili has gone to La Seu to have an operation on her knee, Conchita tells me.

— Has she? I didn't know.

— She hurt herself when she fell working in Burg. That's no work for a woman. She's not fit for it.

Pili has been working as the municipal janitor, doing a week in turn in each of the four inhabited villages in the valley, clearing brush, sweeping paths, tidying round the rubbish and recycling containers, with not much in the way of tools, and no machinery.

Conchita and I talk about the main news of the village that day, the killing of four of the five dogs that have been attacking the sheep in the high pastures beyond the Pass of Sound. The dogs had been there for some time. They had killed more than fifty sheep, most of them Oppen's. For the last few days waves of vultures had been hurrying through the sky over Farrera like scruffy partygoers in ragged anoraks fearful lest all the food be scoffed before they got there. The shepherds said there were hundreds of them sitting on trees and promontories up there, waiting for the next kill. The remaining sheep had been brought down yesterday, as many as could be found from the three scattered, frightened herds that had got all mixed up together.

All the shepherds, the Besolís and Oppen from Farrera, Isidre of Casa Valentí in Glorieta, with hunters from Burg and Tírvia, about fifteen of them altogether, had gone up that morning to get the dogs. They had shot four of them dead and wounded a fifth one. There were a couple of Alsatians and a Husky among the dead ones. They were not Farrera dogs, though some of the dogs of the village had been under suspicion for a while. They seemed to have been abandoned dogs that had formed a pack.

— Do you ever remember dogs attacking sheep in the old days, Conchita?

— Just once. In those days everybody had sheep, the Manresàs, the Bigarrets, the Besolís, the Felips and others. One time El Bigarret put all of their sheep into that bothy they had on this side of the Pass of Sound because there were dogs on the loose. The dogs got in during the night. The sheep tried to escape through the small window at the end. They all piled on top of one another and got suffocated. They all died. I'll never forget the sobs of Bigarret. Such wails! He went round the village crying like a child. *Aiiy mother!* I never saw such despair.

As she says this, Conchita throws her two arms in the air, for she is very expressive with her body, leans forward on the bench, shakes her head from side to side, and looks as if she might weep at the remembered tragedy, but then brightens, smiles and says,

— Such things as happened in this village you wouldn't believe.

In the first few years after Juanito died Conchita had been inclined to cry at the slightest pretext, and to lament how hard it had been looking after her brother after having nursed her mother till the day she died, and her trying to make a living for the three of them. Yet, gradually, over the ten years since she was left on her own, as she has sold her cows, killed the last of her rabbits, strangled her remaining chickens, let her gardens go, and seen her last dog, La Pastoreta, die, it is as if Conchita has reconciled her karma with the dharma of the place, so that now she is a Buddha of beatitude, always cheerful, counting her blessings, glad to be alive, taking every day as it comes. In the darkened cinema of her kitchen she is the last devotee of the Rocky Horror Show of mountain life, who narrates the story, plays out the scenes and remembers the exact dialogue, even though the projector is broken and the film has self-ignited and burned to celluloid ashes.

— Do you ever remember wolves or bears here?

— Not in my time anyway. I don't know if there were ever such beasts here.

There were, in fact, a bit before Conchita's time, and I wonder why she would say there were never any. She must have heard stories, like the one about a shepherd whose dogs roused a female bear in the woods at Juverri. His only escape was to throw himself down a cliff. He knocked himself unconscious and had to be carried back to the village. He always walked a little lame afterwards.

When the locals did kill a bear, they would skin it, stuff the hide with straw, put it up on a mule and process it through all the villages of the valley, to be showered with presents and money by the peasants glad to be rid of such a threat to the herds upon which they depended. I had read that offspring of the European black bears released into the wild on the French side of the Pyrenees had been spotted in the northern part of the Pallars Sobirà. At one stage I had wondered if maybe the damage being ascribed to dogs had in fact been done by bears, but now that the dogs had been shot, the case was closed.

I wouldn't fancy the French bears' chances if they got the taste for mutton.

Outside we hear Marsal breaking into one of the songs that he sings all day, most days, since he got over his long, hard grief at his wife Generosa's death some years ago.

— Listen, Conchita says, grinning and nodding her head in that direction. The artiste.

And she laughs heartily, throwing herself back on the bench, covering her mouth with her hand, and then dabbing at her rheumy red eyes with the handkerchief she keeps up her sleeve, infecting herself again, as she was probably first infected by her own mother, who had the same eye disease, and maybe her mother too, in her turn.

With Marsal's plainchant rising and falling in the distance, Conchita tells me again how I would not believe the things that have happened in this village. Like the time Ermengola Llopetegui was brought back dead from Lleida after what seems to have been a bad case of post-natal depression. Some weeks later one of her brothers went with the rest of the young people of the village to the tavern in Casa La Roca to play cards. He did not return home. The next day the alarm was raised. They looked everywhere for him. Then his mother thought of looking at the cistern on the river above Burg. There she found his clothes neatly folded, with his rope-soled sandals set side by side on top of them, and his body floating face down in the water. The mother was inconsolable. Such cries and sobs! The poor woman was so desolated she made leaps in the air and had to be restrained, Conchita says.

She tells me about the Manresàs and how rich they were. When she talks about families here she goes over all their names in their several generations, sorting out brothers and sisters, sons, daughters, and then their in-laws, often other people from hereabouts. That starts her down a side-track of them and their cousins. 'Nowadays they say it is not good to be marrying so much within the family,' she comments. Her own mother came from Ars to marry a brother-cousin, or first cousin, in Farrera. Many houses would have married into houses with which they already had connections. Nobody thought anything of it. That was just the way.

— Do you remember Joan and Angeleta de Manresà? she asks.

— Yes, I do, but only from the last years of their lives.

— And Maria de Manresà?

I remember her too, the Manresàs' orphaned cousin. She it was who herded their few remaining cows and was reputed to have caches of wine in hidey-holes all over the village. Sometimes when we met her she would be hectic, spittle flecking the sides of her mouth, talking nineteen to the dozen, of which we sometimes only understood the seven left over. A handsome woman though, for I still remember with warmth the stirring of the loins I had one day talking to her, though I kept my loin-stirrings to myself. Conchita tells me that Maria's sister, Trinitat, whom we had not known, had been a dwarf who had hopped about all her life on her two short legs. But apart from her size, Trinitat was very *espavilada*. She could embroider, knit, sew, cook, milk, and make cheese. She lived to a good age, and all her life hopped about,

— Just like a chicken, Conchita says, moving forward on the bench, tucking her arms into her sides, and making as if to hop like a chicken herself.

There is a pause while we both look into the blackness of the fireplace, thinking our own thoughts.

— *La vida fa gràcia, a vegades,* Conchita resumes.

Life is funny, sometimes.

— Do you remember your wedding? she asks.

— Of course I do. As if it were yesterday.

— *Que lujo*, Conchita says: such luxury. Mary looked lovely in her green dress. And all those flowers Colm brought from Barcelona. I had never seen such flowers in the church before. Not in December anyway. And then the feast in Casa Felip. Such dishes! Such cakes as Mary and Barbara made! The priest said if he had known there were such good desserts he wouldn't have eaten so much of the other dishes. It was a great *tiberi*.

Tiberi is from the Emperor Tiberius, whose orgies live on in this peasant word for an opulent repast.

— It was a great *tiberi* all right, she says. And now we're like family. You are people of confidence for us.

A nostalgic tearfulness rises to Conchita's throat, threatens to choke out of her, then dies away again.

— Family, that's what we are. Family.

She tells me about an eldest daughter of the house of Manresà, of a generation or two before we lived here, whose marriage had been arranged to a rich man from the valley of

Cardós. He arrived on the day before the wedding, dressed in such finery, *Aiiy mother!*, bringing with him such a luxury of *indumentaria*, her very word, as you wouldn't believe. That night the bride disappeared. The family hunted high and low but could not find her anywhere, while the fiancé in his wedding clothes paced up and down the main room with the long oak table in the middle of it that sat thirty. The next morning the bride reappeared. She had spent the night in a hay barn with one of the serving boys with whom she was secretly in love. The marriage went ahead anyway.

— *Els rics sempre van amb els rics,* Conchita reflects.

The rich always go with the rich.

— But sometimes it wasn't so good to be rich, she continues. There was one time I heard about, years ago, before the Manresàs you knew and even before Joan's parents. There were bandits about then. They robbed travellers and stole cattle and sheep. There were no police here in those days. The bandits could do what they liked. There was one called Meco of Tírvia who went about with a gang of five or six others. They did terrible things, Meco and Bella of Alins and the rest of them, even raped a woman in a house in Besan when they couldn't find the money, terrible things I remember the old people talking about. They came to the Manresàs' house to steal the bag with the money in it. It was always the head of the house who kept the bag, but when the oldest daughter heard the commotion of Meco and his men arriving, she snatched up the bag and her youngest child and climbed out of a back window and ran away down the mountain. They tortured El Manresà, told him to hand over the bag, but he just kept saying he didn't know where it was. He didn't have it. When he still wouldn't tell them, they took him outside and stretched him out on that big stone at the gate that women used to use to get up on their horses. They tied his hands and feet and then cut his throat. They made his wife collect his blood in a basin. Meco and the rest of them drank the blood. That was one of the most terrible things ever happened in the village. My mother used to talk about it as if she had seen it herself.

It was now dark outside. I had been up in the garden all day and wanted to go home to cook something to eat. Conchita pressed me to stay, rushing at me with a brandy bottle, spilling out more biscuits, saying it was early yet, she was enjoying our little talk. I insisted and rose to go. She accompanied me to the door, telling me to send her regards to Mary, and to tell her that she missed her very much and hoped she would come back soon. She pined for her, she said, and found her absence very hard to bear.

She said Mary was a saint. Conchita has always said Mary is a saint. She is now working on the canonization of Santa Pili too.

As I take my leave and go out the front door, Conchita thanks me again for coming. She says I am to come in anytime I am passing. And that when I am passing, even if I can't come in, always to shout to her, for you never know what might happen, and her a woman living on her own in that old house, like the time she told me about, she reminds me, when her leg went through a rotten board in the floor upstairs and she couldn't move for hours and nobody heard her calls for help.

As I go round the corner on to the upper path, Conchita is still thanking me from the door of the Convent of the Poor Pobladora,

— *Gràcies per haver vingut. Gràcies per tot. Bona nit. Fins demà, si Déu vol.*

Thank you for coming. Thank you for everything. Good night. Till tomorrow, if God wishes.

One Man and his Mule Went to Mow a Meadow

The next day I encounter Marsal as I am going for a walk to Alendo by the path through the valley.

The previous Sunday his son, Josep, a mechanic, and his grandson, also called Josep, had come over the mountain from La Seu d'Urgell to give Marsal a hand, as they have been doing every week since Generosa died. They had cut all the grass in Marsal's lower field along the near bank of the river with the chip-chop, back and forth, spike-toothed, hand-held, petrol-driven mower whose drone had lulled our Lord's Day's rest.

On Monday Marsal tedded the hay, turning and tossing and loosening it to let the air dry it. On Tuesday he raked it into an L of round piles in one corner of the field, like an artist's installation waiting to be photographed. There were clouds coming over the Pass of Sound from the east all day as he worked. Towards evening it began to spit rain. Marsal brought a sheet of black plastic down to the field, struggling with it as it billowed around him in the wind. He eventually managed to pin it down at three of the corners by throwing stones and branches on to it. By the next morning it was only attached at one corner, but it had not rained much so the hay was not spoiled.

On the Thursday, when I meet him, he is gathering the last of the hay and forking it up in hanks on to the wooden frame his mule Castanya carries, leaving only her nose, feet and tail peeping out from the moving haystack. In the spring Marsal's daughter, Remei, had had someone come to cut Castanya's hooves while Marsal was in hospital for a hernia operation. I had thought they would have been sharpened and toughened by the trek up and down the stony path below John's Haggard, from where we have heard her clip-clop, slippety-clop all summer long – a percussive accompaniment to Marsal's singing – but I now see that they still bulge and buckle awkwardly on the ends of her legs like ill-fitting second-hand boots bought out of four different charity shops.

As Marsal stops to greet me, Castanya makes to ramble home, the hay only half-tied. Marsal hauls her back by the bridle and finishes strapping the hay on to the frame with a few laps and knots of the rope, then leads her, her neck straining forward, as he comes over to speak to me, smiling shyly, for Marsal loves to talk, and takes every opportunity to do so. As he approaches, I see that sweat has run in dusty streaks down his face under his Rommel-in-the-Western-Desert peaked cap with its flap at the back over his neck, and I am surprised again by how stooped and small he is.

The week before, Marsal had made his annual pilgrimage to the graves of his ancestors in Glorieta, where he was born, and Montesclado, where his remaining relatives live. I ask him how it went.

— The sea of well. I went to the cemetery in Glorieta. I put flowers on the grave of my mother and father, and on my brother's too. I owe my life to that man. I will always honour him. He saved my life twice.

— How did he do that, Marsal?

— I'll tell you now.

And with that he lets Castanya's bridle go. She stands for a moment with her head down, grazing round our feet, then starts munching her way back to the path, as if she knows this is the last, light load of the day.

Marsal always talks with pent passion, as if the stories are spilling from the open sides of the stone barn of his memory, using his claws of hands, knobbled and knuckled like sun-dried leather gloves, to give substance and emphasis to his discourse.

— It was one time when I was young and I had that disease of the glands, in the neck.

— The mumps?

— Yes, the mumps. I was very bad. My neck was all swollen up. On the third day my brother went to Tírvia to get the doctor. It was late at night. The doctor didn't want to come. My brother said he had to come. He had a horse and cart there at the door. He must come now. The doctor came. He said he thought I would die. He couldn't do anything for me. He left. I couldn't breathe. I was suffocating. My brother said, we can't let him die. Open his throat so he can breathe. Sharpen me up a knife and I'll do it, he said. He sharpened the knife himself, really sharp. He took it and stuck it into me and brought down the swelling. I could breathe. I got better then. I owe my life to our Manel.

— What was the other time, Marsal?

— Well, cunt [*cony* being a forceful oath in Catalan, almost totally dissociated from the vulva it primordially signifies], that was when I was maybe twelve or thirteen. I was minding our sheep on the mountain. It was my first time minding them on my own. They kept running away, up and down, all over the place. I had to run after them. I called them all the names of the day. At that time there was a priest in Mallolís. He must have heard me, because that evening when I got home, my father said to me, 'What's this I hear you were shouting on the mountain today? I won't stand for it.' He gave me whacks with his stick, on the legs and on the back. I ran away. Up those mountains there.

He points to the wall of pine forest below Juverri and the peak of Urdossa.

— I stayed up there for three days. They were looking for me everywhere. A couple of times I heard their shouts in the distance. I stayed where I was. Not a bite to eat, just water from the stream and bits of grass. I ate grass because I was so hungry. Then, on the third day, a hunter from Llavorsí found me. 'What are you doing here?' he shouted at me. 'They're looking for you everywhere. Here, you have to eat.' And he slung the bag off his shoulder, and the wineskin, and he set me down and made me eat my fill and drink out of the wineskin. God of mine, was I glad to see him! Then our Manel saw me from the road. He came down and hugged me and kissed me and said they were all distracted looking for me.

— All just for what you shouted at the sheep? It must have been bad.

— A few curses, that's all.

Maybe that's why Marsal doesn't use bad language, if you don't count the odd *cony* and an occasional *hóstia*, communion host, upon which he generally does not shit, as so many others here do.

— Did you go to Montesclado?

— I certainly did. Everywhere I went I was invited to take something. People are always glad to see me. They esteem me. Everybody esteems me. That man who has built the new house in Mallolís, Casimiro, is a relative of mine too. He invited me in and we had a beer. He's made a good job of that house. He has an orchard planted and a garden started. It was always his family home. It's good to see it being lived in again, even if it is only for the summer.

We latter-day aesthetes think Casimiro's house is an abomination: walls of more cement than stone, roof of thin, cheap, machine-cut Galician slate, surrounded by an Algarve-paranoid wire mesh fence, with a spiked gate at the front, built by the company of Portuguese builders who are slapping up such houses all over these valleys. Still, Casimiro and Marsal like it, though Marsal agrees that it is maybe a bit heavy on the cement, and not very traditional.

— At least it's comfortable, and has all the amenities. What more does a man of seventy-five want? He's seventy-five, Casimiro, four years younger than me.

— And you walked back from there through Alendo?

— Yes. Not as fast as I might have once, maybe, but no bother all the same.

Marsal has been making this pilgrimage every year since he married out of Glorieta into Farrera over fifty years ago. The round trip, down by the Path of the Mother of God of the Ridge to Glorieta, up to Montesclado by the road, along the track to Mallolís, down the winding path into the ravine of the Alendo river, up the other side into Alendo, and back to Farrera by the road, might be twenty kilometres. The day he had made his pattern, his annual round of the holy places of his ancestor worship, had been cruelly hot, perhaps the hottest of the summer so far.

Living on his own since Generosa died, Marsal has recently had half of the roof of his house re-slated, new windows and balcony door put into the ground floor, and a big metal door like on a lock-up garage hung on the entrance to the cellar where he stores the fruit and produce from his gardens, makes up swill for his pigs and keeps his wooden barrel of wine. When he stretches out on the old sofa down there for his siesta, his many cats step over him, or yarm in his face. In one of his barns further down the path he keeps rabbits in a wire mesh cage along the front of the upper storey, under the overhang of the roof, from which some of them have escaped to make warrens in other barns nearby. He has a couple of pale pigs in a dark sty behind the stall where Castanya stands in her own dung with her slipper-hooves growing towards the light of the one small chicken-wired window. In the biggest of his three barns his cows and their calves spend the winter chained to their mangers, dreaming bovine dreams of the long summer they will spend roaming free in the high pastures. Across the path from the front door of his house, on a wide ledge of rock where the first village school used to be (destroyed by one of the bombs in the Civil War), he has a chicken coop where scrawny-necked hens peck and squabble. Along the Path of the Mother of God he tends an acre or more of scattered vegetable gardens and orchards, which feed himself, the pigs, the rabbits and the chickens.

His dog Perrico is usually lying at Marsal's door or mooching around after him. Perrico is a Catalan sheepdog from one of the Casa Maria litters. He may also be part human, for he smiles a lot and is everybody's friend.

One day, on her way home from shopping in the valley, Mary saw a skin and bones of a dog at the entrance to the village. She went back up the long climb from John's Haggard with food for it, then came back down crying because she thought the dog was choking to death on a piece of the bread she had given it. I went up to see. The dog was staggering about in a pool of watery vomit, into which it fell as I approached. Someone said it was Marsal's Pincho, Perrico's predecessor, who had disappeared a few days before. I went and found Marsal in one of his gardens. He came back up with me, carrying a piece of cord he took from a swag of them hanging over the door of Castanya's byre. Marsal tied the string to the collar on the dog's neck. As Pincho tottered along beside him, Marsal said, 'Sure we all have to go one day,' as if he would have preferred for Pincho to go off and die quietly on his own in the woods somewhere. He told me all of his dogs have been called, alternately, Pincho or Perrico.

The new Perrico showed no sympathy for the last Pincho being at death's door, and tried to chase him off.

Pincho disappeared again a few days later, and was presumed dead.

A Late-afternoon Levée

Every year from early May to late October the Besolís come in transhumance with their big herd of sheep from the low-lands near Lleida, where they also rear pigs and have a butchery business. Their house is just across the main street from the barn of Casa Felip. The original house burned to the ground ten years ago when townie cousins to whom they had lent it for the New Year holidays used a jerrycan of petrol to get a recalcitrant fire going. The petrol blew up in their faces as soon as it touched the embers still smouldering from the previous attempts. It seems they had to jump clear from windows and balconies, still in their night attire, and then stand and watch as the house was gutted. At the fire's peak its flames licked at the wooden rafters of our barn, and would have burned it down too, if Oppen and others had not had the presence of mind to get up on the roof to strip off slates and douse the smouldering beams with water. A year later the Besolís had their house rebuilt, straighter and neater, but much the shape it had been before. In a one-storey shed which slopes down the hill towards Casa Marsal, the only part of the old house which did not burn, they keep the accoutrements of their trade: temporary fences, bells tied in bunches, bags and blocks of mineral lick, marking paint, brands, shears, castrating tongs and dehorning devices.

The grandfather Besolí we had known died when he was

ninety-one. He came to Farrera and went up the mountain with the sheep almost every year to the end of his life. He was succeeded by his son, Pepe, who has been succeeded now by his son, Ramón, whose own son, Josep, will succeed him in his turn.

When they are in residence, Pepe de Besolí often goes before dawn with Ramón in their workdog of a blue Land Rover to see the sheep on the mountain, just to check that they are all there. It is hard to count 700 sheep without falling over in a dead sleep, but they know there are black ones in the herd in a ratio of one to every thirty or so. If all the black sheep are not present, others are probably missing too.

A really black black sheep, as well as being a counter on the shepherd's abacus, is said to protect the herd from lightning during thunderstorms.

Ramón and Pepe usually come back down the mountain for their lunch, the main meal of the day – just as it would be in the country in Ireland, where it is called the dinner, as here it is called *el dinar*. Then in the evening, after their siesta – a proper siesta of bed turned down, shoes set out on the windowsill, shutters closed – Pepe de Besolí, wearing a dandy white cap, open-necked shirt, light jacket and trousers gathered tight at his thin waist with a belt, slightly bowed in the legs, supporting himself on his shepherd's staff, accompanies his stout wife, Matilde, on her slow, step-by-step progress through the village. To assist his mother's daily escalade, Ramón has put up a metal handrail on the steep climb from the front door of their house and another on the wall that leads up to the main street. From there Matilde supports herself on the wooden railings along the side of the street, then against the walls of the houses and the church, leaning heavily on the stick she holds out at a forty-five-degree angle like a stabilizer on a catamaran. They stop at intervals to catch their breath.

They usually sit for a while on the low wall at the upper square, where the cars park, looking back down under the arch of the church. Then Matilde heaves herself up again and, arm in arm, she and Pepe move round the cliff that towers at the end of the village, past the white electricity transformer building that is lighthouse and landmark, moving *poc a poc*, little by little, as Matilde keeps saying, out on to the Head of the Ridge overlooking Burg. When they reach the bench that is their meeting place, Matilde subsides on to it, legs spread, leaning both hands on her stick, ready to see everybody and know everything at this late-afternoon levée.

Pepe prefers to stand, leaning on his staff with the polished iron crook on the end of it, just like the one his father used to carry (or maybe it is his father's), and just like his son Ramón's. Ramón usually joins them there for a while on his way up to or down from the mountain, leaning his cheek against the cool of the hook on his staff as if it were an aid to speech. Pepe often stands the same way. His father did too.

In the distance Burg is piled like a settlement of troglodytes on its sandy-hued rock (a different, more solid rock than Farrera's, part of a syncline that runs into Aragon and beyond), the houses clambering up the mountainside, the gardens around the plastered church of Saint Bartolemeu a Yangtze of terraces, each house distinct and named to the viewers from Matilde's bench. Joana, widow of El Noi (The Boy) of Casa Noi, blonde, demure and ladylike with her Pomeranian lapdog, La Tabolina, widow of El Tabolí from Casa Tabolí, and Victoriano, sun-blackened, from Casa Ambrosi, usually walk the couple of kilometres up from Burg, bringing their news.

Various people have their moments on the bench with Matilde, who looks straight ahead, regally erect in her plumpness, attentive like a slightly deaf person who is not letting on, her stick solid under her two hands like a sceptre, her domain spread out before her, and her subjects bringing her tribute of talk.

Marsal sometimes joins them there, usually going on about something in one of the rants on which he gets launched like a rocket heading for a mid-air explosion. The Coté sisters go up when they are here. Montserrat of Casa Bigarret, who is Pepe de Besolí's sister, goes up every evening, and is Matilde's best buddy.

All the locals' cars and jeeps and tractors, entering or leaving Farrera, stop to impart and gather news at Matilde's bench, as at a toll post: who's coming to stay, did the children win the football match, whether it is warm, or fresh, or windy, or likely to rain, who's that in the back of the car, where is such and such a child, did they see so and so, were there many at the swimming pool, did we hear about the dogs, when are the builders coming to start work on our house?

— Sure, never worry, one day you'll get it done, Matilde reassures us. *Poc a poc.*

Black Money

In the summer of 1990, after we bought Casa Felip, builders had come to ask us for the work of fixing it up. Construction work was in short supply then, especially in the Pallars Sobirà. Everyone in Spain was talking about *La Crisis*, with capital L and capital C.

Now, in 1999, there was building going on everywhere in the Pallars. Black money looking for bolt-holes, some said it was, before the euro came in. Much of the money in the Pallars is black, for that is the natural colour of peasant money. A cash economy flows through these valleys, some of it streaming over the passes out of Andorra, where many Pallars families have relatives, to commingle with the new black money the tourists bring that crosses counters and palms in *efectiu*, effective, meaning notes and coins, and none of yer oul' traceable cheques or bank transfers or money orders, *gràcies*.

The Pallars is awash with black money looking for ways to legitimize itself. Developers in Sort are filling in the last open spaces within the town boundaries with blocks of the flats the peasants buy as investments, with a wad of money counted out in large-denomination notes and the minimum credible price declared for legal and tax purposes. Cranes loom over these construction sites like money rigs pumping the black stuff down out of the ether and into four- and five- and six-storey apartment buildings.

Peasants trust cash money – and property – more than anything else. That explains the phenomenon of Andorra, whose peasant founders knew how to parley quaint medieval rights into a low-tax statedom under the protection of the Bishop of La Seu d'Urgell and the King, or, latterly, the President of France. Far from being the romantic mountain principality I had once imagined it to be, Andorra is a vulgar, clamorous, multi-lingual *mêlée* of high-rises, hypermarkets, shopping malls, souvenir shops, tobacco and drinks emporiums, a garish honky-tonk that stretches fifty kilometres from the French border to the Spanish one. In Catalonia itself, the Vall d'Aran, once so remote it had its own language, Aranès (which looks, when written down, like Catalan with a bad lisp), is now an extended holiday city with more than 21,000 tourist beds in hotels, campsites and apartments, three times the year-round population of 7,000.

When we talked to Claude Duval, a French builder and general handyman whom we tried to interest in our job, he told us about how he and a few others were in at the founding of Dizi Rafting, now one of the biggest rafting businesses on the Noguera Pallaresa. They worked as guides, monitors, drivers, trying to do something a bit different, he claimed, though how you can make the fairground ride of rafting different, I can't imagine. For seven or eight years they worked for five or six months a year, at reasonable wages.

During this time the Dizi owner had had to find backers, partners with money, to expand the business. These associates were the usual Pallars godfathers, Claude said, who were creaming it from the tourist boom. When business took a dip one year they decided they would have to economize. Anyway the founder-workers were getting presumptuous, asking for year-round contracts, pensions, overtime, bonuses and job security. One day out of the blue the new bosses sent them sack letters offering 300,000 pesetas (€1,800) as a *fin y quito*, end and over, pronounced as one word, *finyquito*. The Dizi workers baulked at this peremptory dispatch. They started legal proceedings. To help their case, they copied documents to show that the Dizis were coining it, with no tickets issued, no trace of who went down the river on the rubber rafts, so no taxes paid: rafting, the river and the black, black moolah.

The godfathers got shirty and dirty when the workers challenged them. Claude's Spanish wife was threatened, went to the police, but could prove nothing. They were told in anonymous, whispered phone calls that neither they nor their children would ever work in the Pallars again. They should go home to Frogland.

When we had arrived in Farrera in early spring there had been builders at work on another house in the village. On the side of their rusty red crane was painted in wobbly white letters

PAREJA, their name, and underneath, SALÀS DE PALLARS, the town where they were based.

Pareja Inc. consisted of four brothers. They were from Aragon but had been working in the Pallars for years. The brother-in-charge was Manuel, who called himself Manel in the Catalan he spoke in a headlong, heedless, slapdash rush. The other brothers looked at us blankly if we spoke to them in Catalan and replied in Castilian.

We talked to Manel, in Catalan, and showed him the plans. Or rather, he came and talked to us. About his marriage that had just ended; his ex-wife, whom he still loved; the daughter he never saw; how lonely he sometimes was; how it was nobody's fault, really, it was just the way things go. He told us how much he liked working out costs. He would sit up until three or four in the morning with his computer and ready reckoner and the guide to prices per square metre issued by the Chamber of Commerce in Lleida. He could see we wanted to do a good job. He liked the modern style. It was all a question of colour and shape. If you got the combination right, you couldn't go wrong. He could see that Mary had taste. What was that cooking on the stove? It smelled delicious. Had we ever tried lentils with chorizo? He liked cooking, always had, but now he was cooking only for himself and sometimes it wasn't worth the bother.

After longer than he had imagined, the manic midnight oil maybe having run out on him, Manel gave us an estimate. He had simply taken the architect's listing of the jobs to be done and put costings beside some of them. Not very many. Perhaps half. The rest of the jobs would be done according to 'administration'. We asked him what that meant. He said it would be by the hour, whatever it took to do the job.

We told him we would have to look at the figures. We needed to know what we were letting ourselves in for. Manel said that would be fine. Some day soon that suited all of us we would sit down and discuss it again.

After finishing the chalet with its plastic-looking roof tiles, façade of imported stone and second-homer's garage with suburban door, the Parejas, now minus one brother who had thrown up the head, started to build an extension to Andrew's Hay Barn for Michael and Colm. It was to take a few weeks. In the end it took a few months.

In late summer Manel told us he was not going to continue as a builder. The two other brothers were going to jack it in too. It was too far to travel every day. The brothers would look for jobs near Tremp, where they lived. He himself was going to the coast to buy and sell apartments. He had a start with a company he knew there. It would be better than this building lark where you never made any money and it was just one problem after another. They would finish my brother's job and that would be it.

By this time, suspecting that Pareja Inc. would not last, I had contacted another builder, a man called Stilts. His real name is David Walker. He is from Wales. He is called Stilts because he used to perform on a pair when he was younger. He and his then wife, Sally, had happened on Farrera when they were travelling in a truck from England to a street theatre festival in the south of Spain. They had stayed in Farrera for a few days, liked it, and returned after the festival. They bought a ruin on El Castell to build themselves a house. When we had met them for the first time during one of our holiday visits they were clearing the site. They had already been at it for a couple of months. Sally was six months pregnant with their first child. Then one day, when they were at foundation level, Generosa de Casa Marsal went up to El Castell to tell them she had made a mistake when she had described the site to them at the time they bought it. She had mixed up the

families and the houses. What they had bought was not the
site they had just cleared but another one lower down that
was smaller and even more overgrown, with less sun.

After that, we heard they had moved to Boixols, a scattered
townland in the Pre-Pyrenees where other alternative types
had settled. There, over seven years, Stilts had built a dome-
shaped wooden house around a geodesic frame. Now they
were getting separated. Sally would keep the dome. The co-
operative Stilts had started was being wound up. He would
be interested in our job. He needed to make a stake to buy a
plot of land and build another house.

Stilts came to see us with his new companion, Charo, and
her child, Nadir. He arrived in shorts and no shirt to meet the
architect. I could see podgy Joan Albert Adell sizing up his
physique: muscles moulded to the bones on his arms, tanned,
lithe and *mucho macho*. Stilts's Catalan was very fluent, and
plausibly technical when he and the architect had a little canter
through their masons' argot to show what they knew.

We agreed a deal. Stilts would be our foreman. He would
live downstairs in the flat on the first floor of John's Haggard
with Charo and Nadir.

Dani Trillas, tight-curly-haired, in his twenties, came to see
us about getting a start. He had lived on the Balearic island of
Formentera for a number of years, surviving by making wood
carvings and jewellery to sell on a street stall. He had carved
his own didgeridoo. If we took him on he would live in his
teepee in a field on top of a cliff overlooking the village that
he had already sussed out. We took him on.

So without further ado (time is money, Colm kept saying),
and still without a mortgage, we started work.

House of Dreams Old and Dreams New

At seven o'clock on the morning of the thirteenth of September 1999, Stilts, Dani, Mary and I study Adell's plans spread out on the upstairs floor of John's Haggard, and then go up to look at Casa Felip and its barn from every angle, working our way through it space by space, trying to envisage where everything will be, discussing how we will get machinery and materials up to the job.

Viewed thus, the house, the barn below it, and the two terraced gardens above it – twenty metres or more from the ground floor of the barn to the apex of the roof of the house – are built on four or five platforms like giant's steps hewn from the mountain. The cliff itself forms the back wall from top to bottom.

The remaining floors of the barn are roughly sawn planks nailed into big beams perched on stone ledges: strong enough to support loads of the light, dry hay this nave was built to shelter, but giving no structural reinforcement. That is why the front wall of the half of the barn whose roof collapsed two years ago hangs out over the main street like a hesitant avalanche waiting for a loud noise to set it off.

Above the barn, the house itself is a climber who has clung to the cliff for dear life by fingers, elbows, knees, toes and fingernails, and died like that, fixed to the rock by force of will. Less anthropomorphically, it is a quarry of stones held together by river mud and gravel, since cement had not reached these parts when it was built a hundred years ago – or more, for it may incorporate even earlier structures. The wood of the roof is buckled, worm-eaten, and rotted where the rain has come through. On the outside the rough-edged, hand-quarried slates hammered into these boards are covered with a low tundra of vegetation; the west-facing half of the roof browny-green and bluey-grey with growth, the slates of the east-facing side fresher and blacker but also frilled with mosses and lichens that on calm days in the garden I had imagined I could hear digesting our investment, and burping.

At the front, facing the path past Andrew's Hay Barn that leads down to the street, is the *carabiner*'s cabin. Its days are now numbered but I feel withal a great affection for it, as for an aged, frail but still doughty grandmother who will always be missed from her place at the inglenook after the ambulance whose klaxon can be heard in the distance takes her off to the funny farm.

Up the set of stairs that are just inside the door to the *menjador* from the *carabiner*'s cabin is what used to be our bedroom, where Maeve Eulàlia was born. This narrow, low-ceilinged room, duskily lit by its one window, divided off by a thin-skinned wooden wall from the rest of the space under the roof, has always been sacred in our memory of it, but the wall will have to be removed so that we can make two bedrooms and a bathroom on this floor. Our Bethlehem will never be the same again.

The *menjador* had been eating room, work room and pig-killing parlour for the Andorràs, from whom we bought the house. In the far corner there is a wooden-boarded compartment with its own door. Inside this Cartesian black hole low benches run round three sides of the hearth where the ancestors would have made their fire, at all times of the year, for heat, cooking and smoking meat. It too would be demolished, and not much missed.

All through the house there is a pungent, musky smell overlying the all-pervading odour of soot, so strong I see

Stilts's nose wrinkling as he looks at me quizzically, as if to say, What the hell is causing that?

Some months before, at the beginning of the summer, while Mary was in Ireland looking after her mother, I had gone up to stay in Casa Felip for a few nights, one last time for nostalgia's sake in the old house as it was and would never be again. The first evening I was there, as I was settling down on the battered sofa in the *menjador* to read by candlelight, a pair of dormice emerged from somewhere, looked around a bit, then started to play tig along the beams, up and down the walls, round and round the room, in dizzy caracoles, rushing at one another, rolling over, grooming one another's belly fur, before the male got up on the female's back to have a few seconds of trembling coitus, its glazed, transported eyes seeming to be looking straight at me where I sat with the book lying open on my knee.

Dormice, I discovered on the Internet the next day, have high metabolic rates. The temperature must be above an average of twenty degrees centigrade for them to have any interest in mating. In colder climates they may hibernate for up to six months of the year. Dormice in the south of England, for example, fail to mate at all one year in two or three because the temperature does not get high enough to turn them on – which is why the Dormouse in *Alice in Wonderland* keeps falling into the teacup in his asexual torpor.

The common or hazel dormouse, *Muscardinus avellanarius,* is a squirrel-like rodent with a long bushy tail. It has rounded ears, large eyes and thick, soft, reddish-brown fur. Hazel dormice build nests of leaves and grasses in bushes and thickets, often in social groups. They feed on insects, berries, seeds and nuts, and are especially partial to hazelnuts, in which they make a neat, round, teethmark-fringed hole. The European or fat dormouse, *Glis glis,* can reach a length of twenty centimetres, excluding the tail. It grows a thick coat of greyish fur and becomes extremely fat in autumn before going into hibernation. The ancient Romans used to raise it in captivity to eat.

That night, from the bed in our old room, our resident dormice sounded enormous, definitely *Glis glis* rather than *Muscardinus avellanarius*. They seemed to have their bed under the floorboards right next to mine. As I listened to them rustling and shuffling their nest like neurotic bag ladies, the sound exaggerated by the dark, their ratty stink in my nostrils, I wondered how the fat bastards might taste skinned, stuffed with hazelnuts, spitted and roasted, with *allioli* and chips.

After an almost sleepless night I went back to John's Haggard, where the only nocturnal disturbance is the patient chewing of an apparently solitary beetle making *papier-mâché* of our landlord's roofbeams.

The smell of the dormice still lingers in Casa Felip this September morning, but the only sign of the tasty beasts themselves is the nest that they or some other creature had pulled out and scattered all over the floor, like squatters trashing the gaff before the developers move in.

As we continued our inspection we went down a single step from the *menjador* into the one-time store and pantry at the back. Half of this is an open space with a wooden ladder leading up to the floor of which our bedroom occupies one end. The other half has been divided with walls of thin brick into three rooms, each with its glass-paned window in the metre-thick front wall. The first of these windows illuminates a room with a low white sink and a mirror with a bare bulb over it. In the other room there is a cold-water shower and a toilet that can only be flushed by climbing on to its rim to adjust the ballcock in the overhead cistern. At the back door there is a concrete jawbox sink with a tap, the window above it blacked out by the tree of ivy that has rooted in the outside wall.

Ivy also creeps through the cracks and round the frame of the low wooden door which opens into a small garden: a tangle of nettles, docks, brambles and more ivy growing through the rubble accumulated there from years of landslides from the wall of the garden above it. Against the back wall of the house leans the paunch of the round stone baking oven. The ancestors had burned wood in it and cooked their daily bread on the embers, pizza-style. Its smoke would have been drawn into the chimney-hole under an overhanging slate – or some of it, at any rate. Throughout the house the wooden beams and boards of all the ceilings are blackened with the decades of smoke and soot from the main fire and the side fire in the kitchen hut, the bread-oven fire, and another fire there had been on a stone upstairs in the sleeping quarters, whose smoke would have found its way out through cracks in the roof. Up there, under the pitch-pine, hole-riddled, slate-loosened roof, a lot of people have slept. Some years ago Catriona Crowe woke up there one morning after a night at the *festa major* with seven or eight other people sleeping around her, and saw the lead singer of the previous night's band having what she described to the rest of us at breakfast as 'a vigorous wank'. It was always an intimate place, presumably for the ancestors too, making you wonder how they managed to perpetuate themselves at all.

The front wall of this dormitory has settled and twisted around its three skewed openings, a tall one in the middle and a lowish on either side, all with wooden shutters and no glass. When you hunker at one of the low windows, or lean out from the taller one, you are looking down the beetling, bulging, bellying front wall of the house on to the barn roof, a vertiginous prospect that is quite sickening, if you own it.

It's probably settled as much as it's going to settle, I tell Mary. Like ourselves. I'm not sure she believes either assertion.

At half past one in the afternoon we have the first of the workers' lunches that will be cooked by Mary in John's Haggard: potato, thyme and cauliflower soup, then chicken in a cream sauce with rice and the last of the courgettes from the garden. There is fresh fruit salad for dessert. The sun is warm and buttery, low in the southern sky, shining through the big windows, almost reaching the back wall. The conversation is somewhat stilted, for Stilts is wary of us, I feel, as if he has been burnt by disappointment once too often and is determined, as we think we are, to keep this relationship businesslike and uncomplicated. He mostly talks directly to Dani, not catching my eye.

I thought of all the workies' lunches Mary and I have eaten in our many workplaces: at the wine harvests in France; in the kitchens of the Majestic Hotel in Chamonix Mont-Blanc with Tunisian co-workers, bland European kinderfodder for us, hot dishes spiced with harissa for them, until we went African ourselves and had what they were having; with the passengers on Weaver Boats on the Shannon; and at Annaghmakerrig with the artist-workies, where I learned to let the conversations grow like unruly tomato plants whose shoots you don't nip out, so that you get lots of little green tomatoes that will never ripen, and now and then a truss of fat, red fruit full of juice and pith.

There will be a few hundred of these breakfasts and lunches before we're done, so settle down for the long conversational haul, everybody, I hectored myself, trying to relax and let the rhythm establish itself, as I am not very good at doing.

★

A couple of days later Stilts and I went to look at machinery to buy and for hire, hardware shops, timber yards and builders' merchants. We stopped to see the last of his defunct co-operative's works, the tower they built at the Pallars Aventura place on the other side of the tracks in Sort: across a bridge out of the town, over a car park, past a dump, down a rutted lane and through a bent gate into a field with poplar trees along its edges.

Stilts had told me the owner still owed him money. As we were looking at the tower – beautiful masonry work on the arched windows, carved architraves, orange-hued Provençal tiles on the roof – the owner appeared in the distance. He and Stilts talked to one another from a field's length. The owner seemed none too pleased to see us.

We went to Manel Pareja's store in Salàs, where reposed the remains of his builder's ambitions: drifts of white and yellow plastic safety helmets, scrums of green rain jackets, piles of broken blocks and shattered bricks, hardened bags of cement, congealed sand, wheelbarrows with no wheels heeled against the wall, two battered cement mixers, salvaged radiators, coils of cable, twists of rope, congestions of scrap and jumbles of junk. We picked the tools we wanted as part of the job lot we were buying from him: winches, pulleys, scaffolding, planks, chutes for pouring cement, screwdrivers, hammers, planes, saws, a Hilti jack-hammer, a tile-cutter, an angle-grinder. With the dumper we had bought cheap when we first arrived – our very own dumper, I never thought we'd own a dumper – we now have the complete middle-aged builders' starter kit.

The Blind Osteopath of Andorra

Worrying about money, for I can already see that what money we have ourselves is not going to go very far, and unsure, on some days, what we are doing back here in this place of dog shit and dilapidation, I have an attack of my bad back. It lays me up for days. The doctor comes and gives me jabs. They alleviate the pain for a few hours, enough to let me sleep, but the next day it is as bad again as ever.

My bad back is psychosomatic, but real, like my paranoia.

After a week of being bedridden, I am advised to visit the blind osteopath of Andorra who fixed Javier Rodríguez, the carpenter from Alendo.

On the appointed day I ease myself into the passenger seat of the car like a crash dummy that has hit the wall one too many times. I hold myself as erect as I can, wondering if maybe I should get a prosthetic support, and perhaps a folding wheelchair, a disabled sign, a drinking cup with a spout, a plastic bib with a crumb- and slop-catcher at the bottom, and incontinence nappies too, while I'm at it.

Mary drives us down through Burg, whose scabrous dogs stagger stiff-legged out of our path and then stand by the side of the road looking at us the way the people of Burg used to look at us – blankly, as if they had never seen us before. I feel every swerve of the horseshoe bends below Burg, and then the twisting and weaving descent into Tírvia. The old men there watch us pass as if they know I will not be long in joining them in my own crocked shuffle from house to square to bench.

From Llavorsí we drive along the Noguera Pallaresa, where laughing, carefree crews of tourists in polypropylene wetsuits and plastic crash helmets pitch and heave on rubber rafts down the fast-flowing river; through Rialp and Sort, where upright people go about their business; across the Pass of the Cantó, whose stony paths through fields and forests I will now never walk; and down into the valley of the Segre, where the traffic to and from Andorra shines like the carapaces of soldier ants who will still be tramping northwards and southwards long after I am dead. That can't be long now.

The blind osteopath works out of rooms in the Festa Brava Hotel. The straight-backed, pretty young hotel receptionist smiles at me as I hobble up to her desk. Without asking me where I want to go, she tells me to take the lift to the tenth floor and knock on the third door to the right.

The plaque on the door announces that José Palomo y Herranz is a kinesiologist, acupuncturist and physiotherapist.

I have been expecting him to be a big, strong man who would throw me over his shoulder and wrench me back into place. The man who comes out of one of the consulting rooms, dressed in a white coat that makes his thinning hair look very black, as if dyed, is slight, even small. He asks his receptionist (his daughter, I deduce from the cross way she speaks to him) to give him a chart. When she hands it to him he places it across his belly, holding it against him with his left hand, and reads it raised letter by letter with the fingers of his right hand, going over and back, muttering a little.

The door of the consulting room he has just left swings open. The naked man lying face down on the high bed in the middle of it gives me the rueful grin of a fellow sufferer.

As Señor Palomo goes back in there he says to the patient on the table, in English,

— Now you dress. Nex' week we work more on lef' leg. Now is good. You will be hohkay.

His daughter asks me for my details – name, address, passport number, phone number, nature of ailment – typing them into the computer for the braille-printer to emboss the pages for her father to feel.

— Go into the room over there and wait, she sternly orders me, as if her tone were part of the therapy necessary to buck me up and snap me out of it.

In the consulting room Vivaldi's *Four Seasons* plays softly from a speaker up in one corner. On the two end walls are framed Alpine scenes. Against the back wall a Formica table sits between two tubular steel stools. The window on to the street has its venetian blinds drawn, making of the room a shadowed place of afternoon assignation.

After a few minutes Señor Palomo comes through the door, holding its edge and slipping his right hand down until he finds the inside handle, with which he carefully closes it, giving the door an extra push when he has, as if he wants to be sure we will not be disturbed.

He sits on one of the stools at the small table and holds my chart in front of him, facing out. As he reads it with the fingers of his right hand he talks to me in Castilian.

— So you live in Farrera.

— Yes.

— It must be very beautiful.

— It is.

— We went there once. Over the mountains from here, through Os de Civis. It was delightful. I love the mountains. That's why we came to live in Andorra. We lived in Paris for ten years, and then in Madrid, but I always wanted to come to the mountains.

Does his startled-looking daughter describe the landscape to him as they go along? Do they stop so that he can get out to smell the air, feel the rocks, listen to the wind, drink water from the rivers, crush pine needles between his fingers? Does his wife, maybe, read out of a book and tell him how high the mountains are, what they are called, starting from the left and moving to the right across the peaks, so that he can imagine them? Perhaps he has not always been blind, though his eyes have the caved-in look of lifelong blindness.

— Take off all your clothes please, he orders me.

I strip to my underpants and stand facing him.

— Take off everything, he says, without touching me, as if he knows I have kept on my trunks.

I take them off and immediately feel very nude.

— Turn your back to me and come closer.

I sidle up to him.

— Where does it hurt?

I try to explain: at the bottom, all across the lumbar region. I couldn't move out of the bed for days. I had to roll myself along the floor to go to the toilet, and sometimes could not even get that far, and had to lie sideways on the bed to piss into a bottle. It seems to happen when I have *preocupaciones*. This time it came on when I was bending down to lace my shoes one morning and something snapped.

As I talk, and he asks me more questions, his soft, boneless-seeming fingers are counting my vertebrae. He mutters '*dos, tres, cuatro, cinco, seis,*' as he spans up from the coccyx – my hairless, exposed tree-mammal's tail – and then down from halfway up my back, marking the roundels of the spine by using his fingers like calipers, '*doce, once, diez, nueve, ocho,*' until he is pressing where the pain is, asking does it hurt, and it does, like hell.

— *Ponga-se sobre la cama, boca abajo,* he commands.

I lie myself on the narrow table on top of the white sheet, face downwards.

As he positions himself at my feet, I think about how blind people have an enhanced olfactory sense, and hope they don't smell too bad. Undaunted, evidently, he feels between my toes, wiggling the big ones from side to side. His soft, seeing hands move to my Achilles tendon. After pressing the skin there between two fingers again and again, he feels his way up my legs, as Vivaldi erupts into spring, and I wonder if my hole is clean.

He moves to my right side and counts vertebrae once more, as if he has forgotten how many there are meant to be, and works down to where the pain is, pressing gently with his razorshell-clam fingers, as cold as if they have just been pulled from their shells.

— *Ponga-se boca arriba.*

I turn on my elbow, twisting the sheet out from underneath me in a ball, until I am lying face upwards. He tells me to lie on my right side, facing towards him. He takes my legs and gently separates them, talking to me all the while, telling me what he's doing, instructing me. He puts my legs apart so they are both lying easily on the bed, and my arms the same. He then approaches me from the side I am facing.

— *Ponga sus brazos sobre mi espalda.*

I lean up and put my left arm over his right shoulder and my right arm over his left as he works himself under me, holding back a little for fear of toppling him. He braces himself, gets the weight of me limply on his back, and wrenches me sideways, as if to haul me off the bed. I feel something move down where he has been working. Then the other side, the same again, and this time I feel a crunching down in the lumbar region that comes as such a relief I think I am going to fart. He tells me to sit up. He comes behind me and gets me in a neck grip, as if to throttle me, then twists my head. I hear cricks.

— *Ahora se puede vestir.*

As I dress myself he asks what kind of work I do. I tell him we are building a house. I do some gardening. As I hop about to get my socks and shoes on crabwise, he tells me I will have to be careful. I need to lift things with my legs spread. He stands up and shows me how, bending his knees, legs apart. He sits down again, feeling for the stool, and shows me how I need to rise from a sitting position with my hands on my knees, gently, letting my arms take the weight. Then, groping forward, he gets up on the table and shows me how to get out of bed – which is when most damage is done – by bringing myself up on my elbow, first, then swinging my legs out of the bed, one by one, and rising the way he has shown me, hands on my knees. It is all a question of posture. Those who have a weakness in their backs need to be careful. Even labourers used to lifting and carrying things all their lives can strain themselves if they don't pay attention to their posture.

Going out the door after paying my 6,000 pesetas, I hear Señor Palomo (Mr Turtledove, appropriately enough) dictating my condition to his daughter.

Out on the street, I twist my back this way and that way, doing a Monty Python walk, not caring who sees me. The pain has gone. The blind osteopath of Andorra has cured me. His healing hands have made me whole.

Later that afternoon, after Mary and I have been to the cinema, I see my saviour being led along the main street of Andorra La Vella by his daughter, tapping to the right with his white walking stick, as a tessellated rainbow of a halo shimmers round his head.

Saint Eulàlia Intercede for Us

One afternoon, as we were watching the yellow BOMBERS helicopter fly up the far side of the Alendo valley, Stilts told me that he had been in the cadet corps at school for four years. He had flown a few times over the Welsh mountains in battle formations of helicopters that crested the hills and dropped down their far sides like flights of metal raptors. He had ended up as a sergeant-major. They had wanted him to go into the real army after school but he had other plans.

The same day he showed me how the laser level-finder we bought in Lleida worked. Its beam probed the corners like a red-eyed truth-finder, showing the house to be as wildly awry as it always seems in my dreams, yawing in all directions, not a straight wall in the place. But capable of being coaxed upright, bit by bit, we had to trust. Stilts's tough-guy confidence was bracing. He had no doubts at all. He didn't do doubts. Mary and I must have got his quotient, for we seemed to do nothing else.

Stilts told me that when he was young his parents had had an organic pig farm. They put every penny they had into it. There were over 600 sows. In the farm's third year of operation the pigs got swine fever. The disease was diagnosed one day and the next day soldiers came to shoot all the pigs. It took them a day to do it. They used army bulldozers to dig pits to bury the carcasses. As a boy of fourteen Stilts had watched the slaughter. His parents sold the farm and moved to Swansea. They got divorced shortly afterwards. The children all stayed with their mother. She bought first one house, then the house next door, and converted them into flats, doing all the work herself. Stilts helped. At the age of sixteen he built his first mansard roof. Recently, he said, the building had had to be renovated. The only part that did not need to be redone was that mansard roof. Stilts is very proud of his mansard roof, and of his mum. He does not seem to have much time for his dad.

When Mummy Stilts, who is called Angela, came to visit him, we invited her to dinner in our house. She looked as we must look: a greying hippie gone conventional, though she had that English, I mean Welsh reserve the Irish can only imitate, if so inclined. I didn't even try. I asked my usual twenty questions with supplementaries instead.

Over the years, she told us, she has done courses in cooking, furniture restoration, computers, Scottish dancing, property development, book-keeping and Spanish. She held down two jobs, one with a chiropractor and another distributing medical support garments. She had recently started to rebuild a cottage in the country, after selling a five-bedroomed house that had got too big for her after her children left home.

She had been to school with nuns, she said. Mercy nuns, she said they may have been. How come she did not know? Mary and I wondered afterwards. Surely that is the first thing you know about school nuns, what order they are? Perhaps not, if you're Welsh. Irish people would always know.

By the beginning of November the *carabiner*'s cabin of so many lives and pasts was no more. Stilts and Dani spent a week demolishing it, first of all the roof, saving all the old slates they could, though most of them fell to mossy powder when they were touched, then the beams, for firewood. The concrete floor succumbed in jagged lumps to the jackhammer and sledgehammer. The slab of concrete reinforcing over the door of the haggard was brought crashing to the ground with a thud that shook the barn wall and raised a cloud of dust.

So much had happened in that gimcrack space, and now it was just sooty rubble. The word-filled, song-filled, life-filled void it leaves will always be there for those of us who knew it, an 'invisible, untoppled omphalos', as Seamus Heaney calls the place from which the tree in which he had played as a child had been felled and cleared.

Talking with Javier Rodríguez, the carpenter, about the windows we needed, I wondered if we should have triple glazing. Javier is from Salamanca in Castile. He is handsome in a northern European kind of way, fine-featured, light-haired, pale-skinned, inclined to burn in the sun, the only one of our friends here we can count on to have sunscreen when we go on excursions together. He said triple glazing would be excessive. The winters are not that long and not that cold. You need a bit of air circulating about a house anyway. This was not Lapland. It was Spain.

He was right, of course. The people who built these houses with no insulation, wooden windows and draughty doors did not come up with the snug villas of the Swiss Alps because they were too poor to do so. They just built as well as they could with the material available to them, then hunkered down in their chimney corners and bore with whatever the few months of winter sent. For eight or nine months of the year they were out in the fields, warmed by the sun, singing and dancing and laughing away.

Javier agreed, but said he didn't imagine they laughed very much. Or sang. Or danced.

Mary decided we would have the traditional windows with divided panes all the old houses have. The back door would have six panes of glass. The new window out to where the *carabiner*'s cabin had been would be a single, undivided pane to give an uninterrupted view of the middle and nether villages and the church of Saint Roch. She did drawings for Javier of all the windows and doors with the new skills she had learned from her interior design course, and the ruler-slapping that entailed gave me more cause for strange joy.

I am already preparing the garden for next spring. It is a good place from which to keep an eye on the works without getting in the way.

From up there, the eye that roams over the landscape and slakes its thirst for spectacle on the Twisted Mountains to the west, that avid eye ever hungry for news, event and incident, strains after every human movement: Marsal singing as he skelps cows and calves through his fields; Oppen with his pack of dogs and herd of sheep heading down towards the hermitage church (now sheep shed) of the Mother of God of the Ridge; mushroom-pickers stopping their jeep to get out and scour the fields on the road to Alendo; the hamlet of Alendo itself; and the spirit-jolting wonder of the church of Santa Eulàlia, which was wedded to its side-slanted cliff in the eleventh century.

This hermitage church – so called not because hermits once lived there but because of its isolation – sits within the low walls of the cemetery that encloses it on the southern side, while the body of the church backs on to an upthrust of rock from the cliff below. Its single apse is a child-round womb with one rectangular belly button of a glassless window facing up the Farrera valley towards the east out of which the sun rises. Up close, its roof sags on weather-stained timbers. Its walls lean. The bells of its double belfry sit on stones under the rotted beam from which they fell years ago. Its door hangs on bent hinges. Its interior walls shed their madonna blue in leprous licks. No Mass has been said there for decades. But its power of place is palpable, still.

For the *festa major* of Alendo on the tenth of December, Javier Rodríguez and his wife, Anna Mestre, have a dinner in their house there to which they invite all the villagers in residence, and some who make the journey from farther afield. Maeve Eulàlia and I once came from Ireland to attend, and were treated like Magi out of the far west. This year Mary and I walk round from Farrera, our boots crunching on the frosted snow, reminiscing about our wedding on this date all those years before, and wondering how it was that life's wheel had brought us back to this same point on its slippery rim.

Javier and Anna's house is radiant with warmth and welcome through the laced curtains of the front windows as we arrive, and, on the inside, mellow with old wood, hung with Christmas festoons and greenery. There are two rows of tables laid up the centre of the *menjador* with salads, sausages and dips set out in big bowls among baskets of bread and *porrons* and bottles of wine. The main dish is *carn d'olla*, a traditional stew cooked in a cauldron big enough to hold the football of minced meat that is fished out, cut up and passed round.

Along with the dessert and coffee we make up *goigs* in honour of Santa Eulàlia. *Goigs* is pronounced something like *goytchus*. It means joys, acclamations, imprecations. In Catalonia there are tens of thousands of them in existence, often printed in elaborately illuminated editions, and still sung for the feast days of the saints to whom they are dedicated when people meet at the sacred places where communities mark their boundaries and the passage of time − as we are doing here in Alendo in the depths of winter and as is done in the height of summer at the hermitage church of Santa Magdalena at the eastern end of Farrera's territory.

When the *goigs* are written out and rehearsed we process by the light of torches to the church. Nightlights are lit on the sole altar, where the statue of Santa Eulàlia with her two staves of a cross and her bouquet of plastic madonna lilies stands. In the otherwise bare sanctuary – rooted to the rock of mother earth – there is no sign of Jesus, his Father, the Holy Ghost or any other male saint or god.

We stand with candles in our hands and sing the *goigs* in raggedy chorus under the baton of Lluís Llobet, our choirmaster: invoking Santa Eulàlia's aid to put up the price of lambs (the Little Shepherds), get Farrera a high-speed Internet connection (the computer-owners among us), bless the children (all of them), tarmacadam the road to Alendo (the carpenters), and send money to finish the Irish people's house (us):

> Santa Eulàlia we trust in you,
> protector of our lovely valley,
> to get us money and get us through
> our act of building folly.
> Buy us slates and flushing toilets,
> as well as pipes and chimney flues,
> tiles and floorboards, bricks in pallets,
> and we will always pray to you.

To Belfast and Back

The floor of the *menjador* of Casa Felip and its rotten beams have been stripped out. More firewood, to join the man-high pile of it at the door of John's Haggard, brought down by Dani in the dumper and carried up the steep slate path to the terrace. We keep the stove in the sitting room going all day. It gives out enough heat so that downstairs is at least tolerably warm, even if upstairs, where I type this, is always freezing in the mornings and only really heats up when the sun strikes the big windows at the front, shining in on my feet in the thick woolly socks I use as slippers. It speeds up my typing as it excites crickets to stridulate their back legs, though I am beginning to doubt whether anyone will ever want to publish, or read, for that matter, my angry memoirs. One day I used the word-finder on the computer to find all instances of 'fuck' and 'bastard': thirty-five of the former, twenty-three of the latter. Catriona Crowe, who is always right, has told me I should try to be more patrician. Patricians don't say 'fuck'.

After paying Stilts and Dani with the last of our cash and wishing them Happy Christmas, Mary and I go up to look at the works on our own. The house is a skeleton. There is a concrete floor at the back where the kitchen will be. To create this space, almost a metre's depth of clay and rubble has been dug out and slim-slow-slidered down the alley between our barn and the Cotés' house next door, along with tons of clayey debris from the soon-to-be patio at the back.

We discuss whether we should have a set of steep and high steps from the middle of the patio straight up into the garden, or whether we should dig out more of the earth and have the steps going up a new back wall, which would have the effect of doubling the usable area and reinforcing the terrace above. The new roof, when we have a roof, will form an overhang here, so we agree we should make as big a space as possible.

— Then you will be able to run out of the kitchen, skip up the steps and dig fresh vegetables straight from the ground and pluck fragrant herbs from the living bush, I tell Mary.

— I'm not so sure about the skipping, she replies. I want the steps to be low enough not to be a strain on the knees. We're nearly in our fifties, Benny, don't forget.

Mary calls me Benny as a pet name, and Bernie sometimes with a sarcastic American accent as a means of calling me to my senses. Being Benny today, I hold her in a long embrace in the middle of the building site our youthful dream has become.

House-building is an anxious, trying business, we are discovering. I wonder does the formula which says you lose one degree of annual mean temperature for every hundred metres of altitude also apply to the emotions? We are both, I think, very tired from the lack of financial oxygen.

We borrowed more money and went to Ireland for Christmas by the last Irish Ferries boat leaving France. It had been having mechanical problems. It had not made two return trips. There was doubt about its being able to move at all from Cherbourg, where it was stuck, as the Irish Ferries girls in Dublin, Cork and Rosslare reported when we called them from phone boxes along the way. It had to get a certificate of seaworthiness from the French authorities.

It was a relief to see its Irish cattle-boat livery at the port when we arrived, black smoke rolling from its funnels as if bonfires of tyres had been lit in its boilers. The crew looked as if they had used the enforced sojourn in Cherbourg to go on a pre-Christmas piss-up. The ship seemed to have been on its own batter. Its opaque, salt-sprayed windows wept rusty foam from their joints on to the sorry Santas, crossed hollies, cracked bells and streaming ribbons that had been daubed on to them. We had the ghost ship almost to ourselves: just us, a few other intrepids of the retired type, glossy continental bourgeois heading for their holiday homes in west Cork, I imagined, and truckers who kept to the truckers' ghettos, those roped-off areas of special privilege where the men of the road swop tales of *fellatio* in Vintimiglia, checkpoints in Czechoslovakia, boredom in Bologna, lechery in Lisbon. We looked for our friend Joe of the Juggernaut, just on the off-chance, but he wasn't there.

I thought to myself that if all else failed I would become a trucker and have my own rig, with dangling phosphorescent skeletons and both our names entwined across the top of the windscreen on a strip of green plastic:

BENNY AND MARY — NO DREAM TOO HEAVY TO CARRY.

When we got to Rosslare a raddled-voiced fellow came on the tannoy to tell his fellow crew members to get their 'asses ashore and have a Happy Bloody Christmas'. After passing through the feeble spittle of the foot-and-mouth douches, we exited the port into an Emerald Isle grey and gusty with rain and wind. Wexford town looked like Andorra when we got lost going to meet Colm and his family. We inched our way in the car up the main street through crowds carrying gaudy bags, shops ablaze with light and ablare with jingle bells, the economic boom a mist of money droplets in the air, with us feeling we were the only ones who were poor, dodging from cash machine to cash machine like pickpockets, for I had discovered that if you run really fast from one to another you can sometimes wrong-foot them over your credit limit.

Over Christmas in Belfast people kept asking us what we were doing.

I said I was writing my memoirs. We were setting up a business having artists and others to stay in the houses of friends in the village. There had been quite a lot of interest so far. We'd find the customers, help to look after them, and take a percentage of what they paid, like travel agents. We expected the first guests to arrive next summer. We were also building away at our own house. Getting on very well, in fact. We would be living in it soon. I didn't say we only needed roofs, floors, windows, doors, plumbing, electricity, heating, and about £150,000 sterling more than we were ever likely to have.

Mary spent long hours with her mother, Kathleen, all the days we were there. They have a literally touching relationship, close and tender. Mary cajoles her mother out of her glooms when she says she is no good to anybody, she'd be better off dead, she is only a nuisance. Mary pooh-poohs her fears as she tucks her up with cushions in her winged armchair, puts a blanket over her legs and wraps her feet in an electrically heated slipper like a big, squared-off tea cosy. She arranges her mother's arm from the side that disappeared on her with the stroke so that at least it looks more comfortable, even if Kathleen doesn't know it's there. When Mary has her mother's hair done and her lipstick on, so that she is fit to receive guests, the big room with its windows on to the gardens of the nursing home is like a salon where Kathleen holds court. Her family and friends are all very attentive to her. She loves to have an audience for her drolleries, bursts of schoolgirl Irish, waspish retorts to her fusspot of a sister, and teasings of me, when I am there, for sitting on the edge of my seat ready to bolt at the first opportunity.

My own mother, Sadie, is patient and kind with my father, Henry, the gravity of whose Alzheimer's she has been masking for years. He has stopped working now. The two workshops out the back of our house are dark, dingy and depressing. Without the work that was the mainstay of his life for so many years, he seems cut adrift. He takes long, seemingly random walks – who never went for walks – to the Falls Park, up the Glen Road or along the Andersonstown Road in search of the shop where he buys his lottery tickets. He sometimes gets lost and has to be conducted home by someone he meets who takes pity on his confusion. The police brought him back in their armoured jeep one of the days before Christmas when he went into the barracks to ask them if they knew where McDonnell Street was, the street where he grew up that was slum-cleared two decades ago.

We all know this can't go on, but can see no other solution for the moment than that they should go on living in the house where they have always lived, until there is a crisis.

We got back to Farrera on the thirtieth of December, to be joined by Maeve and Eoin. As so often in all these years, there are moments of tension, and sudden blazes of frustration and impatience at how long it seems to be taking to find the way out of the confusion of the past, followed by sometimes tearful, intense discussions out of which we all realize, I think, that we have more of our journeys to go before we can stand together in calm and confidence looking out over the wide sea that awaits us. Moving away from Annaghmakerrig has not unlocked any magic door of release from its memories for any of us, though I feel that after all our searching, now together, now separately, and coming back on occasions like this to report our findings to one another, we may already be smelling the salt-laden air that blows through the labyrinth's cave-entrance. One day soon we will see its light and go towards it, hand in hand, to stand on the sandy, sun-soaked shore of the future.

To have our children with us is a great, great joy.

On the thirty-first, just before midnight, we went up to the square, each with our ration of twelve grapes. There were about thirty of us: second-homers brought in on the Yule tide, Alex and her children, Oppen, Anna and Roger, Llobets, other Loughlins, Colm, and Marsal with his millennial reminiscences. For each knell of the midnight hour struck by Arnau Llobet up in the bell tower of the church we ate one grape, counting out loud. We all roared at the stroke of twelve as Arnau made the bell ring and resound through the darkness that surrounded the village. We kissed everybody and every-body kissed us, then stood around for a while and talked, looking up at the stars.

It didn't take long for Farrera to feel as it has always felt: edgy, provisional, promissory, like the new millennium.

On the sixth of January we went down to Llavorsí for the coming of the Three Kings. Spanish children get their presents on the day of the Kings rather than on Christmas Day. It was Eloi Loughlin Rapalino's first year to have his name on one, brought down in advance by Michael and Verónica. The kings and their attendants were played by bigger children, or young adults, the sons and daughters of Farrerans, some of them, whom Eloi said he recognized. He wondered how they had become kings. We told him it was only for this one day, and that one day he would be a king too.

Singular Pigs

In February, for my fiftieth birthday, as our finances dipped into a light coma, we went for a few days to the province of Huesca in Aragon, thinking of poor Katharine of that once kingdom, whose mother tongue was Catalan when she went to marry Henry VIII.

Our object was to visit the Romanesque churches of the valleys of Taüll and Boí, soon afterwards declared a world heritage site by UNESCO. It is the scale of these exquisite edifices – measured out, you imagine, the way builders still talk here, in fingers, palms, arms, steps – that makes them so touchy-feely, close and human. No two are the same, even

though they were all built in the same few centuries at the
turn of the last millennium. Elements recur: rounded arches,
bulging apses, Lombardy chevrons, sculptured doorways, and
their most gracious features, pillared belfries with many
windows – to give light, of course, but also to make the
structures light. Each church conjures something new out of
these morphologies, twisting and adjusting them around its
rock, promontory or eminence, for they are all thrillingly
placed among the mountains, and are visible from miles
around, like *goigs* sung in stone, in perfect harmonious pitch
with their surroundings.

Everything done in the late twentieth century has been
crass speculation. Hulking blocks of holiday flats and thuggish
gangs of terraced houses have muscled in around the village
of Taüll as if to overwhelm it by brute force of numbers.
According to the big signs proclaiming their qualities, they
are fitted with jacuzzis, finished with hardwoods, ornamented
with stone fireplaces, bestowed with terraces and balconies.
These second homes lie empty for most of the year, making
the nearly deserted original village all the bleaker now in
February, while the flighty, playful tower of Sant Climent
looks on in eleventh-century fright at these ghouls that have
gathered to gorge on its eternal soul.

On our way back we went to Isil and Alòs d'Isil in the valley
beyond Esterri d'Àneu, at the northern end of the *comarca* of
the Pallars Sobirà. The predominant vegetation there was
stunted oak, still holding its dead leaves, making the landscape
a burnt brown over black leafmould, as if a fire had passed
through, among outcrops of mossed rocks, streams bursting
their banks into puddled, saturated fields, the river in spate:
the west of Ireland on a wet day.

In Alòs d'Isil we went to look for a *casa pairal* that had

intrigued Tere and Claudi. It was easy to find, occupying as it did a couple of acres in the heart of the village. It sprawled like a forbidden city around a vast courtyard with stables and barns and a couple of enclosed paddocks opening off it, as we could see when we peeped through chinks in the tightly locked high wooden door. Along one range of the house, hanging out over the street, was a two-storey, glassed-in balcony of jalousies, where you could imagine the heiresses of all this would have sat and looked down at suitors as they arrived at the gate. Perhaps the swains sang up to them like the ones in Farrera did, according to *Events, Customs and Legends of the Pallars Sobirà* by Joan Bellmunt i Figueras. The Farrera lotharios sang in Castilian, it seems, because the village schoolmaster at the time was Castilian-speaking, and must have taught them the song:

> *Debajo de este balcón*
> *hay una piedra redonda,*
> *donde nos sentamos los mozos*
> *cuando venimos de ronda.*

> *En tu puerta planto un pino*
> *y en tu ventana una vara,*
> *para que el sol no te quite*
> *la hermosura de la cara.*

> Underneath this balcony
> there is a circular stone,
> where we lads sit
> when we go on our round.

> I am planting a pine at your door
> and putting a branch in your window,
> so that the sun will not take away
> the loveliness of your face.

The heiresses had certainly all left. There was no sign of life within the citadel. The rest of the village was otherwise far gone in desolation: rain running off corrugated iron roofs to dribble down grey stone façades with gaping windows and rotted wooden balconies. A man wearing a sack split down one seam over his head and shoulders, the only human being we had seen in the village, looked mournfully out at us from the door of a byre where he was crouched on a three-legged stool, with his cows in stalls behind him. As we went past we said '*Adéu*', 'to God', as if it were a wish that he might have an easy passage to wherever the rest of them had already gone.

There were a dozen cars and jeeps, bearing Huesca, Madrid, Castellon and Barcelona registrations, parked in the square where we had stationed our Toyota Carina with its Monaghan number plates. These vehicles belonged to the wild-pig hunters we could hear hollering in the woods above the village. Just as we were getting into the car we saw a boar surge up a steep slope of furze and scrub in bursts of strong-shouldered pushing, then pause, listening and panting, until it was spotted by the hunters, who hallooed, yelled and sicced their dogs on it, until there was a chorus of man-cries and dog-howls chasing the pig towards the guns of men we could see lurking at the far end of a small wood the pig would have to traverse.

We did not stay to watch the execution.

A few days later I saw a wild pig (*porc senglar* in Catalan, from the Latin *Porcus singularis* – singular pig) as I made my way to Alendo through the fields and over the river. It squealed and grunted as it blundered out of the brambles and under-brush of a copse under a cliff, leaving a smell behind it that you could bottle as a biological weapon. It was stocky, with tufted ears, hairy all over, blackish and whitish striped on the back as if the paint had run, black underneath, and quite nifty on its feet as it half-ran, half-jumped away from me. There were signs of more of them everywhere in parts of fields where they could not be seen from the village, as if they were soldiers trenching out of sight of the enemy.

One evening some weeks later, as we came round the last corner into Tírvia past the hermitage church of Saint John, patron of fire and renewal, smoke billowed round the car from a fire burning in a concrete pit beside the weighbridge where the forestry lorries check their loads. We stopped to see what was happening. There were three dead wild pigs laid out on a slab above the firepit, all facing in the same direction, biggest to smallest, Daddy Pig, Mammy Pig and Baby Pig: holocausts to the old gods of the forests and the mountains who had taken refuge behind the wooden door of the sanctuary of Saint John. Curved tooth-tusks protruded from the ends of the pigs' bathplug muzzles, giving them a surprised, caught-in-the-act look. Their too-dainty-and-delicate-seeming-for-their-size hooves glinted in the firelight as if their legs had been shoved into shiny metal chair-leg ends. Hunters in camouflage gear with bandoliers of bullets slung over their shoulders swaggered through the smoke while lean dogs with long ears yawed back and forth sniffing the air, as if expecting the hunt to resume. The chief *bomber*, who also seems to be the head hunter, told us the fire was to burn off the pigs' bristles before they were quartered to be divided up among all the men who had participated in the day's sport.

The wild pigs lie up in the woodlands and scrubby patches near the villages during the day and emerge at night to forage in gardens and pastures. They use their snouts to go over the ground for roots, bulbs, worms and grubs. Their diggings leave the fields pitted with patches of rocky subsoil that make them difficult to work. The peasants have always hated and persecuted them, but now that there are so few peasants left, the wild pig population is increasing spectacularly.

Of recent days Marsal had made half a dozen scarepigs from plastic bags draped over crossed sticks and stood them in a line along the run of the dung drain in his field by the river. At night he goes out on to the balcony that overlooks his gardens, sometimes rising from his bed to do so, and stands there in his long-johns, rattling pots, clapping his hands, guldering and shouting 'I shit on the mothers that bore you!', throwing things out into the darkness, including a chamber pot I found lying on the path after one of his outbursts: a crazed Canute trying to hold the tide of wilderness at bay.

He says that the nights he goes out to shout, they don't come; the nights he doesn't, they do.

God Bless Enric of the Deutsche Bank

After the debacle with the Banca Catalana, on which we had wasted months, we had gone round the rest of the banks in Sort to ask them for a mortgage. They had all said no, except the Caixa Catalunya, whose nail-biting manager had held out some hope.

As I climbed up the sweep of steps to the sunny, Italian-looking Plaça Major, a Mediterranean interlude in this mountain town, where the Caixa Catalunya has its offices in the one-time palace of the Counts of Pallars, I noticed a plaque to the memory of Doctor Josep Mir i Rocafort (Fassman) – 'Hypnotist and Creator of the System of Applied Mental Dynamism'. As I gave Josep Maria Capmany i Ungla, the new manager in whom all our hopes reposed, Adell's plans along with details of our prospects, I tried to fix this brother nail-biter with a hypnotic, dynamic Fassman stare. As he listened to my spiel, rather distractedly, I thought, he gnawed a thumbnail that was already red and bloody.

After a few weeks he said his regional director '*no ho veu clar*', does not see it clear, which is polite Catalan for no way, José.

We went to Barcelona. I touted our dossier to all the banks on the Plaça Catalunya. In one of them a sour-faced young woman who looked like Solbank Mercedes's wee sister just said no, after looking me up and down from grey head to scuffed shoes. The rest of them did not see it clear, except a zesty young fellow in Bancaixa, who said he would send on the dossier, we seemed to have a lot of assets, the business plans were interesting, a mailing list with seven thousand names on it must have some value, they were a new bank looking for clients in a very competitive marketplace, so he was sure they would study our proposal favourably.

A week later they said no, too.

By now I was looking up mortgage offers on the Internet and sending off e-mails with bits of the dossier attached.

No, no, no.

I phoned banks and building societies in Ireland. No, we don't do loans in Spain, even if they are secured on properties in Ireland.

Amidst the classified ads on the back pages of *La Vanguardia*, next to the massage-parlour and brothels section with photos of naked women with their nipples blanked out by stars, I found offers of emergency loans, debt consolidation, and mortgages for people who had been rejected by banks.

By now in a state of advanced desperation, I phoned one of these places. It had an address on the Ronda Universitat in Barcelona, where I knew there were a lot of detective agencies.

As I explained our predicament to the hoarse man on the other end of the line, I could hear traffic on the street outside his office through what must have been an open window, for it would have been very hot and muggy in Barcelona then. As we talked, I imagined him sitting at his cluttered desk, phone crooked under his unshaven double chin, belly bulging through his string vest, wiping his brow with the bandana with which he had just been cleaning his gun and his gum-shoes, looking over at the blowsy blonde broad in the wide-brimmed hat, black sheath dress, high heels and sheer nylons who was buffing her long red nails on the sofa under the window. In his bored, laconic replies he sounded as if he would rather be out rifling boudoirs, or sneaking polaroids of couples in flagrante delicto from wardrobes in hotel rooms, or following suspects from an unmarked sedan, or getting on to the sofa with the blonde and sweating out the afternoon with her to sounds of sirens, howls of the mugged, the dying falls of the screams of the terminally indebted as they leapt to their deaths from high buildings, and the clackety-clack of his fan.

He said if he could get us a mortgage the interest rate would be at least 10 per cent. I said I'd phone him back.

Then one day, as I was idling on the Internet, I found a website announcing the arrival of the Deutsche Bank in Spain. They were offering the cheapest mortgages I had seen. I phoned the head office in Madrid. They told me there was a new office in Lleida, our provincial capital. I phoned and made an appointment to see the manager.

The first good sign was that Enric Farré, the manager, called me *tú* and Mary *tú* and the two of us *vosaltres*. All the other managers had called us *vosté*, a Catalanization of the Castilian *ustéd*, short for *vuestra merced*, your mercifulness, which takes the third person and is thus a way of keeping a formal distance, and being able to say God buy you, loser, if the negotiations don't work out.

Enric, for he was so genial we already thought of him by his first name, said sure, he could not see why not, maybe not 35 million pesetas, perhaps 12. We thought 12 million would be better than no millions, which was all the millions we had.

Our weary, world-worn dossier, now rendered into my best Castilian, went to the Deutsche Bank headquarters in Madrid. They hummed and hawed for weeks, not seeing it too clear either. I sent more e-mails, in the second person, to Enric, clarifying, pleading, almost whining, unable not to seem needy when we were as needy as we had ever been, for snowdrifts of bills were accumulating round our mountain refuge, whose door we would soon not be able to open. Then one day an e-mail arrived from Enric, saying yes, and the computer broke into a joyous, root-tooty-toot fanfare.

A few weeks later Enric visited Farrera with his wife, from where they were staying in their caravan at a campsite in Ribera de Cardós, to leave us a draft of the mortgage agreement. Enric was not wearing socks with his light shoes. They both looked burnished with Deep-Down, Well-Being Glow Factor 10. As we had tea together in John's Haggard they told us about the piano lessons they were doing together. Every year they did a different course, to keep their minds active. We discussed caravanning. I told them my father had had a number of caravans during his life. As a garrulous, funny man he had always enjoyed the camaraderie on the campsites. New audiences for his old jokes, he used to say. He had had to give it up recently because he was not fit for it any more. Enric said he liked caravanning himself because you met people from different walks of life, and you could always move on to another site if you wanted a change.

I didn't tell them that Mary had said at one stage, when the mortgage seemed doubtful, that if Enric didn't give us one, we would burn down his caravan. We had tried to work out which one was his a couple of times as we were driving through Ribera. He would never know the lucky escape he had had.

After the tea we went up to Casa Felip. Enric, the only one of all the bank managers with whom we had talked who had actually come to see the place, gazed into the enormous rubble- and wood-filled hole of the barn, which looked like the aftermath of another Civil War bomb blast, and said,

— *Déu n'hi do.*

Which means Jesus H. Fucking Christ.

On the signing day, as Mary and I made our way to the Deutsche Bank office on the Avenue of the Field of the Riverbank, we stopped to watch a pair of storks repairing their nest of twigs on top of a plinth in the middle of a busy road. Each time they tucked a new stick into the nest they did a little hopping dance, clacking and scissoring their long beaks at one another, then using them to caress one another's necks with proud love of their spiky home on this prime site over-looking the city of Lleida and the river Segre, where they fished for a living.

In the bank we had to wait an hour for the notary. When he arrived we were closeted in Enric's office with Enric explaining to us how the contract we were about to sign was all in the bank's favour. If we missed payments we would be punished with loadings and the cost of sending us notifications. If we defaulted they would take the house off us.

The Castilian-speaking notary asked us if we understood Spanish. We said we did. He then read out the document to us, explaining one or two points, and asking us a few more times if we understood. He told us that when we signed the deed the money would be ours. The property would remain ours as long as we kept up the repayments.

He then signed with a fat-bodied, broad-nibbed Parker, which he handed to us to make our marks.

We were to receive the first tranche there and then, the second when we had a certificate from the architect to say 80 per cent of the work was done, and the final pay-out when we had a certificate of completion with a Stamp of Habitability from the Department of Housing of the Generalitat de Catalunya.

After the signing, Enric was to give us 1,967,567 pesetas in cash, with which we were going to meet the most pressing bills. He went into a cubbyhole at the side of the room and brought out a pile of bundles of notes, each packet lapped with a note folded over. He then counted each packet all over again, flicking back the notes one by one, counting them out loud, then solemnly folding each 100,000-peseta pile back into its mothernote, smoothing them down, then setting them out on the counter, in twenty separate packets, and laying the coins out, side by side, in a neat row, down to the two light alloy one-peseta pieces, as though he and we were involved in a ceremonial exchange whereby the money was transubstantiated by his priestly powers into all the things we might do with it, and he was enjoining us to use it well, and to bring it back one day, fructified and multiplied.

— *Argentum vobiscum*.

— *Et cum spiritu tuo*.

Catalans have a reverence for money, talk and joke about it, are unembarrassed by it, and handle it in a way that is all their own. Foreigners get them mixed up with the caricature of the easy-going, *mañana*, *mañana* Spaniards with their sombreros, siestas, soulfulness, picturesque poverty and crumples of low-denomination notes spilling drunkenly from their shallow pockets. That is not the Catalans, at all, at all.

Catalans have purses.

That afternoon I bought one myself, to be more like them.

Farrera Fabulosa SL

At around the same time as we got Enric's mortgage we formed a company called Farrera Fabulosa S[ocietat] L[imitada] as a means of employing people, and paying tax and social security. Up until this we had been doing everything on the black, which was just more to worry about. We did have building insurance, but I still kept wondering: what if one of them fell off the roof? Were they being careful with the chainsaw? Would it be worth a man's while to cut off a finger or two and then sue us for every penny we had?

I had other ambitions for Farrera Fabulosa, written out in a twenty-page business plan that Mary looked at on the computer screen one day. She went pale as she scrolled down through it, stopping after a few pages.

— Let's just get our house finished, she said, then you can try out your big ideas.

To form the company we first of all had to get the constitution of an Irish company we had already incorporated translated into Spanish. We took the translated text to a notary's office in Barcelona. There it was typed out all over again and put between pompous, velveteened covers with the name of the notary in Gothic letters on the front. When it was ready, we went to his office for him to sign it.

— You will have to wait for Señor Nuñez y Navarro to finish signing for another client, the receptionist told us.

It seemed that was what notaries did for a living. They

signed. As we sat in the busy foyer we could hear the receptionist saying that this one was signing and the other one was signing and somebody else was waiting to have something signed.

An hour later the notary took us into a consultation room and read out the constitution of the company to us, having first of all enquired if we understood Spanish. At the bit where it said we could build bridges, highways, dams, railways, blocks of apartments, factories, offices and churches, a fat worm of a slimy rictus slithered over his face. After tugging back the sleeve on the right arm of his chalk-striped suit as if about to do hard physical work, he signed with a flourish: 75,000 pesetas (€450) worth of signing with his golden pen.

A week afterwards, with the already much be-stamped deed of the company in hand, I went to Lleida to complete the formalities. It was a ferociously hot day.

First of all I had to go to Hacienda – Housekeeping – as the Spanish tax office is called, a ten-storey modern building just beside the columnar monument where Mary and I had watched the storks building their nest. There were young ones in it now, the tips of their beaks just visible when the parent birds landed on the stork-pad to disgorge fishes and frogs into their imploring gapes.

In the cool hall of Housekeeping I had to take a ticket, number 973, for my place in the queue. The red-dotted electronic scoreboard above the inside door showed number 869 was being attended.

At twelve noon, with only three hours to go until closing time, other people sat around watching the numbers change, very, very slowly. I went for a cup of coffee in a nearby bar. When I got back they were on 907. An hour later it was my turn. No, it wasn't this desk, but that one over there, where there was another queue. When I got to the head of that queue the woman behind the desk seemed none too happy, as none of them seemed terribly happy, though why they wouldn't be with their permanent and pensionable employment in these offices, where the air-conditioning was so delicious after the heat of the day outside you would nearly pay for the luxury of standing in it, was beyond me, as I stood there oozing nervous sweat, profound impermanence and utter unpensionability.

Our Lady of Cool unfroze a little when she heard my Catalan. Catalans have the notion that their mother-tongue is a minority language – and therefore appreciate foreigners making the effort of learning it. As I went from office to office I would veer from Catalan to Castilian, on the principle that if the person returned my Catalan *bon dia* with a Castilian *buenos dias*, then the latter was the language to use, rather the way Protestants and Catholics sniff one another out in my own schizophrenic country, though without the same frisson of danger, since, as far as I know, nobody gets murdered or kneecapped here for speaking the wrong lingo. She told me that as a foreigner I could not sign for the company. I needed to go to the police station to be registered and get an NIE, Número de Identificación de Extranjero, a foreigner's identity number. She explained to me where the police station was, and listed the documents I would need: my passport, three photographs, a copy of the constitution of the company, and proof of being resident in Farrera.

In the police station, where national identity cards were also renewed, there was a fluid, disorderly, noisy queue which seemed to consist of people who all knew one another, as if entire neighbourhoods of the city had had their cards go out of date on the same day.

When I got to the top of the queue the policeman told me I was in the wrong place. I needed to go to the Department of Governation, in another part of the city altogether. It was three o'clock. The offices there would be closed. I would have to go in the morning.

I stayed the night in the Hostal Mundial. My room had an enclosed balcony overlooking the main square of this most provincial of provincial cities, which always makes me think of Camus's Oran, especially in the flagrant heat of the middle of the day, when nothing stirs. The mile-long principal street of Lleida, which meanders through this square from the railway station to nowhere much in particular, closes up dead for four hours, as if the plague has just passed, and then opens again between five and six in the evening as Catalan heaven, where everybody is resurrected as a shopkeeper or a shopper.

The next morning, in the already torrid heat of 9 a.m., I went to the Department of Governation in a building down by the river which looked like a maritime consulate in Honduras or Belize. Among the palm trees and canna lilies in the little park in front of it black people and brown people wearing djellabahs, burnooses, saris, big-mama costumes with matching head-dresses, Adidas bottoms, Nike tops, and whitish-looking men in pre-wrinkled suits (Romanians? Bulgarians? Belarussians?) stood talking and puzzling over papers. They all held sheaves or folders of documents, groups and families of them, for no one seemed to be there on his or her own. Inside the building a straggling queue was being dealt with by a policeman wearing a gun, truncheon and handcuffs pendent from his easy-going midriff, speaking in bluff telegramese, as if to dim relatives.

— Where papers? Show. Not today. *Mañana.* Need piece paper, like this, from police station in place live, he told them, holding up a pink strip.

Those who had the requisite slip he directed to a room with glass doors off the foyer where forty or fifty people sat in rows on plastic seats, silent and stolid, as if merely getting into that room had been their object, as if this was the European Elysium they had come so far to find.

When I got to the top of the enquiries queue the policeman took me by the arm and led me to the separate section for citizens of the European Union. I was the only one there. A woman gave me three forms to fill in. When I brought them back she said it would take a few weeks to process my NIE. They would let me know by post when it was ready.

I went home.

Five weeks later I was notified that my NIE was ready. I set out very early to make the two-and-a-half-hour journey to Lleida, which is at the far end of the province from Farrera. In the Department of Governation the black and brown and whitish people were all still there, as if posed by a continuity director on a film. At the true whities' desk they gave me a single sheet of paper with my NIE on it, surrounded by the stamps of all the places it had been and all the people who had seen it and expressed their approval of my being granted this exalted status for which the refugees and the refusees would have sold their first-born.

Back at Housekeeping a woman took the constitution of the company from me and typed details from it into her computer. She wrote a number in pencil at the top of the front cover, then handed it back to me and told me to go to another desk. The woman there entered more data into her computer. She then sent me to a desk at the front where I had to pay I can't remember how many pesetas, but quite a lot, because I had to go out to a bank machine to get more cash.

Once I had the receipt I went back to the desk where I had started five weeks before. There I was given a NIF, Número de Identificación Fiscal, a tax identity number for the company.

It was now closing time again. Outside it was hotter than

ever. The storks on the nest on the plinth were fanning their wings to shade their young ones, who had got very big. They would probably fledge and leave the nest soon.

All this time I had been dealing with the Spanish state. The next morning I had to go to the tax office of the Catalan government. It was even cooler than in Housekeeping. There were no queues. I paid more pesetas and got another stamp on the constitution.

At the Chamber of Commerce of the Province of Lleida at the other side of town I left the constitution and the various documents now attendant upon it so that they could enter Farrera Fabulosa SL in the register of companies. Two weeks later I got the call to go back and collect the registration, on payment of another swatch of pesetas.

On the way home Mary and I went to the regional Social Security office in the riverside town of Balaguer further up the Segre to get registered there too.

And we were in business – above-board, straight-up, honest injun, legit – at last: just in time to go broke, by the looks of it.

The Assumption of Saint Sadie into Heaven

In early July 2000 Michael and I learned that our mother, Sadie, had had a stroke. She just fell over in the garden while she and our father were having tea. We went back to Ireland in a hurry, by Easyjet through Liverpool, where we spent the night sleeping on benches in John Lennon Airport while waiting for the early connection to Belfast.

Sadie had lost her speech and all mobility. She seemed to recognize us when we arrived at the hospital, though she had no way of communicating beyond a lift of one eye and a girlish gesture of lifting her right hand to the side of her mouth. When we came to her bedside, she looked from one to the other of us, her eldest and her youngest, knowing us but possibly not able to put names to us. The doctors had told us that after her stroke Sadie's understanding of language would be severely disrupted. She would see things and know things and perhaps get the tone of what was said to her, but it was as if she had awoken in Russia or China for what she might comprehend verbally.

Our father, Henry, collapsed one day when he was visiting her and had to be brought to a heart ward upstairs. They put a pacemaker in his chest. When I went to see him after the operation he was up on his hands and knees twisted in a tangle of tubes and wires, struggling to get down off the high bed. He had no idea where he was. He wanted to go home to McDonnell Street, where he had not lived for fifty years. He thought I was his brother, Johnny, who had died ten years before.

We had to find a nursing home that would take him, since now, without Sadie, he would not be able to fend for himself. After looking at and smelling all kinds of dismal and not so dismal establishments, we got him a room in the clean, airy, friendly Fruithill Nursing Home only a few streets away from our family home. We had to use strategems you might try on a child to get him to stay there. He called it his digs, or the fold – from hearing Sadie talking so often about a fold, for it had always been her hope to end her days in one – but kept wanting to know when he would be getting out of it. He would sometimes pack his bags and be standing at the door with them when you went to see him, and you would have to start all over again to persuade him that the fold was the best place for him. Every day he walked the quarter of a mile to his own house. We would hear the click, click of the steel-tipped soles and heels of his shoes as he came flat-footed down the street, one of the symptoms of Alzheimer's being a tendency to shuffle. He was anxious and fretful all the time. When were we going to see Mammy? He seemed to think it was his own mother we were going to see. In the ward with Sadie he was plaintive, edging up close to her on his chair, holding her hand, calling her love, telling her she would get better, as if pleading with her not to abandon him.

She didn't get better. All five of her children took turns to sit with her, and just keep talking, about everything and anything.

One night, when I was there on my own with her in the private room on the twentieth floor of the City Hospital where the nurses had moved her when they knew she had not got long to live, I started to tell her what we were doing in Farrera, sitting up close to the bed in the low light of the lamp on the bedside table, holding and patting her hand. About the building work, and the lads we had on the job, how Eoin was enjoying working on what would one day be his own house, the ideas Mary had for embellishing it when the structural work was finished, about events in the village, people she had met there the three times she had visited with Henry – all the time thinking how infrequently I had ever been able to tell her I loved her, and telling her now, making up for lost time, how much I loved her for how she had always been there, without reproaching me ever, no matter how foolish I had been, as I had been remembering in my memoir. Here I'm recalling my homecoming after a year of travelling on the continent while in my early twenties:

I felt exhilarated to be in Liverpool, with an afternoon and evening to spend before the boat sailed for Belfast. I had I don't know how many pints of bitter in brass-and-glass English pubs. If it looked interesting I would swerve into it, until I had the last one in a Yates Wine Lodge where the few other customers were on half pints of fortified wine.

I bought a naggin of whiskey to take with me. I drank it on the top deck of the ship while it was dropping through the lock out into the Mersey. My intention was to sleep out on the deck in my sleeping bag. I went down to the bar for one last pint. After the cold deck the bar was fuggy with tobacco smoke and the heat of bodies, full of British Army squaddies on their way back to the war.

Up at the bar I fell into talk, or inept banter, with one of them, who seemed to be the centre of a circle of drinkers, a corporal or a sergeant maybe, for I have a memory of stripes on his shoulder, though I can't remember how many of them there were.

— Well, off to Paddyland, are you, to kill a few papes for Queen and Country?

— Ye wot?

— It's good to see Her Majesty's troops getting limbered up for service in the last colony. I suppose when you get there they won't let you out except for rampages.

— Ye fucken wot, mate?

— Get it down ye now. You never know when you'll get the next one.

Trying to be funny, perhaps. I don't really know what I said. I must have been very pissed.

I remember a smirk coming over the soldier's face. The rest of them stepped back to see what he might do. I don't remember the actual moment of getting lamped.

The next thing I do remember is waking up on a bench on the deck to a grey dawn through facial swellings, with the Harland and Wolff shipyards sliding past, and a woman standing near me saying, in broadest Belfast,

— I don wanna say this, son, but ye wer askin fer it. I never seen anybady as drunk as you wer las night. I said to my fren, didn I,

*Marg'et? that wee lad should just go an have a sleep. And then I saw
ye going inda the bar wi all em soljers and I jus thought ye wer mad.
Is anybady meetin ye aff the boat? Luk at the state of yee. I's jus
shackin. He shudn a hit ye. Sure ye didn know wat ye wer doin.*

I went to the Casualty Department of the Royal Victoria Hospital
on the Grosvenor Road to get two stitches put in the wound on my
neb and a big white bandage over it.

Thus appeared the prodigal son to his parents.

That morning long ago my mother had just given me a hug.
She had never mentioned the incident again, and now, on her
deathbed, when I reminded her of it, she just moved her hand
up to the side of her mouth, as if she would have liked to
smile at her first-born, her blue baby who had grown up to
be such a silly man, if she could just remember how to smile.

Sadie died in late August, having never had the peaceful
years in a fold she had so often talked about, just the constant
worry of my father and his failing memory, his endless rep-
etitions, his boredom and his restiveness.

Eoin and I left Belfast two days after the funeral to go back
to Spain. Mary stayed on to be with her mother, who remained
frail but full of spirit, having shed all her worries, to the point
where she no longer knew or cared about money, or had any
interest in going to see her house, and lived in her room in
the nursing home as resignedly and, for the most part, as
happily, it seemed, as Conchita lived in her chosen, scaled-
down world.

As soon as we arrived in Farrera, Marsal came to the door of
John's Haggard to give me his condolences, with a sweaty,
stubbly kiss on each cheek.

— I accompany you in the sentiment of your loss.

— Thank you, Marsal. That's very kind of you.

I sat with him on one of the benches on the terrace, in the sun.

After talking about death, and how it would come to all of us – there was nothing we could do about it except enjoy the time we had left to us – we got on to Marsal's diet, one of his favourite topics, where he tells you what he eats and how healthy he is and what age he is, and thereby proves the efficacy of his regime.

— I don't drink. I don't smoke. I don't eat meat. I don't abuse myself.

— What about a drop of wine, Marsal?

— I drink wine, all right.

To drink wine is not really to drink, as eating pork from your own pig is not really eating meat, since you are not buying it from a butcher.

— There's nothing wrong with a glass or two of wine, I agreed. In our northern countries the doctors are even telling people a glass or two a day of red wine is good for the heart. No harm in it at all.

— Host! Marsal replied, thinking this over. A glass or two? I drink a *bota* or two a day. Here, would you like a taste?

His greasy goatskin *bota* was like a recently dead, clammy mole in my hand when he proffered it for me to take a glug. A few drops dribbled down my front, as always happens when I use these things. He had a long, expert drink himself, spilling not a drop.

He told me that one night the winter before when he had an attack of bad circulation, perhaps a premonition of a stroke, and his leg went dead on him, he got up out of bed, hobbled outside, plunged his head into the trough at the door, drank a couple of litres of water, and then walked to Alendo and back. He slept like a log after that and has never had a twinge since.

A Sandstorm

While we were in Ireland Stilts had tried every way possible to get Pareja's rickety red crane – left behind to settle an unpaid debt and now hired by us from the legatee – up to Casa Felip. Its wheelbase was a foot too broad to go up the path. That meant we would have to take off the old roof and put on the new one by hand. Just like they did in the old days.

The wood for the roof came from the sawmill in Rialp, on a big lorry with its own crane. It took us two hours to offload it. As the driver used the crane to lift each piece or packet into the air, Stilts and I guided the loads to set them down along the side of the road: massive trunks for the main supports; long, planed, squared-off beams for the rafters; bundles of boards for the two layers of wood that would go on top of the rafters; along with all the floorboards for the *menjador* and the bedrooms upstairs.

Stilts contrived a two-wheeled contraption on to which one end of the main beams was tied while the other end was secured to the dumper, to be brought under the arch of the church, through the village and up to Casa Felip. It took days just to get all the wood where we needed it.

Scaffolding was set up inside the house itself. The beams for the roof would be carried in across this by all six members of the crew: Stilts, Andy (a South African Rastafarian), Dylan (a pale-faced Irish builder from our previous parish of Aghabog), Eoin, Jan Taanmann (son of Barbara Taanmann of Tressó), and Teton, who was living with his girlfriend Maria and a pregnant Alsatian in a tent in the field at the back of the house (Dani having left the job months before after crocking his arse in a bad fall when snowboarding on spring ice at the hippie ski station of Tavascan).

Manpower instead of crane-power.

The slates of the old roof were stripped off, first the west side, then the east. The ones we might reuse were set aside in graded piles. The two big cracks down the front wall of the former dormitory had already been pinned together with iron staples, a double appendix operation in stone, then thickly rendered on the inside with roughcast: the more binding in the marsh of those walls of stone, mud and peasant spit the better. The new beams were fitted in the places of the old, each resting place rebuilt in cement and stone. When all the beams were in, meshed iron reinforcing was tied all round the tops of the walls and then cement poured and pounded into it to make one heavy, hipped hat that would press down on the house's head and spread all the new strains and loads we were putting on it.

The men were sauntering and casual about this steeple-jacking, but careful, using cords and harnesses when necessary. They carried in all the cross-beams, then sawed and planed them to make them fit into the main beams, before nailing and screwing them into place. The first layer of boards was nailed on to the cross-beams, until first one side was tight and tied, then the other. Lathes were nailed on top of that again, where the next layer of wood would be secured. At this stage you could walk up and down either side of the roof, as I did often just to admire and be a little frightened by the redstart's view of the village and the valley.

They sprayed on a layer of yellow polyurethane insulation foam that looked like a fungus attack from Saturn. A layer of boards was nailed over this, then one more array of batons over which the butyl rubber rolls of waterproofing would be laid. The slates would be nailed to these batons in a system, of which Stilts was very proud, that minimized the number of nail holes in the felt. And right enough, when I looked with the eyes of knowledge he had given me at other works in the vicinity, the local builders usually just banged the slate-nails directly into the felt, making rusty iron channels for the water to run down and rot the wood.

Stilts is a clever boy.

Sand-blasters came from Sorra Brothers in Olot in the province of Girona to clean the black carbon crust from the old ceilings of the kitchen and *menjador*, which we had not replaced. The back axle of the van in which they brought the machinery and the bags of sand was buckling under the weight of the five-hour journey across the Pyrenees. They parked it on the lower path to Casa Felip and ran the hoses out from there.

Pep the Sandman, the older one, had been sand-blasting for twenty-five years, he told me as I watched him put on his deep-sea diver's breathing apparatus and throw the helmet with shoulderflaps over his head like a judge donning his wig. His mate, Manolo, remained on the surface in the back of the van working the controls on the compressor that drove the sand through the gun and fed air to Pep so that he would not asphyxiate.

The sand-blasting did have some effect. Pep explained that you can't blast too much at old pine or it just digs holes. After they had blasted away all day, there were still flecks of greasy fireblack on all the beams, but at least there was now a sense of the wood.

At dusk they came down to John's Haggard to be paid and have a drink. As we sat out on the patio, Pep talked about his twenty-five years of working in a sandstorm as another man might speak of his travels.

Cashless Cashless Cashless

Money didn't appear when it was meant to appear. It had taken a minor eternity to get the Deutsche Bank mortgage. Each of its first two tranches was spent in a whirl of catching up with debts, so that we could walk out of the door through the piles of them cleared to either side, until they started to drift again. Everything cost more than we had imagined. Labour costs got out of hand, with six men to pay. I spent a lot of the time I begrudged from my painful memorializing juggling what money or prospects of money we did have: 800,000 pesetas borrowed from Goodfriend; top-slicing and other reliefs from the Revenue Commissioners in Dundalk, County Louth; my share of an insurance policy Sadie had had; IR£3,000 lent by the Sailor Poet. I spent days on the phone getting payments deferred, bluffing a month's credit here, another few weeks there. We ran up an overdraft in Ireland. Our credit cards were eaten up by disapproving mouths in the wall that went titsch-titsch, gulp.

I saw myself, as I had seen myself before, as the owner of a rundown circus who sells the tickets, spins the plates, acts the clown, vends the popcorn, tames a couple of mangy lions, and still goes bust.

Life became just one worry after another, not the least of them my father, about whom we had many family conferences by telephone and e-mail. Making me think of how troubled his own early days in business had been:

My father used to talk about his foolishness and naivety then – the lachicos he had working for him; the dirtbirds who stole as much as they ever made in his workshops, or threw stuff they had botched down behind the benches or into the bins; the brothers who made claims on the business they could turn into drink; the dirty tricks other businessmen pulled, and good Catholic businessmen too – the bitter aloes of his misanthropy, so many years in the making, that had started out funny and ended up tragic.

At one time he had had three workshops producing picture frames and fancy goods, as they were called on his letterhead, a big van on the road selling them, and a hardware shop on the Falls Road, with a workforce of a dozen or so. His main workshop in Distillery Street was a whitewashed-brick end building of three storeys. In the many rooms in my father's mansion of enterprise there were workbenches with the framing blocks of solid metal he had made in his latter days in the Aircraft Factory – where he had done an apprenticeship in the 1940s – like a prisoner of war fashioning the means of his own escape, along with the other tools he bought and has had for fifty years: a mitre machine for cutting the forty-five-degree angles of picture mouldings, a big curved guillotine to cut the cardboard backs, a circular saw, a bandsaw, compressors, spray guns, and a collection of the delicately balanced, wooden-handled, diamond-tipped glass-cutters that only he was allowed to touch.

Among the smells of fresh woody cardboard, methylated spirits, paint thinner, printer's ink, workers' tea, and dust from the plaster statues that Dominic Traversari made for the shrine boxes, the prevailing odour in Distillery Street was of the cow gum that was used by Sophie to glue the protective brown paper backs on to the Sacred Heart altars.

The Sacred Heart reared us, you could say, for my father made thousands of them over the years, for the Catholic Book Company of Berry Street, Paddy Kearney of Cullyhanna and the Laws of Ballymena, Mary's aunts.

In my father's shop on the corner of Spinner Street, opposite Reid's fish and chip shop, the Sacred Heart altars hung on the pegboard walls along with The Blue Lady *and* The Last Rose *by Tretchikoff and framed prints of views of the Giant's Causeway, the Lakes of Killarney, the Meeting of the Waters, the Ring of Kerry, the Glens of Antrim. On display stands throughout the shop there were the fancy goods H. Loughlin and Co. Ltd themselves produced — plywood toy forts and crib sheds for Christmas, wooden clothes horses, low tables with metal legs and Formica tops — among the other stuff in which he dealt, fireguards, coal scuttles, tins of paint, rolls of wallpaper, china ornaments, and paraffin oil out of a big tank at the back where nails, screws, locks, tools and other items of hardware were stacked on the shelves that covered every wall. Upstairs in Spinner Street, and in all of his workshops and stores, there was stuff he bought at fire sales and closing-down sales, though much of what he bought — tinfoil biscuit wrappers, Second World War gas masks, blurred prints, stuff he thought he might one day sell or do something with — was never used and never sold. Fifty years later some of these optimistic purchases still sit on shelves in his garage, pouring down trickles of dust if you touch them.*

Then he went bankrupt, put in the stocks of Stubbs Gazette, his hives of industry swept away by a deluge of bills, tax demands and court judgments that I scarcely remember, for we were kept safe away from all of that in our cul-de-sac off the Glen Road, to which eventually his business retreated. For all that his rage and despair might have vented itself on his family, at a time when, I now recognize, the duns would have been circling his kraal like duiker dogs, there was always food, coal for the fire, five shillings for school dinners, whatever was needed. Only later would I learn at what cost, sometimes, that sufficiency was procured, though I had a sense, as children always do, of all the trouble there was.

My father salvaged enough from the wreckage of his business to build first one workshop in our back garden and then, some years later, another one.

Out there, in our backyard (mutatis mutandis, for he had started his picture-framing business in the yard of his parents' house in

McDonnell Street), he worked and worked and worked and worked and worked and worked and worked and worked and worked and worked and worked and worked and worked and worked and worked and worked and worked: no end to his work, evenings, nights, Saturdays, Sundays.

Wondering if I were not repeating a pattern that would inevitably lead to disaster, by the time the lads finished at 5 p.m. on those Fridays in late autumn, after the long, expensive, energy-sapping summer that was sweeping us into a premature and bitter winter, I looked forward to the peace of Friday evening and all day Saturday and Sunday like a weekly ride in a glider. As with the sacrosanct siesta during the week, when you know that shops, banks and creditors have shut for three or four hours, so nobody will phone you, or call to see you, or otherwise annoy you, the close of business on Friday was a liberation into weekends, just like everybody else's, for the first time in twenty years, for it had never been so at Annaghmakerrig, when I would work in the office, buttle people to their rooms, labour in the garden, hustle and hassle, obsessive as I was, like my father before me.

But just to prove to myself that I wasn't, sometimes I did not go up to the works for a day or two, and ate a quiet breakfast on my own so as not to have to join the workers when they came down for theirs. Over those months, without seeing a pattern in it at the time, I read Jorge Semprun's *The Long Voyage*, about his journey to Auschwitz by train after being captured fighting for the Resistance in France in 1943; Primo Levi's *The Periodic Table*; Ian Kershaw's two-volume biography of Hitler, sub-titled *Hubris* and *Nemesis*; and Victor Klemperer's *I Will Bear Witness* and *To the Bitter End*, his diaries of surviving the war in Dresden as a Jew married to an Aryan.

Victor Klemperer never gave up on his house, either, through all the vicissitudes of the war. The pre-war diary entries record every *pfennig* he spent on acquiring it, the renovations he had done, his dealings with the work people and his anxieties about being able to pay for it with the loan he had to raise on the security of his professorship and the steady, well-paid academic future he seemed to have. Towards the end of the war, when he had lost everything – house, job, savings, and almost his life – he was able to flee Dresden when it was fire-bombed, and watched it burning in the distance. He spent months living in the countryside, having torn off his yellow star, finding there was still kindness in Germany, even in the midst of cataclysm. When the war ended he went back to reclaim the house that had been stolen from him by the Nazis.

Perhaps my reading was too salutary, as it has always been, for as Mary imagined the worst, at long range from Ireland, where she spent eight months that year, and I read these books about how much, much worse it could be, I was lulled into a drowse of Micawberism, trusting that it would all turn out for the best in the end.

Mary came back from Ireland in November, her mother being stable, holding her own, as we said to all the people in Farrera who enquired after her.

Nadir broke his arm so Stilts was not at work one day, then not the next day either, raising questions like how many days' sick leave you get for tending to your current companion's son's triple fracture in his arm? Mary and I began to think we may have been too soft with him. We agreed that we both in our different ways have always tried too hard to have people like us. Mary says I am extravagantly inclined to think the best of everyone. I thought I had learned it from her.

Two weeks after her return, Mary and I had one of our synchronized bad mornings, after a shared night of tossing and turning.

We squabbled all the way to Sort. Sort was all mild, prosperous and businesslike.

We fought our way back up Heartbreak Mountain. Mary said I had to take my courage in my hands and stop this charade. We had no money. We had no immediate prospect of getting more money. There were not going to be any paying jobs for Farrera Fabulosa Ltd. The men were only fiddling about because we could not afford to pay for the materials they needed. The works must stop.

At lunchtime I told the men we were suspending the works, in hopes that we might resume soon.

In the afternoon I walked round to Alendo to see the final two windows Javier Rodríguez has made for us. That meant we would have all the outer doors and windows in, the floors laid, the new roof on, the pharaonic patio built, the garden cleared, the stone for the front patio quarried, and altogether, maybe, 70 per cent of the work on the house done. On the way back I felt all the little weathers along the road: an accumulated warmth from the day in the sheltered, south-facing places, a down-flow of cold air from a north-facing ravine, and a dampness rising from the river, far below.

All of which felt highly significant at the time.

We had to get the house certified as habitable, in order to get the last lump of the Deutsche Bank mortgage.

We went to see Joan Albert Adell in his busy office on the other half of the floor his flat occupies in a straight-up-and-down block in a new suburb of Barcelona – a strange place for a specialist in the Romanesque to live, we remarked as we drove into its raw Wild Westness. He made no problem about signing the completion certificate, even though he was not able to come to see what we had done, which was just as well, since it was far from completed. He was bad with his nerves. He had developed a limp since the last time I saw him. I told him I knew how he felt.

Stilts decided he would move back to Boixols, where someone wanted him to help them build a sod-roofed house. Mary and I were glad that all was ending civilly, for there had been some prickly passages in our living with our foreman and his family under us in John's Haggard, with just thin wooden boards between our intimacies.

After we stopped the works, I went up to Casa Felip on a day of heavy rain – one of those remorseless downpours that you think are never going to cease because you are in the clouds with the water as it falls – to see how the drainage was working. The roof was a joy, glistening with the water running over the slates that we had salvaged and recycled. From the inside the house felt very snug, with its gutters babbling like happy water-babies.

To get as far as we had had cost us at least twice what our medievalist architect had estimated, and we had only worked on the house. We had not touched the barn, except to strip the slates from the one remaining good side of the roof.

In early December we met Claudi in Tàrrega, after he had been to Guissona to check that their closed-up restaurant and house were safe. We went for lunch in Vilagrassa (Fat Town), where the day had a Mexican Border feel to it when Claudi handed me an envelope containing $10,000, a loan we would repay when we sold the cottage we owned at Annaghmakerrig.

That was what paid off all our workers, in cash, and settled a few other hashes as well.

Fin y quito.

I knew all along that expression would come in handy.

IV

Festa Major

And the cheers and the jeers of the young muleteers
Who hadn't got a penny,
And who weren't paying any,
And the hammer at the doors and the Din?
And the Hip! Hop! Hap!
Of the clap
Of the hands to the twirl and the swirl
Of the girl gone chancing,
Glancing,
Dancing,
Backing and advancing,
Snapping of a clapper to the spin
Out and in –
And the Ting, Tong, Tang, of the Guitar!
Do you remember an Inn,
Miranda?
Do you remember an Inn?

Hilaire Belloc, 'Tarantella'

Round the Houses

We would start building again when we had the money to do so, whenever that might be. In the meantime there was life, and in August, the *festa major*.

There had been no mention of a *festa major* during the first year we had lived in Farrera. I have no memory, either, of the Mass there must have been in the church on the fifteenth of August for the feast of the Mother of God, Farrera's patron. The first revived *festa* was in 1979. In the photos Claudi took you can see Conchita, Juanito, Generosa, Marsal and the Manresàs, along with a few émigrés who had returned for the Mass, standing around in their Sunday country best among the newcomers with their braids, beads, beards, smocks, kaftans and jeans. As some of the *jipis* played guitars and bongos, the old villagers and the new villagers drank wine from *porrons* and ate *coca*, a flat, sugared, anise-flavoured bread that is a requisite of all Catalan special occasions. A record player was set up on a chair in front of Casa Ramón, overlooking the village square. In the photos you see it in the background with its lid open and can only imagine the tinny sound it must have made. They all danced to its music anyway. The next year Claudi and Tere killed a pig they had reared and invited the whole village to a feast in the *menjador* of Casa Felip. Tere says they danced so much and so hard they could barely see one another through the dust stirred up by their pounding feet.

The first poster was designed and printed in 1981 by El Viejo, The Old One, who was twenty then. This year Pili

Sarroca has designed the poster. She has used an old photo of
Conchita with her arms stretched out to two of her cows, all
of them – the Queen of the Byre and her Heavenly Kine –
smiling into the camera. Pili has drawn flower motifs on to
Conchita's skirt and got the printers to stretch it to reach the
bottom of the poster, so that Conchita looks as if she is on
stilts. Corinthian pilasters down each side and a baldachin
with fleur-de-lys across the top complete an image that is
wonderfully, if perhaps unconsciously, camp.

Camp means field in Catalan.

Of recent years the *festa major* begins with a *cercavila*. This is
something between a revel and a reveille. In some Catalan
mouths the word can seem to be pronounced *circavila*, as in
around the town, but in the *Gran Diccionari de la Llengua Catalana*
it is spelt *cercavila*, which could also mean *in search of* the town.

This year, around midnight on Thursday the twelfth of
August – for complicated reasons I have only imperfectly
understood to do with the fact that the fifteenth falls on a
Sunday – Eoin and I, Mary being still in Belfast with her
mother, mosey up to the square under the belfry of Saint
Roch from a festive dinner in Andrew's Hay Barn at which
we have been overlong, according to the young people who
are sitting on the low wall rattling and shaking us a sarcastic
welcome on the pots, pans, tins, football corncrakes, cornets,
drums and bottles with which they have been making noise
for an hour already. There is embracing by people who have
not yet seen one another, kisses on cheeks, by-plays of pats,
rubbings of backs, graspings of arms, holdings at arm's length
and drawings over of children or other friends, as knots of
retrouvailles ravel and unravel, and the racket from the noise-
makers rises and falls, synchronizes, disperses, and briefly dies.
It starts up again as Estefan Sambola, owner of a bothy at

Tressó and a recent recruit to the mixum-gatherum of village society, smiling broadly, wearing a docker's donkey jacket and a sailor's shore-leave knitted black hat, strides into the square carrying his accordion, wrapped in a sheepskin, over his shoulder, like an emissary of Pan.

In a moment of quiet Lluís Llobet tells us to look up at l'Estudi. There, on the third floor, crowded on to the balcony under the wooden eaves, lit by flashlamps and candles, are the English composer Nicola LeFanu, her Australian composer husband David Lumsdaine, their son Peter, and Douglas Birtram, Peter's friend. They sing an Anglo-Strine rondelay, merry and bright, that spills a spangled confetti of harmonies over the lamplit faces looking up at them.

They then sing a piece from the libretto of one of Nicola's operas, as translated loosely into Catalan by Lluís:

> *Ells d'aquí, ells d'allà,*
> *Tant els pobres com els rics,*
> *Ells del nord i ells del sud, de l'est i l'ouest.*
> *Beneieu nos, Senyor, beneieu nos a tots,*
> *Beneieu, beneieu, la Festa Gran.*

> Here and below
> Most and least
> North and south and west and east
> Bless us Lord, bless us all
> And bless this feast.

After they descend and come among us, to applause and more hugs and kisses, we move off in a strung-out gaggle down the street. Michael, youngest of my siblings, has the sleeping two-month-old Dani, the youngest of all our family, strapped before him in a baby-carrier, two Irish redheads leading our rowdy ramble. Verónica carries the almost two-year-old Eloi

over her shoulder wrapped in a blanket. He peeps out of it
like a creature at the mouth of its burrow, scanning the crowd
for all the people he knows, as if, at this his first ever fully
conscious *festa major*, he wants to be sure of not missing
anybody or anything. We turn off the main street, down the
steep hill towards the lower village, then go in through the
big wooden doors to the flagged entrance hall of the Besolís'
house. I stand at the back with Colm, watching the body
politic squeeze up against the walls, four and five deep: permanent villagers, second-homers, friends and relatives of both,
with more outside pushing in, and more arriving behind them.
Pepe de Besolí looks out at us over the half-door of the house.
A polished wooden yoke hanging above the door frames this
picture of transhumance man with his staff, looking as if he
never puts it down and maybe even sleeps with it by his side.
In the background we hear Matilde talking her way *poc a poc*
down the stairs as she comes to stand beside her husband. The
two of them smile as they look out, Pepe's smile straining
every pore on his age-tightened face, as if they too can't quite
understand how there have come to be so many of us. Their
twin granddaughters, Mercé and Anna, who have just learned
that they achieved top marks in their *batxillerat* exams, come
out with a tray of foil-wrapped biscuits and two bottles of
chilled *cava*, which they open and give to the crowd, and as
they do so are felicitated on their success – *enhorabona*, in the
good hour.

After some persuasion, Ramón de Besolí's wife, Rosa,
sings Lluís Llach's 'L'Estaca', 'The Stake', with fervour – and
perhaps an unintended irony, Colm and I think, for it is strange
to hear this protest song, this anthem of our own youth in
Catalonia, this call to pull down the old dictator, here in the
house of peasants who would have been, at the very least,
conservative and cautious during the Franco years.

When Rosa finishes, and we have applauded, Estefan slings his accordion off his shoulder and takes it out of its sheepskin. He plays 'Spancel Hill', and then a medley, many of them Irish tunes, rocking back and forth on his long legs, braced as if on a boat, his black-capped head moving in rhythm with the music, finishing with 'When the Saints Go Marching In', the rest of us clapping along, and whooping at the end.

We move back out the door and on down the hill to Casa Marsal.

At the first calls Marsal appears from his front door, waving at us as if he has never seen us before. His face is scrubbed and shaved, his hair wetted and slicked to one side. He is dressed in a brown suit, with a white shirt buttoned up to the collar above a black corduroy waistcoat. He holds up two bottles of *cava* and a packet of biscuits. They are roundly cheered and then passed over to be opened.

He takes a folded-out sardine packet from his pocket and hands it to Cesca. She tells us, in arch surprise – for Marsal has been discussing his performance for days with everyone he meets – that it is a list of the songs Marsal has prepared. But first he wants all the children to gather round him so that he can sing them his song of the seasons. The children go to sit along the low walls on either side of the path to his door. Perrico the dog sits in the midst of them, smiling, as if he might sing too, if he were only asked.

Marsal's songs all have the same air. I think he makes up most of them himself, usually in Castilian, to the basic tune he learned when he was in the army. The one he sings now to the children is like an incantation, swerving up and down. It says life in the mountains is very good, as we work and look after our gardens and our fields and our animals. The year is divided into four seasons, spring, summer, autumn and winter. In the spring the birds return that have been away, swallows and cuckoos and nightingales. The sun shines and the earth warms. We plant our crops. We rise with the sun and go to bed when it does. In the summer the sun is hot and we sweat as we work. In the autumn we collect fruit from the trees, vegetables and potatoes from our gardens, and we kill our pigs. In the winter there is snow and cold and wind and ice but we sit at the blaze of our fires and eat all the good things God has given us to enjoy. We must work hard and give thanks and love one another, because life is short and if we do not love our fellow human beings we will not get into heaven when we die.

We applaud boisterously, with me trying out my Belfast guttersnipe's whistle, as Marsal bows and smiles.

Conchita takes an unconscionably long time to come out of her Grimm house further down the path along which our tide of giddiness has bumped and swerved, for the *cava* is beginning to have its effect, on top of whatever else the young people have been having. Her closed door is like the curtain in a cabaret, teasing us, making us wait, though the more charitable think she is just being shy. By the time she emerges, holding out two bottles of *cava* and a platter of biscuits, her audience is sitting up on the outcrop of rock under the high street light, standing back along the path and clustered around the door, honking, whistling, clapping, and shouting out in acclamation:

— Con–chi–ta! Con–chi–ta! Con–chi–ta!

She waves, giggling and smiling, hiding her mouth with her hand, as she stands in the open doorway beside a spray of the tall yellow flowers that grow there. She has tied the flowers to the trunk of the ash that was a sapling twenty-five years ago and is now a tall tree that makes a Hansel and Gretel forest glade above an array of other plants in red, yellow, blue and green plastic pots. The light above the door shines down on her hair, freshly dyed an auburn that is almost orange, held back with a mother-of-pearl comb, the first time in a long time I have seen her without a scarf on her head. She has a fringed red shawl over her shoulders on top of a blouse with bright red splotches on a ground of pale blue. The blouse hangs out over a long black skirt with black- and white-spotted pyjama-like trousers underneath it. As the women shout at her – 'How elegant! How swank!' – Conchita grins coquettishly, turning from side to side so we can get the full effect.

— Con-chi-ta! Con-chi-ta! Con-chi-ta! A song! A song! A song!

At first she says she cannot sing. She is too old. She is suffocated. She has no voice. She has a cold.

After more shouted persuasion, quaveringly, clearing her throat, she sings 'La Linda Mora', about a Spanish girl taken captive by the Moors who meets a fellow countryman one day at a well and tells him to let her people at home in Andalusia know that she still thinks of them.

The applause is tumultuous, with more cries of,

— Con-chi-ta! Con-chi-ta! Con-chi-ta!

When the noise dies down, after some more urging, she says she will sing 'El Girineldo', her party piece.

The year before, Verónica and I wrote down the words of the song from Conchita's dictation. I have printed out a couple of dozen copies, which I now pass around.

We think the song may be medieval. It is in a courtly Castilian, about a serving boy who seduces the king's daughter. The king meets Girineldo in the palace and asks him where he is coming from, so sad and so pale. Girineldo says he has just been smelling a rose. It has drunk up all his colour. The king tells him the rose he has been smelling was born of his blood.

At first the king wants to kill Girineldo. The young lovers

feel the cold blade of his sword in the bed between them. Then the king, though it is not explained why, says he will buy them a house apart where they will live honourably. 'Before you were my servant / Now you will be my son / Beloved little Girineldo.'

Our operetta chorus sings along, linking arms, swaying back and forth, reading off the hymn sheets: under the aegis of the Mother of God we are a company of saints gathered here to witness Conchita's annual apotheosis and ascent into heaven, for which she has to steady herself by leaning against the wall, swooningly just touching it with the tips of her freshly painted crimson nails.

The congregation moves up the dark path behind Conchita's house to the steep steps that lead down to the patio of John's Haggard. I run on before them to go into the house and get out the two bottles of *cava* I have chilling in the fridge. By the time I come out again the company has settled on the two wooden benches and along the walls of the patio, up the flight of steps and along the wall of the terrace where we have our clothes line.

After a botched attempt at 'The Foggy Dew' with Estefan as unrehearsed accompanist on the accordion, I sing 'El Rossinyol', a French peasant girl's lament at having been mis-married in Catalonia. My rendition is charitably acclaimed by the kindly throng, as it is every year, for my always limited repertoire has long since ossified to bony relics of the *chansons d'antan*.

Eoin stands back into the light and shyly sings a Celtic supporters' song. He seems very tall among the Spaniards. My heart fills, as it always does when I see him in such situations, with tear-welling appreciation of his straightness, his honesty, his fortitude, and his beauty. I never thought I would have such a handsome son, having always thought of myself as jug-eared, scaby-eyed, big-nebbed, *plutôt laide*. He is mostly Mary's doing, I think, and as I watch him I have a sharp pang of missing her.

The friends he has made among the young ones of the village crowd round to congratulate him when he finishes. None of them can or will sing. Eoin grins over at me, knowing he has done his Irish duty.

We move on to Casa Manresà. Specky twelve-year-old Josep, a great-grandson of the first Manresàs we knew, comes down from the balcony to pass round biscuits and *cava*. A couple of times a year such descendants of the once most powerful house in the village come to spend a few days there. We meet them as they go up to or down from their sporty cars that squat like sleek, smooth-skinned toads on the main square, carrying skis or pushing mountain bikes, depending on the time of year, bulging out of their Lycra, looking urban and rich, the lush fruits of the Manresà capital that was extracted from Farrera and invested in businesses and educations in the lowlands.

But all their money seems not to have taught any of them to sing, for no one sings in Casa Manresà, as we stand in the yard, suddenly at a loss, the hubbub quietening as it washes against the mystery and reserve of this mass of stone. Colm and I wonder what it might be like inside. Every year we stand there wondering, until we can wonder no more.

We move off up the path at the back of Casa Joan, go under the arch of the church and through the square, then up the narrow alley, also recently paved with river stone, that leads to Casa Vinovis, Cesca and Lluís's house, where we cram on to their tiny patio. This is overlooked by the covered wooden balcony that is also the front door of the house, like a gallery in an Elizabethan theatre. From there Lluís hands down two bottles of *cava* and a tray of buns Cesca has made. He then reads the Catalan translation of a poem in Hebrew written by an Israeli poet, Ronny Someck, the winter before at one of the translation seminars El Centre d'Art i Natura organizes:

> *De bon matí els cavalls vénen a jeure*
> *en un racó de la catifa de neu que Déu ha posat*
> *damunt la hivernació de les muntanyes.*
> *El galop, l'han deixat a l'estable,*
> *i a les busques del rellotge de la creació*
> *el temps, com les ferradures, s'ha glaçat.*

> In the early morning the horses lie down
> on a corner of the carpet of snow God has laid
> over the mountains' hibernation.
> They have left their gallop in the stable,
> and on the hands of the clock of creation
> time, like their horseshoes, has frozen.

Lluís's younger brother Jordi, whom I asked the year before if he had a girlfriend yet, plays a Handel rondo on his violin with his boyfriend, Joan, on the cello. Jordi's nephew Arnau holds the sheet music up in front of them in the light of a torch. At the end, after we have applauded, Jordi says it would be OK too if we laughed. Nobody does.

By the time we get to Andrew's Hay Barn, Colm, Michael and Verónica already have the *cava* open and are passing it around with platters of the bite-sized round quiches Francisca, Veronica's granny, recently arrived from Argentina, has spent all day making.

They form a chorus – Colm, Michael, three Scottish boys who have just turned up, nobody is quite sure from where (a campsite in Alins, somebody thinks), and Nick, aka DJ Tal, who is also Scottish and is on the festival bill for tomorrow night.

The summertime is coming,
And the leaves are sweetly blooming,
And the wild mountain thyme
Grows around the blooming heather.
Will ye go, lassie, go
And we'll all go together,
To pluck wild mountain thyme,
All around the blooming heather,
Will ye go, lassie, go.

Then, without any preamble, as the applause dies down, Fafá Franco, a Brazilian woman who is also staying in Andrew's Hay Barn and will perform at the *festa* tomorrow as Madame Hair Lacquer, starts whirling in her fantastic red, frizzed hairdo with glittering tiara, in a space that widens as she dances, and sings a song in Portuguese that everybody seems to know:

Mama I love,
Mama I love,
Mama I love to suckle.

Give me a dummy tit,
Give me a dummy tit,
So baby won't cry.

Sleep little male child
Of my heart,
Hold on to the feeding bottle
And join in the chorus.

I have a sister
Called Ana.
From so much blinking her eye
She ended up with no eyelid.

Mama I love,
Mama I love,
Mama I love to suckle.

Back on the main street, reeling from our surprise visit to Rio de Janeiro, more of us now than at the start, we stop at the Cotés' house, just beyond the ruinous barn of Casa Felip that, to my relief, does not fall on us as we go past ('*Festa Major* Marred By Mass Murder As Irish People's Wall Falls On Revellers' is the headline I imagine). The Coté sisters, Magdalena, Asumpción and Rosa Maria, bring out *cava* but cannot be persuaded to sing. Estefan, who bought his bothy from them, plays more tunes on his accordion.

We move on down the street and up past the cattle trough, where a thick black pipe splutters and gurgles and writhes in the long cement basin like a disgruntled water snake.

On the terrace behind the House of the Cattle Trough, under the overhanging roof, with the lighted living room and kitchen for backdrop, two chairs are set out with music stands in front of them. A full set of drums stands beside them. Chairs and benches are arranged in rows in front of the slate stage in this nightclub whose back wall is the cliff. Francisca is conducted to a chair at the front.

Joan Lloret i Quirante, twelve years old, son of Paco, the botanist, and Teresa, the music teacher, comes out from the kitchen with a violin case under his left arm. He sits down on the stool facing one of the music stands, holding the case across his knees.

His mother sits down beside him with her accordion strapped to her front. Joan takes the violin out of its case. It looks full size on him, but may be only three-quarter size. He sits quietly waiting for the audience to settle. When they do, he plays, reading off the sheet music his mother turns for him, first a tango, then a waltz, and then 'Greensleeves'. Everyone is very attentive, except the Scottish boys, whom we can hear noisily bringing up the rear below us on the main street. One of them is wearing a Rangers scarf, I notice. He and Eoin are talking to one another, all smiles, as if to say, fancy a Celtic fan and a Rangers fan meeting here of all places.

Joan moves over to the stool behind the drums and weighs the sticks in his hands. From the garden of Casa Felip a few days before I had heard him practising and the sound had brought back to me all the other drums I had heard banged in less sunny Ulster summers. After hefting the sticks again, he twirls them into place between his fingers and plays a rather tame burst of percussives, as if he is afraid of hitting the drums too hard and breaking them, while Teresa vamps along on her Orangey squeezebox, which might be what is making the Scottish boys so uppity. At the end, after tip-tapping it out, Joan rises a few inches off his stool and gives all of the drums and cymbals a big clatter and roll and blatter that gets everybody cheering, as if a wild beast has just escaped from its cage.

When Joan finishes, the Scottish boy with the Rangers scarf, Keith, we think his name is, starts muscling his way forward. 'I want to have a go on the drums,' he says as he passes us. I tell Colm this maybe isn't a good idea, the drums are brand new, and maybe wouldn't be up to an assault from a man who has been drinking whiskey with his *cava* out of a litre bottle in a brown bag. But we don't feel we can intervene. Anyway we did not invent or invite the Scottish boys. They are nothing to do with us.

We watch as Keith makes his way towards the drum kit. The stool almost falls over as he sinks heavily and awkwardly on to it. He takes the drumsticks from Joan, and – Jesus, what a relief – Keith Moon come back from the dead, he gives the drums a professional pasting, cymbals thrashing, the bass drum moving forward on the slate floor as if wanting to escape, setting off an explosion of clapping and dancing. He ends in a long crashing riff that chases the drums bucking and skidding almost into Francisca's lap.

As we leave, I see Joan looking at his drums in a whole new way.

We go back through the village and climb the steps to the square outside the double door of Casa Maria. We call, 'Oppen! Anna!', ring the bell on the end of its long rope, holler and rattle, cheer and jeer, but nobody comes out. The little shepherds are not in festive mood, the price of lambs being what it is, Oppen having a bad back and a sore knee, much hay still to be saved, wild dogs loose on the mountain again – what's to celebrate? We can only remember other years when Oppen would appear on his balcony to play his accordion with a bravado and a braggadocio all his own.

At the House of the Barracks Cisco and Lala bring out *cava* and biscuits. Neither of them can be persuaded to sing, as we crowd round them, not so much persuading as importuning and bullying.

— No way, Cisco says.

Estefan would play a tune if they would dance together.

— No, I can't dance, Cisco says, even though we know he can.

As Estefan gets going, Joaquín from Ecuador grabs Lala from the Dominican Republic and they give it a swirl and whirl on the dance floor of dried dung under the moon-grey street light. *Aiiy Caribe!*

At Casa Llucio Claudi and Tere produce bowls of black olives, which are refreshing for their saltiness after all the biscuits. With their son, Joel, their daughter, Acarona, Joaquín and his wife Montse, a gutsy Catalan woman with a delightfully coarse, hoarse smoker's laugh, they form a sextet under the light above their door, with the stone wall and low slate roof as scenery and set behind them, and sing a number by Maniatica, a Spanish group beloved of Joel, doo-ing and dah-ing and clicking their fingers like a skiffle band.

Further along El Castell, at Casa Caterina, the *cercavila* peters out, as it does every year, for us, because the young people in summer residence there have no songs, and instead are doing loud noise, cavorting and horseplay, which seems to suit the Scottish boys, who are in the middle of the leaping, messy mob, making sure the *cava* reaches them on its rounds, with swigs of whiskey from the bottle in the brown paper bag as chasers.

Eoin and Keith are sitting on a bench amicably discussing Celtic–Rangers encounters.

After watching for a while, Colm and I mooch off down the steep, rock-strewn path towards the cattle trough. There we bid goodnight to the people of Alendo. They are going to walk back there. We threaten to go with them, to hear their song. We haven't had it yet. It's not too late. They could sing it there and then, if they liked.

But they don't.

Next year, they say.

They say that every year.

La Hora Tràgica de Farrera

The next morning we clean up the church square for the dancing there will be that night and the next. We sweep and hose down the half of it that is trampled earth and wash the mud and dust from its other half of roughly cut black slates that have lost their cement joints and now look more like stepping stones than paving stones.

There is a rhythmic, African-sounding *huh-uh, huh-uh, huh-uh,* as Arnau Llobet and his friends come marching down through the arch of the church carrying a birch tree they have cut in the village woods – a giant, rustling, green, hairy insect with a dozen legs. They put its pared end into a deep hole in the middle of the square and secure it in place with wedges of wood. When the tree is up, Arnau (once the most intrepid, noisy, wild gang-leader of a child, now a stocky teenager in hang-round-your-arse trouserbags, and still the chief wrenboy at every village rout) climbs up into its branches to show how strong and steady it is.

Somebody finds the plastic garlands that are recycled from year to year. Arnau goes up into the bell tower of the church to drop down the ends of them to helpers below. They are festooned from the bell tower to the tree, from the tree to the balcony of Casa Ramón, and from the balcony of l'Estudi to a big stick nailed into the wall at the far end of the square. After some searching, a string of coloured bulbs is found and slung from church tower to balcony to balcony. All four balconies which overlook the square are bedecked with multi-coloured Chinese lanterns with electric bulbs in them.

The stone platform in front of Casa Ramón, on which the bands will play, is draped with a red tarpaulin. Beside the bandstand the bar is set up in the downstairs room of l'Estudi. It is a rude affair of planks laid on concrete blocks, covered with blue crêpe paper. Framed posters from all the previous *festes majors* are hung around the walls. One of Pili's posters of Conchita adorns the door, as it does many doors and walls around the village.

The stock for the bar arrives in the back of Javier Rodríguez's white carpenter's van. We help to carry up the couple of cases of whiskey, gin, vodka and rum, trays of minerals and mixers, and a couple of dozen barrels of beer, along with refrigeration units and the apparatus for two beer taps. Having two beer taps is intended to be an improvement over previous years, when the one and only dispenser would be sure to go on the blink, causing the beer to froth out soupy and tepid.

In the church, through the afternoon, after a puppet show for the children performed in front of the altar, Fafá, aka Madame Hair Lacquer, has her hairdressing and face-painting workshop. The pews have all been cleared back and set along the walls. There are three tables with big mirrors encircled by stands and clothes rails on which Fafá hangs the painted bits and bobs she uses to make the hairdos. People go into the church looking normal and come out paranormal. Peter Lumsdaine-LeFanu has his shock of hair done up into a purple Mohican. Colm has his head shaved, one side of his face painted black and the other half white. Children become cats and dogs, tigers and lions. Women turn pompadour. Men go punk. I stay me.

There is a lull for a couple of hours around ten o'clock, the sacred hour of the *sopar*, when everyone retires to their own houses to eat, and to look at Madame Hair Lacquer's hairdos in the privacy of their bathrooms and, some of them, recant.

Around midnight, the weather threatening a summer thunderstorm, we go up to the square. The Colombian group Mambalú is setting out its instruments. They take them in again when it starts to rain, try once more, throw a cover over them, and then, after half an hour of gazing out the door, seem to say to hell with it, and just get started, despite the drizzle, and the thunder and lightning we can hear and see rolling through the valleys beyond the Pic d'Urdossa, to the south. We seem to be on the edge of the tempest. Its worst might pass us by.

Under the shelter of the arch of the church, heads – variously shaved, hairy, Rasta, wasted, callow, mostly young, in their teens and early twenties a lot of them, male, female – huddle to roll spliffs in the Spanish fashion, dope and tobacco kneaded together in the palm of one hand, then inverted into a single skin and rolled into a neat cone, as if they were cowboys doing it one-handed on the back of a horse.

The square is *de gom a gom*, chock-a-block. Michael gets a big red-and-white golf umbrella for Francisca. She and Matilde are discussing livestock and other matters. A lot of people from Burg are there too: the mayor, Jordi de Bernat, and his wife, Roser, Da and Ma Bernat, La Tabolina and others of Matilde's Companions of the Bench, and Paquito with his indefatigable Chupa-Chup. Conchita is regal and aloof, mantilla spread over her hair, holding a black lacy fan in her right hand, with which she gives herself the odd flap, and a battered, patched, fringed white parasol with twisted spokes in her left. Colm has taken up his station on the stone that juts out of the wall beside the entrance to the bar, from which he will not budge the whole night. I join him there from time to time for the pleasure to be had from seeing how many people we recognize, speculating as to who is doing what with whom among the young ones, and guessing what the elders might be saying to one another: the tittle-tattle of village life. He asks me who is the woman with the face like thunder standing on her own beside the arch. I don't know so I ask Tere. She tells me this is the famous Pamela, a descendant of Casa Cargol (Snail House), now in ruins, who had taken it upon herself to clean the church of Saint Eulàlia and put up pictures of Saint Joseph, Saint Ambrose and others. The bitch, I said, interfering with our mother cult. She was a bit of a Holy Josephine, Tere said. She'd wanted to become a nun but no convent would have her.

The band features a man on the pan pipes, two men on bongos held between their knees, and a big, broad fellow with tall bass drums, all dressed in loud shirts. It is fronted by a woman in a long skirt with cascades of flounces that she whirls around her as she sings songs redolent of tropical nights, luscious fruit, blue seas, frigate birds and languorous heat-waves, such as we are not having. She keeps encouraging us to dance, doing swirls in her long ball dress, turning her back to us to lean over and wiggle her magnificent Caribbean *culo* to show us how, as Lala gives little yips of pleasure and launches into bouts of salsa and merengue, the saucy dances of her homeland, while Cisco smiles through his beard and shimmies a diffident countryman's two-step beside her.

All through the evening the bar does a roaring trade, tended by relays of volunteers under the supervision of Paco, the botanist, assisted by his wife Teresa as roper-in, making sure everyone does their turn. Their friend Belén, who does a very long stint, looks very fetching with dampish locks of her blonde hair falling into her eyes and one strap of her black bra lying loose on her upper right arm as she pours plastic goblets of beer from the only one of the two taps that seems to be working.

The Colombians finish around 3 a.m., when the older citizens have long since gone home. DJ Tal wheels his sound machine out to the door of Casa Ramón and starts playing the selection he has been making over days with headphones clamped to his ears in a bedroom of Andrew's Hay Barn. The first tunes he plays have a fast, driving, Irish-sounding fiddle underscoring. Eoin and I start doing *céilí* swings, and every-body else joins in, swopping partners, arm into arm, river-dancing under the deluge that has now set in, so soaked it doesn't matter any more.

After a few numbers I decide wet fifty-year-olds like me

should be in their beds. As I go through the arch of the church on my way home I see that Merlin has set up a pancake stall with a two-ring gas burner on top of a spindly table. He has a queue of customers – the hash-hungry, mostly. His sisters, Tina and Poma, are behind him beating up batter in a bowl.

At the front door of the church I see the Coté sisters, with Lluís Llobet, Ramón de Besolí, Rosa de Besolí, a couple of women I don't recognize, and Pamela. They are all in a flap. The sacristy has been desecrated, they tell me. The priest's vestments have been taken out and thrown all over the place. This is what comes of having carry-on in the church. It is an outrage.

I agreed it was a disgrace. Had much damage been done? They said it wasn't the damage, it was the scandal of it. A stop would have to be put to carry-on in the church, even if it was for the *festa major*. The women were all standing in and around the door, their arms crossed defiantly, as if to repel Vandals and Visigoths. They had obviously been talking it up among themselves for a while, because, now that I remembered, I had seen Verónica coming into the square about an hour before to whisper and confer with Fafá, presumably when the outrage had first been discovered.

Well, it was all too bad, I said. Why not just lock the church and see what could be done in the morning?

There was no key, they said. Marsal had the key and he was at home sleeping. Well, let's go and get the key, I said. We couldn't do that. He was an old man. He needed his sleep. We couldn't go waking him at this hour. Just then DJ Tal moved into heavy-metal mode (house? techno? acid? hip-hop? How would I know?). Whatever it was, it was very loud.

Ramón said he would go and get a chain and a lock. There was no hole to pass the chain through, I observed. He would have to bring a drill and make a hole. The easiest thing,

I said again, would be just to go and get the key from Marsal.

No, no, you couldn't do that. It was too late. Poor Marsal. He wouldn't hear you knocking.

I felt everybody was more interested in keeping the drama going, drilling holes, getting locks and chains – maybe even standing guard all night with cuirasses and pikes – than in merely locking the door.

I was about to go home and leave them to it, when I thought I might as well go down and see if I could rouse Marsal.

Merlin had two pans of pancakes going now. DJ Tal seemed to have turned up the volume again. Perrico and another dog were having a fierce, muddy scrap beneath the stone bandstand. As I made my way through the still-dancing diehards and looked up the steps towards the bar, faces of bachelors from Burg and other villages were framing its door as if it were the entrance to the dance in the Parish Hall, Tubercurry, County Sligo, on a wet Saturday night.

At my second shout Marsal stuck his head out of a small window above the TELÉFONOS sign.

— What is it? Who's there?

— We need the key of the church to lock it, Marsal. We just want to be sure it's safe for the night, with all these strangers about the place. I'm sorry for disturbing you.

— Sure, sure. No problem. No disturbance. Hold on till I get it.

He pulled his head back in. When I looked up I could see Pamela, who had been the most indignant defender of the church, looking down at me over the wall of the main street, her arms crossed under her breasts and a sour puss on her that Fafá might have painted.

— Here, Marsal said when he reappeared at the window under the stone inscribed with 1903. Catch.

The keys made a metallic tinkling as they fell. I caught them in mid-air, glad of the light that was still on over Marsal's door so that Pamela could see me doing it.

I held the big iron key out before me as I walked back up through the dancing crowd like a hunted priest with a pyx containing the Blessed Sacrament. I showed the key to the Capitoline ladies at the door of the church as a sign of my solidarity with their sodality. Magdalena de Coté took it from me, almost snatching it, saying there was a special technique for closing the door. She stuck the key into the lock, upside down, while my mind went all Freudian on me. Her sister Asumpción pushed the iron latch-piece into its hole, put her shoulder to the other door and then flipped the latch, which brought out my Jungian. Magdalena turned the key in the lock with an iron clunk that echoed in the empty church. The key was withdrawn. Rosa de Besolí took charge of it. They were going to clean out the church in the morning. They would return the key to Marsal after that.

I went home. As I lay in bed unable to sleep, regretting that I had not actually gone into the sacristy to see what the blasphemers had done in the Hora Tràgica de Farrera, I could hear DJ Tal's music still throbbing away, like the din of a barbarian army camped without the walls.

Late the next morning, when I went up to the square, I found Estefan using our dumper to collect the rubbish and dirt and dust the holy women had brushed out of the church, along with the leftovers of the hairdressing workshop that Madame Hair Lacquer and her helpers had gathered into plastic bags. I went inside. The cracked, uneven floor was swept and clean. The altar cloths had been washed and pressed and put back over their respective altars. There were candles lit on the side altars and on the big candelabra in front of the main altar. The pews were back facing God in neat rows.

All the statues had been dusted. Saint Roch was resplendent in his place on the main altar, dressed in a princeling's blue half-cloak with stars on it over a long brown gown whose hem he was lifting to show a shapely leg, while Saint Sebastian the centurion and Saint Godelic were smirking in their niches near the door, as if they had all had their night of debauch too. The church smelt of Conejo disinfectant. The sacristy, when I went into it, smelt of lavender polish. The presses and the drawers were all closed. The priest's vestments for the Mass later that day were hung up on one of the clothes rails Madame Hair Lacquer had used the day before for her props.

As I was going back out through the church I smelled attar of roses. I looked up. Saint Pamela was suspended there in the middle of the nave, her face and head made up as a Madame Hair Lacquer special, crowned with a halo of cardboard and tinfoil, arms crossed, bosom voluminous under the folds of her seamless, heaven-blue robe with gold-tooled fringings. Her right foot with red-painted toenails in a thin-soled sandal trod a serpent coiled over a half-moon scimitar.

She was making a faint humming noise.

Nobody else seemed to notice her.

Around four o'clock in the afternoon we went to the Meadow of Llaone for a picnic. A large party of Andorràs, the people who had sold us Casa Felip, had installed themselves at the end of the road, near the ford of the Juverri river, under the shade of poplar trees. The Andorràs come every year for the *festa major* from their dispersal in the lowlands. They bring folding tables, plastic chairs, sunshades, tablecloths, cutlery, crockery and food in the back of their 4 x 4s, which were lined up now along the road like a wagon train at rest. The fires by the river were still smoking where they had cooked *carn a la brasa*, meat grilled on embers, the very thought of which, with *allioli*, the creamy garlic and oil sauce, causes the eyes of even the hautest Catalan bourgeois to mist over with nostalgia for his imagined peasant roots. They were on the dessert course – fruit, flans and cake. They invited me to join them, making room beside Josep, the eldest son, with whom we had had most of the dealings to buy the house, opposite his mother, Olegaria, who had signed the contract of sale by affixing her fingerprints over spidery writing. Of the rest I recognized Isidre, the cross-eyed brother, and another brother who lived in the Penedès, the wine-growing region west of Barcelona.

The Penedès brother explained that he and his wife made their own *xampany*, 'champagne', about seven or eight hundred bottles a year, from their own grapes, grown on a couple of hectares, the stuff they were drinking now out of unlabelled bottles. They gave most of it to their family and friends for occasions like this. His wife said they tried to produce it as cheaply as possible. There was no point in putting labels on the bottles. They'd looked into all that. It would only put up the cost. Anyway everybody they gave it to knew what they were getting, the best of stuff, produced 'biologically', the wife said, using the word with the happy laxity they do here, to mean organic, traditional, natural, good.

— Would you like a taste?

— I would, please.

They poured me a plastic goblet full. The *cava* tasted like all the *cava* I have ever had: bubbly.

They asked me about the works on Casa Felip. They would be finished for the *festa major* next year, I said, with my best face forward. They asked about Mary. I told them she was in

Ireland with her sick mother. I could see they approved of her dutifulness, for families are anchors still in the seas of the peasant diaspora. I asked about their children, who were now in their twenties, like ours, and had better things to be doing than to be eating charred chops and looking back at the village that no longer concerned them. And more such chit-chat, all the time thinking what salt-of-the-earth, decent people the Andorràs are, like good-living, well-to-do Protestant folk at the Field in Ballymoney on the Twelfth of July.

— *Moltes gràcies pel xampany,* I thanked the Andorràs.

— *Bon profit,* they replied.

A crowd of newcomers arrived, disgorging their picnic spread from bags, baskets, boxes, and even our dumper – that most versatile and useful vehicle. Michael had used it to transport the paraphernalia necessary for the entertainment of two children and an Argentinian granny. The granny had her own chair set up in state under a red-and-yellow-striped Catalan flag of a sunbrolly on a metal stem. Dani was in a lobster-pot playpen. Eloi toddled from one group to another. Eoin looked after his tiny cousin like a big brother, picking him up when he fell, talking to him in Catalan, all smiles and his grandfather's dimples, which Eloi has too. Colm had bought insulated green satin Heidesecker bags for keeping your *cava* as cold as when you took it out of the fridge. We had flutes of it to accompany more of the pampagranny's quiches and her home-made pasta, with salad, sausages and cheeses. The Llobets fed hordes, as they always do, for Arnau and his mates turned up. The LeFanus had sandwiches. Marsal passed round his greasy goatskin *bota*, all the while praising its contents – a good strong wine, he told us, that his family brought in *bidons* from Tarragona twice a year to fill the barrel he keeps in his cellar. He took out bread, tomato, oil and garlic from his shepherd's satchel. He insisted we try some of the sausages from last year's pigs. Other dishes did the rounds. Chocolate melted from hand to hand. The Pacos gave us all coffee.

After the meal the familial hubbub lulled me to sleep. I had a dream-vision of Saint Pamela in a see-through negligee, her folded arms making her diddies bulge with big, round, red areolae that glowed like traffic lights in the dirty dark of my mind.

Just before 6 p.m. Marsal and I left the picnic to go to the Mass in the new-broomed church. It was attended by all of the old elders and almost none of the new soon-to-be-elders, except me, a convert to the Catalan Protestantism that masquerades as Catholicism, which I find congenial to the Belfast atheist from papish origins with Prod tendencies I have become. In his homily the priest made no reference to the outrages of the day before. He just talked about the need for us to love one another. Every year, for we only have the pleasure of him once a year, he tells us to love one another. Mary, who is a sporadic Mass-goer to the churches in Llavorsí and Tírvia, says he says the same every Sunday. I took Communion. The blood-gorged wine was a welcome change from all the *cava* of the last few days. At the end the priest called us brothers and sisters, reminded us to love one another, and told us to enjoy the rest of the *festa major*.

When we went out on to the little square in front of the church there was *coca* cut up into wedges set out on a table, with *porrons* of *ví rancit*, rancid wine, which is in fact sweet. I noticed that even the most gentrified of the revenant older sons and daughters of the village – back for the Mass and the chance to meet their former fellow villagers – used the *porró* without leaving a spot on their best bibs and tuckers: the fat-bottomed glass vessel raised at arm's length, the twirling thread of wine from the narrow spout aimed into the mouth, the back of the other hand held under the chin to catch stray drops. Even after all these years, I still haven't got the hang of it. They must learn it in the cradle. Perhaps that's how Catalan babies drink their milk.

Afterwards, in the sunshine freshly washed by last night's storm, Estefan de Tressó, as he was billed on Pili's poster, played his accordion for an hour and a half from a stool up on the bandstand in front of Casa Ramón, his ascetic face in a half-trance as he swayed back and forth in rhythm with the music, smiling out at us and in at his own saintly visions. It was a *thé dansant*, only nobody danced, and there was no tea. We all just stood around the square and listened to this man from beyond the Pass of Sound who could play the accordion like one of the ambulant musicians of old: as Conchita told me, the only music they had in those days was from an accordionist who travelled to all the *festes majors* in the locality. She said Estefano, as she calls him, was very like one of them.

— *I molt natural també,* she declared him, one of her highest commendations of anybody or anything.

And very natural too.

The Cortxo Band were to play for the dance on the last night of the *festa*. When Eoin and I went up to the square after midnight they were already launched: two saxophones, two trumpets, rhythm guitar, bass guitar, keyboards and drummer, giving it their baby-blue best. The oldest of them was nineteen, somebody told me. Their speciality was ska, but they played jazz, waltzes, tangos, sardanas, some of them swaggering with confidence while playing by ear, two fellows studiously reading their notes off music stands, the drummer off on his own, and the guy on the keyboards giving it the lip between

numbers. They played until they had exhausted their repertoire, parts of it twice over, finally stopping sometime around
four in the morning.

After they finished the boys from the band and their girl-
friends smoked joints of fragrant grass. They gave us one.
They were using their sound system to play CDs, loudly. We
continued to dance. Pili of the Poster was the best dancer. She
is rather dumpy, but has perfect rhythm. She danced with the
carefree abandon of a Fraga cowgirl just in from a long drive
on the range of Aragon. The previous morning, as her contribution to the preparations, she had put up ashtrays made of
biscuit tins and chicken feeders all over the square, with notices
done in luminous paint urging people to use them and not
flick their butts all over the place. Now, as she broke off from
her dancing for skirmishes of butt-cleaning, I joined her as a
butt-gathering heron stalking across the square picking up one
fag end at a time, fastidiously, between two fingers, and then
high-stepping-in-shallow-water across the uneven paving
stones to one of her butt boxes: my own Dance of the Retired
Janitor. Eoin joined us, laughing so much that he almost
fell over.

And then, suddenly, it was 6.30 a.m. Jordi Llobet came out
of l'Estudi to announce that the bar was closing and would
not open again for a year. Everybody protested, but nobody
asked for any more drink. Catalans don't drink very much. I
had not seen a single serious drunk in the four days of the *festa*,
apart from the Scottish boys, who had not returned after the
first night, and were probably still sleeping it off in their tent
in Alins.

The boys from the band were now playing CDs of Spanish
music that all the Spanish people seemed to know, for they
were shouting out the choruses as they danced, while we Irish
just grinned. A fellow with a gingerish toupée, a remnant of

the Tubercurry crowd, took a great fancy to Tere – a handsome heft of a woman, raven-haired with liquid brown eyes, wearing a nimbus of the candid capability of a daughter of peasants from the hard, dry Segarra. Senyor Toupée cut her out from the rest of us, like a cowboy singling out a steer, and talked to her animatedly under the light of a streetlamp to the side of the square. His intense pleading was interrupted by peals of her laughter. When she came back she reported that he had told her he had as much property in the valley of Cardós as he wouldn't look at fifty million pesetas to sell and she could have it all if she married him.

I told her lads from Tubercurry were always like that, except that there they would probably drink their farms instead of dangle them for dowries before damsels.

Tere had told Senyor Toupée she was already married. He immediately turned his attention to Acarona, whose summer this had been to become a gorgeous, tall, strong-featured, Levantine-looking caryatid dressed in tight black leotards with holes at the knees. She had to lean down to hear what Tubercurry Tommy had to say.

I told him he should try the Internet. I had met a man recently from the valley of Cardós who had found a wife on the Internet.

Then I knew it was time to go home.

We had found the village. It had taken four days. But it was there all right, still living in its past and present tenses.

V

The Fleas that Tease

Never more;
Miranda,
Never more.
Only the high peaks hoar:
And Aragon a torrent at the door.
No sound
In the walls of the Halls where falls
The tread
Of the feet of the dead to the ground
No sound:
But the boom
Of the far Waterfall like Doom.

Hilaire Belloc, 'Tarantella'

A Village Meeting

Thus three years went by: two more *festes majors*; two more brief bouts of building; the deaths of my father and Mary's mother, who at one point were head to head in adjoining wards of the Royal Victoria Hospital in Belfast; disentanglement from the last ties to bygone, irremediable lives in a distant parish; the first guests in Claudi and Tere's house and other houses under our auspices – people we had known at Annaghmakerrig and some we had never met before, including a necrophiliac nun; leaps and bounds of self-knowing that we have shared with our children, who always tell us they love us when we talk to them on the phone, or when they write to us, as we tell them; rejections by a dozen publishers of early versions of this book; our complete absorption into the slippery *culebrón* of village life; excursions, visits, parties (any excuse, it sometimes seems, will do), Colm's comings and Colm's goings, and other occasions when communal wounds are cauterized; Tony Dumphy's return to spend a week's holiday checking that all his shepherd's landmarks were still as and where he had left them; Conchita's perhaps last, and very reluctant, departure for the winter lowlands.

And local politics.

Because there are fewer than a hundred registered voters in the municipality, which consists of Farrera, Alendo, Mallolís, Montesclado, Glorieta and Burg, the *ajuntament* of Farrera has an open council. That means anyone who is registered as being *empadronat*, having their domicile here, ourselves now included, can attend the plenary meetings that are held every three months or so to discuss and vote on the issues put before it: the purchase of light bulbs for street lamps, repairs to the secretary's computer, the price per cubic metre of timber to be auctioned from the thousands of acres of commonly owned forest, the location, style and text of signposts, headage payments for sheep and cattle, building permits, rights of way, hunting licences, road improvements, rubbish collection, snow-clearing, subsidies for the annual festivals of the various villages, street paving, the water supply – everything, in the minutest detail.

In Spanish municipalities with more than a hundred registered voters a group of councillors is elected, they choose the mayor, and between them they make all the decisions.

In our municipality only the mayor is elected. Shortly after we returned to Farrera, Jordi de Bernat presented himself for re-election to a third term as mayor, not as an independent, as previously, but as a member of Convergencia i Unió, the hydra party that has ruled Catalonia since it regained its autonomy after Franco died. Javier Rodríguez, standing for the Platform of Progressivists of the Pallars, gave him a run for his money, but lost by three votes.

A couple of months later we had a meeting in l'Estudi of Farrera to select a village representative to liaise with the new mayor, who was also the old mayor grown crusty and autocratic with far too many years in power, we felt. All four inhabited villages in the municipality were to elect their own representatives.

The meeting was to start at 11 p.m. I was the first one there – punctual to a fault, I was finding. The mayor and Roser Bardina, the municipal secretary, arrived soon afterwards. Other people sauntered in. At nearly midnight, with a turn-out of almost every adult alive in the village, Jordi de Bernat said we were there to select a representative who would be the channel for any ideas or criticisms or grievances we might have.

The grievances were then discussed for a couple of hours. The lack of lights on certain village streets and alleys. The state of those streets. The muck and clobber when it rains or snows. Whether the main street should be paved with stone or tarmacadamed. The fickleness and filth of the water supply. The diarrhoea and sick stomachs it caused. The mess the Andalusians had made with their machines when putting in the new water pipeline and sewer. How they had had to come back and do parts of it over again. The dogs. The dog shit. The door of the bell tower of the church that has been off its hinges for years. The amount of money spent on improvements in Burg. Skirmishes between believers and unbelievers in El Centre d'Art i Natura. Marsal told us how in the old days they had no money, no outside contractors; they did all the work themselves. He told of how he had built the road to Alendo with Esteve of Tírvia and how they were cheated of half of their *jornals* at sixteen *duros* a day; of digging the pipeline to the village from the Spring Wells of the Wet Hollows beneath the Pass of Sound in a heat that would boil your tripes; of how the people themselves had rebuilt walls as and when they fell, and had cleared the snow in winter with shovels, each family doing its own part of the street. People then knew how to work. Not like now.

Every time the door opened Perrico came in to smile at us, until he was chased out.

At about two in the morning the mayor said,

— Right, that's fine, we will look into all of these matters. We are here now to elect a representative for the village.

Barbara Taanmann and Verónica Rapalino declared themselves as candidates, each making a little speech. Baltazar Mandonguillo, who was living in La Caravana, and had arrived at the meeting grinning and woozy-looking in a Long John Silver pirate hat, said that if we could not arrive at an agreement, he would be prepared to take on the job and would hope to be able to work with the mayor in a 'humanitarian' way, dealing with him as one human being to another. Jordi de Bernat looked nonplussed. I saw him whispering to Roser. I think he did not know who Baltazar was. There was more discussion, in the course of which Baltazar fell asleep, nodding sideways on his chair, so that I thought he was going to end up with his head on Jordi de Bernat's lap.

The assembly looked about evenly divided for Barbara and Verónica. I walked about and checked people's voting intentions. If it were pushed to a vote, Verónica would probably win, but then there would be a schism as wide as the valley itself. It was suggested that perhaps we could have two representatives, Barbara and Verónica.

Everybody thought that was a good idea. Baltazar woke up and asked what had happened.

At three o'clock we went out into the dark street, for the street lights had come on during the day and gone off in the evening, as they have a tendency to do.

A year or so afterwards I went to my first municipal meeting, held in the ground-floor office of the *ajuntament* in the old schoolhouse of Burg.

The meeting was due to start at 10 p.m. but didn't get under way until eleven with the reading of the minutes of the last meeting by the secretary. I had to strain to catch her quiet voice in the anarchic, echoing acoustics of the tile-floored room. The mayor's brother, Joan de Bernat, who is always grumpy and malcontented, perhaps from driving the county council bin lorry all week, perused a farming paper throughout.

The mayor's edicts since the last meeting were read out: the granting of Paquito's fiancée's application to be *empadronada*, a licence for the hunting club of Tírvia to shoot wild boars in our woods, the denial to the Tuareg 4 x 4 Sporting Club of the right to pass through the municipality, permission for the Orfeo of Lleida to camp out at Tressó – a long list of items. They were all approved.

Every bill due to be paid was read out. They were all approved.

Then El Centre d'Art i Natura was discussed.

Its director, Lluís Llobet, had been hounding the mayor to get him to sign an application for a grant that would pay his wages. At an early stage of its gestation, Jordi Viñas and I had persuaded the mayor to take on El Centre d'Art i Natura as a municipal initiative because we knew that would make it easier to get capital grants and assure basic running costs, though in theory the centre was to break even and not cost the municipality *un duro*. Jordi de Bernat, as mayor, is president of the board of the Centre, though he never attends any of its meetings.

Jordi de Bernat thumped the table. He would show who was boss. If Lluís didn't like it, he could lump it. They would look for someone else who might want to do what he does for 50,000 pesetas less per month (which would cut his salary, which he hadn't been getting for months anyway, in half). As the mayor, and the man who gave the orders, Jordi de Bernat said he would not be talked to like that. He would not have his father persecuted either, for a few days before Lluís had gone to the House of Bernat to look for Jordi de Bernat and, on not finding him, had given Da Bernat the forms and emphasized to him the urgency of his mayoral son signing them and having them sent off. Jordi de Bernat would teach Lluís a lesson, he said, because *he* was in charge here, *he* was the one who *mandated*. He punctuated his fulmination with big closed-fist thumps of the desk beside him, pulling it closer each time to give it another thump, with all the strength of a man who has worked in the fields all his life and has thumps to spare.

His blows reminded me of how much he should have been grateful to us hippies, for our arts centre had benefited his own village, as well as ours. In the mid 1990s Jordi Viñas and I had found the first lump of eurodough with which to renovate l'Estudi in Farrera as accommodation for El Centre d'Art i Natura. The following summer, when we were there on our holidays, I had asked Jordi de Bernat if I might attend the plenary meeting of the municipality where the use of this money was going to be discussed, as an observer, as it were, since I was not then *empadronat*, and he had said to me,

— *Però no hi pot anar tot Déu.*

But we can't have just any old Tom, Dick or Harry turning up.

We had watched then as half of the money was spent on the renovation of the old schoolhouse in Burg. The big red sign saying this money from the European Regional Development Fund was for the establishment of El Centre d'Art i Natura de Farrera had its face turned to the wall. It was then hemmed in by piles of sand and pallets of cement for the year the job lasted. Some one of us was meant to mention this to Jordi de Bernat; I don't think anybody did. The work was finished. The rest of the materials were taken away. The sign went with them. Its legible face had never seen the sun. There has never been an artist in the School of Burg.

From Ireland I had written the mayor a letter about this seeming sleight of hand. All my Catalan advisers, to whom I e-mailed it before I sent it, thought the letter was perfectly justified. It was an outrage what he had done, and typical too. A good scare would do him no harm.

Now, when I spoke up for Lluís, Jordi de Bernat mentioned this letter, which he still had at home, he said, as if he got it out every once in a while to have another read of it.

In the end calmer counsels prevailed. The mayor would sign the application for the grant. Lluís would have another few months of meagre salary assured before he had to go on the dole again.

All other business was concluded by 2.30 a.m. Javier Rodríguez said that was early.

Afterwards everybody stood around and chatted as if there had not been a raised voice all night. In Ireland we would have been reaching for our big huffs and our Mausers.

More Waaater

I knew I was becoming integrated into this little community when the mayor shouted and thumped the table at me.

Over water, of all things.

I had gone up to look at the water supply during the first months we were back in Farrera. The attempt that had been made with heavy machinery to capture water from three or four sources at the Spring Wells of the Wet Hollows underneath the Pass of Sound had made the catchment into an upland marsh. Hardly a drop oozed out from the collection pipe into the little breeze-block water hut. No water at all got from there through the mile and a half of buried pipe to the new cistern at the village. For years what had been intended to be the secondary supply from the river had been the only supply. It came from a pond at the foot of a small waterfall downstream from the plashy ford where the animals drank. After rain it came out of the taps muddied, at best, and brackish sometimes with organic matter and whatever the cows, horses and sheep excreted into it.

I went up again at the end of that first summer to look at the springs on the mountain with Ramón de Besolí, Marsal, Oppen, Lluís Llobet and Michael. Everybody had a different theory of not only where the best springs were but of how the system worked, the mistakes that had been made, how the pipes ran, where they were all gathered into the one tube, how the line to the village had got blocked, where the blockages might be, and what would be required to fix it.

Nothing was done for two years. Everybody said we had to get a specialist company up to look at it, propose a solution, and present a plan and an estimate of the cost of the necessary works for approval by a plenary meeting of the *ajuntament*. No such company came. The water got worse. It was discussed vociferously at every municipal meeting.

I kept saying we should do it ourselves. I could organize it. I had done something similar in the village I used to run in Ireland.

The improvement of the water system at Annaghmakerrig had been a saga too. At first we had used a group water scheme from Drumgole Lake to fill the old galvanized tank on top of the greenhouse wall. The tank had lost its lid, if it had ever had a lid, and was open to the elements. It was curtained with pondweed grazed by snails and crustaceans, which bunged up the inverted lead colander meant to filter the outlet to the house. A few times in our first years I had to go up, undress and dive down into the tank to snatch the colander off the bottom, clear the molluscs and slime out of it and stick it back over the outlet again. The artists were shocked at the wildlife that came out of the taps and swam around the sinks. The water was not just an embarrassment, it was a health hazard. After much study we set up a self-enclosed system which passed water from Annaghmakerrig Lake through an ultra-violet zapper, a carbon filter and a sand filter at one end, then through the artists and us, and back out the other end into a deep bed of fibrous peat and Dutch mussel shells from which it trickled, filtered and purified, back into the lake again. Simplicity itself, even if it did take weeks of work by men and machines, and about £30,000, to do it.

The water supply to Farrera could be tackled in a similar way, I kept saying, without going into the details as above. I didn't want to be a complete bore. But I did want clean water.

Nobody listened. I seemed to have got backs up with my presumption to know such things when for the least little matter *tècnics* were sent for: wet-behind-the-ears young fellows straight out of *tècnic* school who pondered whatever it was, drew up dense documents with fold-out plans, added thirty pages on the security precautions to be taken (which never were), charged a mint, and still got it wrong, as far as I could see.

Then on Christmas Eve 2001, when we were away in Ireland, the few people left in the village discovered there was no water at all in the cistern above El Castell. In the cold spell that had lasted nearly two weeks the supply from the river had frozen or got blocked. The cistern had emptied. Nobody noticed until it was completely dry. On Christmas Day they had had to get a man with a digger to come and look for the blockage. They reckoned it was somewhere on the first long section down to an inspection point where the water normally bubbled over. They brought up hundreds of metres of thick black pipe and laid it over the ground between the river and the register. That got the water flowing again, as dirty as ever.

Nothing more was done for seven or eight months. In late October there was a noticeable fall in the pressure from the taps. I went up to look at the cistern. It was less than a quarter full. Only a thin trickle came from the river supply. It must have got blocked once more.

I went up the mountain with Ramón de Besolí, who was about to go back to the lowlands with his sheep. He showed me where a black pipe was gushing water directly from the most copious of the springs at the Wet Hollows. It should be possible to connect this flow directly to the water hut, by-passing the marsh, and from there to the pipeline down to the village, though this had probably silted up and would need to be cleared and opened again. The steady three or four fingers of water from this one well would be more than ample to fill the cistern and keep it replenished, at least in the winter months. When the water table sank in the summer we would have to try to connect other springs.

Our neighbour Mateo de Casa Coté said he would come up to give me a hand next day, when Ramón would have to start transhuming. Mateo has been working for ten years on making a house out of the byre where Conchita once kept her cows. He is Castilian-speaking but mixes an orally learned Catalan liberally with his Spanish. We speak SpaCat together in our neighbourly relationship of greetings and exchanges of everyday banalities. He had recently sold his handyman's business in Mataró on the coast and was spending more and more time in Farrera. He has done a few urgent jobs around the village out of the goodness of his heart, such as spending three days unfreezing Marsal's water supply during the cold snap before Christmas.

Mateo put all the tools we would need into the back of his brand-new four-wheel-drive Mitsubishi Montero Turbo 2800, of which he was immensely proud. As we turned off the road to Andorra on to the rough track up to the Pass of Sound, I saw him wince as the overhanging rose and bramble bushes rasped the jeep's metallicized skin. We stopped to cut back the biggest branches with a handsaw but our brush-clearings were not very effective. There was more scraping as he tried to edge the jeep round the ruts of the track to avoid the most pernicious of the bushes.

We stopped where the black pipe that had restored the river supply was joined to the original pipeline. The water was not bubbling over in the register as it usually did. We followed the pipe, undoing it section by section, until we found the blockage in the last section just below the intake on the river. One shake of the pipe was enough to clear it. We cleaned a congestion of dead leaves and twigs from the filter in the pool. At least there was now a supply of river water.

There were 25-metre lengths of black plastic pipe lying in fields below the inspection point, left over from the Yuletide Emergency. We tied four of them to the towbar of Mateo's Mitsubishi. As he steered, all the while explaining the jeep's features to me, how much he had paid for it, and the discount he had got for trading in his last one, through the back window I watched the writhing tails follow us over the river, through meadows, round stone walls, streaming and sliding over all obstacles.

We stopped just below the water hut at the Wet Hollows. From there we hauled the four lengths of pipe one by one over our shoulders up the side of the mountain. We connected the first one to the outlet from the best spring and then jointed the others to it with the connectors we had brought. The water was gushing and spouting like a porno orgasm, but we were 75 metres short of the hut. We would have to come back on the morrow and haul up more pipe.

On the way down we hacked back as much as we could of

the offending scrub on the last stretch of track. Mateo's jeep still got scratched.

The next day we went back up the mountain. The three lengths of pipe we hauled up with us completed the connection of the water as far as the hut.

We emptied out the cement-walled tank inside the hut by pulling out the handy bung that let the water into a drain that cascaded into the river, then bucketed out a couple of feet of gunge from the bottom of it. We made a hole in the back wall to let in the pipe from the spring. I used it to clean and hose down the shiny grey cement of the basin. I put the bung back. The tank filled to brimming with the spring-born water of dreams and advertisements, frothing and sparkling with bubbles of oxygen. But it was not going down the outlet pipe towards the village. It was just pouring into the overflow and running away uselessly into the river.

About a quarter of a mile below the hut we opened the tap on the inspection valve that should have diverted any water there was in the line into the river. No water came out that we could see, for it was not obvious where the outlet was in the eroded bank. We got out a shovel and a pick and started to dig to find the end of the pipe. It was cold and wet standing in the river. The bank came away in clayey slews. I could see Mateo was fed up, feeling the forthcoming scourging of his Mitsubishi as a personal martyrdom.

We went down the mountain to consult with Oppen. He was sure the outlet was just there below the road. He had often seen it working when there had been water in the line. But there had been no water there for years.

The next day Claudi came up with Mateo and me to dig out more bank. We found the outlet. A rusty brown trickle emerged, then stopped altogether. The blockage must be somewhere between here and the hut above. Oppen told us we should look for where the terrain had shifted. The time before when it had blocked it was because the bank of the river had moved and twisted the pipeline closed.

We decided we would have to get a digger up and make a few exploratory holes.

Mateo said he was completely pissed off with all this messing. He would not be coming up any more. On the way down this time a thick rose branch gave the Mitsubishi a valedictory score all along the left side.

A couple of weeks later Oppen phoned me to say the digger was up there. It had made a few holes already but had not found the problem. I wondered to myself why he had not phoned me before. I said I would go up with him in his jeep. He told me he would have to have his breakfast first. It was half past eleven in the morning. Afterwards, on the way up, it became obvious to me that Oppen has developed the delusion common to countryfolk that because you have lived in a place for a long time you know more or less everything there is to know about it, things nobody who has not lived there all that time could possibly even begin to grasp. I told him that when Mateo and I had unblocked the river supply we had found the problem on the last section we opened, the one nearest the intake on the river. At the Wet Hollows the best place for the digger to start digging would be just below the hut, where we knew there was water, until we found the point in the pipeline where there wasn't any.

Oppen said nothing.

When we got to the place where the inspection point was, I saw why. He had already had the digger dig four big holes, starting from the bottom up – the wrong way round, in my view. One of the holes was a crater in the middle of the river. In all of them the digger's forked bucket had ripped up the pipe and broken it.

Mr Fucking Know All, I thought quietly to myself, for I am trying to practise forbearance, humility, tact, diplomacy and other such qualities necessary for living in a small village, qualities with which I do not seem to be naturally endowed.

Now we would have to get ten or twelve joints and more lengths of pipe to reconnect all those breaks. And we still had not found the problem.

Oppen went off and left us to it. He had more pressing business to attend to with his sheep.

I got the digger to make two more holes up the hill. There was water in the pipe in the one a couple of hundred metres from the hut and none in the next one more or less the same distance further down.

It started to rain. The rain was turning to sleet. It might snow.

The next day the new Javier, Javier Martínez, who has bought Alex's house on El Castell (she having moved to Cantabria, where the sea air is more salubrious), came up with me to work with the digger man at repairing the breaks. All morning it rained, sleeted and tried to snow, as the digger gouged and back-filled, its pods sucking out of the muck like aliens hatching from their eggs. By the middle of the day Javier and I were soaked to the skin and chilled to the bone. The digger man was warm and dry in his covered cabin. When he stopped to eat the lunch he took out of a canvas bag, Javier and I walked down the mountain to Farrera to change our clothes, put on waterproofs and have a hurried bite to eat. Oppen gave us a lift back up. He addressed all his remarks to Javier in slangy Castilian. Most of them that I could catch seemed to be to the effect that I wouldn't know my arse from my elbow in matters of water, or anything else.

By dusk, the river threatening to wash in and drown us as we worked behind the muddy dam walls the digger kept piling up, Javier and I were making the last joint. We went back down the mountain squeezed in with the digger man in the cabin made for one

The next morning, having dreamed of cool, clear water all night, I went up to the cistern above the village. There was water flowing through the pipe from the Spring Wells of the Wet Hollows. That small, lightsome victory gave me an instant buzz of elation.

I knew it was many years since the cistern had been cleaned of the accumulation of leaves, soil, cow piss, horse shit and whatever else had been washed down with the river supply. At the last municipal meeting I had put in an estimate for cleaning it. The mayor had said no.

Like a ratty teacher dealing with a stupid but insistent pupil (what is it about living here a long time that makes people so grumpy?), Oppen showed me how all the valves on the cistern worked. We opened the big one that would discharge the cistern into the sewage pipe that flows into the river below Marsal's big field. It took all morning to run the water off.

In Catalan being grumpy is called having bad milk. It sometimes seems Oppen's milk has soured from all his set-backs, the struggles over land and grazing rights, marauding dogs, unreliable machinery, one problem after another, over many years. A shepherd's lot is not always a happy one. He has all my sympathy, but I keep feeling I should take him aside and tell him about my troubles – my varicose veins, bad teeth, lack of money, rejections from publishers, heartaches, itchy balls (the water here is very hard) – to see if he would have the same sympathy for me. I have had to accept, though, that Oppen is not my friend as once I thought he was, and that I am grown too old, grumpy and buttermilked myself to beg for his favour any more.

When the level inside the cistern had sunk to a metre or so

from the bottom the flow became sluggish. The outlet seemed to be blocked. I climbed down the ladder into the cistern. There was a black, putrid sludge at the bottom, popping and breathing like the crust of a septic tank. The outlet to the taps of the village was only a few inches above the living muck.

And we had been drinking this?

With Javier Martínez – who is strikingly handsome, like a flamenco dancer or a bullfighter, tall and lithe, his long black hair tied behind his neck in a ponytail – outside at the gulley trap using his hands and a piece of pipe to keep the watery crap moving downhill, and me inside the tank up to my knees in the noisome bog working and stirring at it with a yard brush and square-faced shovel, we kept the flow going until there was only a thin, liquid layer of malodorous mud left. We turned on the water supply from the Wet Hollows and splashed around buckets of it as we scrubbed the floor and the walls, letting it all run down into the outlet on the bottom, where it sucked away with a slurp that echoed in the chamber of the tank. We threw bucketfuls of diluted disinfectant over the walls, then brushed and sluiced them down once more. Outside it was getting dark. The cistern was beginning to feel like home, we had been in it so long. It would be big enough to hold an audience of thirty or forty for a candlelit show, making me think we should bring up the rest of the village to see how lovely it was. When we climbed out it was dusk. I turned on the supply from the Spring Wells of the Wet Hollows. The falling water echoed in the tank, music to our proud ears. Javier did a few steps on the concrete top, clicking his heels and going '*Olé! Olé!*' with his arms spread like the wings of a butterfly sipping nectar.

We left the cistern to fill during the night. The next morning it was brimming into the overflow at the top. When I took off the metal cover of the hatch I could see right through the water to the bottom. I counted the twenty-four rungs on the ladder: all present and correct, to the last one, making a lucent, refracted picture of H_2OK.

At home in John's Haggard I kept turning on the taps to see the odourless, colourless, life-giving liquid pouring out. There was the smack of a wet kiss as it drained out of the sink. It was a pleasure to have a piss into its shining mirror, watch it grow yellow, pull the chain, hear the water flush, that dulcet sound, and then look to see how clean it was once again. You could drink it straight from the toilet bowl.

After it was fixed, nobody in the village so much as mentioned the water to me or Javier.

Not one person in the village, apart from Claudi and Tere, said thanks.

I have always been brusque. If I want to do something or say something or go somewhere, I just do or say or go. All those years of being Father Abbot at Annaghmakerrig had made me even more arrant. There had been so much to be done and there I did not have to consult anyone. I was the boss.

Here in Farrera it is different. It often seems to be a village where hippie laissez-faire and ancestral peasant anarchism have miscegenated to create a muddle: the houses that were built without planning permission; the corrugated iron roofs; the rubbish thrown down banks or heaped into ruins; the three different styles and colours of street lamps, grey, white and yellow; the four kinds of new stone paving; the cat's cradles of electricity and telephone cables strung from wooden poles and metal poles of various sorts across house fronts and barn walls – every intrusion or extrusion of modernity another scar on the once beautiful face of the ancient unified aesthetic, born of necessity, that had attracted us here in the first place.

I had said this publicly, more than once, to the obvious

resentment of the long-time residents, who took my strictures as criticisms of them. Now I was given to understand that I had broken rank in some way. I had not called a meeting to discuss the water situation, again, as it had been discussed dozens of times before. I had not negotiated a contract with the mayor. I had just told him that we were doing it and that we were going to charge a reasonable price for the work based on the hours we put in (money we would only be paid eight months later, after much to-do and mayoral table-thumping). I had just gone and done it. That, it seemed, was not done.

There had been only two village meetings since the one three years before when the village representatives were elected. I suggested it was time we had another. Verónica, as village representative (Barbara having retired from public office to her independent republic on the other side of the mountain at Tressó), was worn out from trying to deal with Jordi de Bernat. She said she hadn't the energy to call a meeting. If I wanted to I could call it myself.

So I did.

I wrote out an agenda and made copies for everyone. The water. What more needed to be done to ensure a reliable supply in the summer. How we would have to bury the pipes we had used to connect the spring to the water hut, or at least insulate them so that they would not freeze in winter. The need for a sewage filtration system so that the village effluent would not be running straight into the river. How to stop wandering cows and horses breaking into gardens. The muck of the streets. The lack of lighting where we lived in the lower village. The need for parking at the entrance to the village so that tourists' cars wouldn't be passing through it on the road to the dead end at Alendo. The rationalization and putting underground of the tangles of electricity and telephone wires.

The elaboration of a long-term improvement plan for the village. Et cetera.

We got stuck at point one. The water. My way of doing things was objected to. There had to be procedures, I was told. Oppen left the meeting in high dudgeon, banging the door behind him. The rest of us argued for four hours. And got nowhere.

Over subsequent days there was a lot of huffing. With my sensitive ears, big and flapping to begin with, and now bat-tuned to supersonic acuity from twenty-five years of living in country places, I thought I could hear Mausers being cleaned and oiled.

Then there was a fire.

A young couple, Israel and Carolina, with their two children, had moved into Casa Joan on an informal arrangement with the absentee owners, who were allowing them the use of the house rent-free in return for them doing bits of repair work. In early December, a few months after they had installed themselves, we were invited to a tea party there for which they and their friend, Estefan Sambola, had made cakes. All the children sat around the table in the *menjador*. The heat from a stove in the middle of room, whose tube passed through a wooden wall into the chimney of the old kitchen, made the room warm and homely, and rose up through the open staircases to take the chill off the upper storeys. On the top floor Carolina had set up the equipment to make leather belts and bags. Israel and Estefan, who were going to work together, had arranged all their tools on shelves they had built on the wall above a wooden bench arrayed with vices and clamps.

There was a feeling that a new family was being welcomed to the community. Carolina and Israel said that if they could find a house or a site they would make their home here. A couple with two young children would give even more life to the village. The cakes were delicious, too.

A few days after the tea party Mary and I were settling down for the evening to watch Fellini's *La Strada* on video. I had watched it at least a dozen times already, while Mary had been in Ireland. I told her it was about us and our vagabond lives. She was the graceful, talented, resourceful Gelsomina and I was the one-trick, bullying, dissolute Zampanó.

Gelsomina was still innocently collecting driftwood along the seashore, while back at her house Anthony Quinn was negotiating to buy her from her mother, when Mary said she smelled smoke. Our own fire was closed up. There couldn't be a fire lit in the flat below, now Michael's office, since there was no one there. Mary opened the window that looks out over the east end of the village. A swirl of sooty smoke blew in along with a flurry of snow from the storm that had been blowing all day. We heard distant shouting. The bell of the church started to ring, frantically, as if someone were pounding it with a hammer. Then we heard, from somewhere up on the main street,

— Fire! Fire! Fire! Help! Help! Help!

We dashed out the front door and up the steps to the top terrace. Over the wall I saw the shadowy figures of Lluís Llobet and his son, Arnau, being beaten back through the front door of Casa Joan by smoke and flames as they tried to spray inside with two fire extinguishers. There was a crash as the kitchen window beside them broke. A belch of flame shot out. They ran down the steps, still holding the extinguishers.

— There are gas canisters in the kitchen, Lluís explained breathlessly. We couldn't get them out. They must have exploded.

By the time I got up to the main square all the street lights had gone out. There were people running everywhere.

The ethereal, disembodied-in-the-dark voice of Cesca was crying,

— *Més aiiigua! Més aiiigua! Més aiiigua!*

More waaater! More waaater! More waaater!

I tried to help with unrolling the reels of hoses for the couple of hydrants that had been installed after the fire in Besolís' house that had almost done for ours. I couldn't connect one bit to the other. Someone took them from me, reversed the lower section and joined the two of them. I had been trying to connect the hose end.

Michael climbed up to the roof of Casa Joan, on to which you can almost step from the upper square, and played the spout of water from the hose on to the flames now surging up the front of the house, roaring, growling and snarling like a hungry, bad-tempered beast.

Ghostly figures, scarves and handkerchieves pulled up over their faces against the smoke (the pyrophiliac Catalans know how to go dressed to any fire event), formed a line to pass buckets of water from the tap on the ground floor of l'Estudi at the other side of the church. Most of it spilled before it got through the arch. I thought the best thing I could do was go up to the cistern to see how the water supply was holding out. I met Oppen coming down with the big spanner for the valves. He handed it to me without a word, like a beadle passing on his rod of office.

The cistern was still full to the brim.

As I came down again I could see red and blue lights flashing at the same point in Burg where Joe's juggernaut had got stuck. It looked as if the fire engines could not get past the schoolhouse. The snow must have compacted and frozen on the road.

Back at the square, we saw Israel arriving. He threw himself on the ground, tearing at his clothes and hair.

— Everything we have is in there, he howled. Everything, everything, everything.

It was amazing how quickly we learned all there was to know. Carolina was away in Barcelona selling her bags and belts. Israel had left the stove burning – safely, he thought, for he had checked it before he went up with their children, Jova and Naïni, to El Castell to have dinner with Javier Martínez and his wife Rebeca. Everything they had in the world was in that house, including stuff they had been storing in our barn that I had asked Israel to move only a few days before. The fire was moving through the roof into the house next door. It might catch the church, which was just across the way and in the line of the wind, if the fire brigade didn't get here soon.

I was worried about the fire spreading to John's Haggard, which is separated from Casa Joan by only the few metres' width of the square. I walked down the long way past Conchita's house. In the dark alley below the Bastida, Javier Martínez grabbed me by the waist, trying to hold me back. I shouldn't go any closer. It was dangerous. The front wall might collapse. There were gas canisters in there. He seemed a bit hysterical, the way fires make people. I told him I would not go too close. As soon as he left me, I went as close as I could, standing under the arch of the alley as burning timbers from the roof tumbled into the square in front of me. I was relieved to see that the cruel, gusting, southerly wind was still fanning the flames upwards, away from John's Haggard (where we had everything we owned in the world). Any sparks that fell on to its snow-covered roof were extinguished immediately.

As I watched, what I supposed had to be the second gas tank caught. It did not explode in one go but spat long whooshes of flame out the kitchen window, four or five times.

All three fire engines did get through in the end. They were volunteer firemen from Esterri, Sort and Llavorsí. They connected their hoses and used the tanks of water they carried on the backs of the wagons to boost the supply from the cistern, which I spent the rest of the night keeping full by letting in water from the river supply. By one in the morning the fire had done its worst. Casa Joan had been gutted. All its floors had collapsed, carrying Carolina's sewing machines, leathers, studs, fringes, buckles, braids, rivets, and all Israel and Estefan's tools, with them. The roof and the top floor of the house next door had also been burned. In the powerful lights the firemen had rigged to their portable generator, it was a sorry, wet, black slough of despair.

The next night all the villagers gathered in l'Estudi, where we had had our fraught meeting about the water a few days before. Israel had gone to meet Carolina off the bus from Barcelona to tell her what had happened. She was in floods of tears when she came into the room.

Verónica, who was once again the village representative in control, had an agenda written out on a blackboard: what needed to be done immediately so that the *damnificats* of the fire could get through the first days of their loss. A list of foodstuffs was passed around so that we could all sign up for what we would buy them. We would put out a public appeal for clothes, tools, toys for the children, and anything else that might be useful. They would be put up indefinitely in the apartment on the second floor of l'Estudi until somewhere else could be found for them to live. There was a feeling of solidarity, a rallying round this young couple who were new blood we did not want to leak away.

In the discussion that ensued, Oppen said the fire had showed the futility of the *ruqueries*, the donkeyish stupidities, of fighting over the water.

A Living Museum

In the late spring, after all the *follón* (the noun from the Spanish verb *follar*, to fuck) over the water, I drove to Esterri de Cardós to see a house and farm that were going to be turned into a living museum.

The road climbed up a wide side valley off the main Cardós valley, through a succession of three neat villages where flowerpots brimmed with geraniums on windowsills and balconies. Many of the houses had verandahs tucked under their roofs, like rooms with the front walls missing, and some had dinky bow windows with lace curtains neatly swagged across them. All the villages looked clean and well kept (faraway villages being always kempter than one's own).

In Esterri, Augustí Esteva, the man in charge of making the living museum, was talking to the mayor, Josep Borrut, and then had to rush off to do a radio interview from the office of the little hotel the mayor runs with his wife. While I was waiting, I had a walk round the village, where I had been once before with Jordi Viñas, who is part-time municipal secretary there. In the square I was awed again by the spectacular verandah on the side of the mayor's house. It was almost as big as the house itself. Its beams, some of them curved just as they had grown in the forest, were jointed into one another and cross-supported in a way that could never have been drawn and must simply have been imagined and then constructed. All its complex weight seemed to come to a point and be supported by a stone head with a flattened skull and bulging eyes built into the wall underneath it. I was tempted to remove the headpiece just to see what might happen.

As I was talking to the mayor's wife about the weather and

the rainstorm that had lasted all night, Austí appeared, running, apologizing for the delay. He got into the passenger seat of my car to drive up the tarmacadamed road through perched fields to Ginestarre, a kilometre higher up. We parked at a squat, ugly barn of a church, the rounded apses of the Romanesque predecessor it had absorbed still trying to fight their way out from under it. Austí pointed out a stone set into the wall to mark its reconstruction. At first glance I thought it said 1690. In fact it said 1620. Being from Belfast, I always see 1690 as the only date of consequence in the seventeenth century, and measure everything else by its yardstick.

From our vantage above the church, Austí pointed out the roofs of the house and outbuildings of Casa Bringué, soon to become the living museum. It was a gallimaufry of gables, angles, chimneys, lean-tos – perhaps a dozen different slopes, their slates still glistening from the rain of the night before. He explained that it had been the *casa pairal*, the strongest house in this village of a dozen or so houses altogether, where only one person now lived.

Austí was carrying a large iron key that looked like the murder weapon from an Agatha Christie story. It let us into the haggard of Casa Bringué, a courtyard overlooked by a timber hayloft. As he walked me through the Escheresque complexity of buildings, Austí said,

— Here we will have the teaching area; there we need to reinforce the beams; over there we will have live animals again; this is the house that will be put back just as it was.

A team of workmen had already been archaeologizing to find the original layout of the stores, granaries, larders, byres, barns, pigsties and other rooms: 1,650 square metres of floor space between all its different levels. Austí said they were respecting and conserving every beam and bulge of the place, touching nothing that did not have to be touched, and not

even using weedkiller to keep down the grass that was muscling up through the cracks in the floor of the haggard, from
which they had removed tons of ancient manure to reveal the
enormous stone slabs that he reckoned had been brought from
a quarry ten kilometres away.

He took me through the house itself: the chimney room
where they would have sat out the winters in the smoke, the
larder with its empty shelves that would once have held all the
family needed to survive the winter, the two ovens where
they had made bread with flour from the three big wooden
bins standing alongside them, the bedrooms that were like
cabins built within the space enclosed by the Lego of roof
beams. From the two verandahs at the front, with their carved
wooden balustrades, there were vistas of mountains, cultivated
fields, oak woods, and the rain-wet roofs of Esterri below: not
as spectacular a view as Farrera's maybe, but lovely in its
quieter way.

The last Bringué, from whom the municipality had bought
the house and all its land, was a bachelor who was now in his
eighties. He had left Ginestarre fifty years before to go and
work in a plastics factory near Barcelona. Since he had not
married and had no issue, he was glad to know that his family's
homestead would now be preserved intact, just as he had left
it. Because Senyor Bringué had sold the house and barns with
all their contents, Augustí and Co. were cataloguing and
photographing everything *in situ*, room by room – over a
thousand objects, he told me – before removing all that could
be moved to a big store room downstairs: straw palliasses rolled
up, wooden beds and metal beds, willow baskets, gridirons,
agricultural and domestic implements, tools, trunks, boxes,
cases, presses, stools, tables, benches, old clothes, and mounds
of worn shoes, some of them with no soles.

Augustí, who is from Barcelona, kept saying *we own this,*

ours goes to there, this is part of ours, over there is ours too, in the way Mary says we all talk about Farrera these days: a declension of *I own, you own, he owns, we own, they own.*

Suddenly, standing amidst all this impedimenta of past lives, I had a vision of what we were doing in Farrera as a form of madness: a romantic folly into which we had poured every peseta, and now euro, we had, which we had still not finished, might never finish indeed, for perhaps it was unfinishable, like Augustí's project. In that moment of illumination, and panic, I saw us as scavengers after a social cataclysm, dreamers stumbling around in a dream that has ended but from which we alone cannot awake.

In the early 1900s there were over 20,000 people living in the Pallars Sobirà. Now there are scarcely 5,000 year-round inhabitants. The pragmatic peasant Catalans just left, pulling the doors behind them, abandoning their dark, draughty houses to the dormice and the bats, with nary a backward look, and got on with making money in the lowlands, for which vocation they had been toughened and readied by their 2,000 years of subsistence in the mountains. The human absence is gradually being filled by brush and scrub, yet everywhere you look the landscape is tinted with a poignancy that would make you weep, if you were inclined to lament the fate of our rapacious species in one of its most extreme outposts.

The various cultural and commemorative undertakings that have sprung up in the Pallars Sobirà – El Centre d'Art i Natura de Farrera; the museum of salt in Gerri de la Sal, where they don't make salt commercially any more; the folk-park exhibit of the old water-powered sawmill in Àreu; the Ecomuseu in Esterri d'Àneu, its name a butterfly net for the *Zeitgeist*; the Archives of Sort, which store the documentation those who fled left behind; the interpretative centre with which the Foundation of Territory and Landscape of the Caixa

Catalunya has violated a virgin valley near Son del Pi; Jordi Viñas and his ecological group Lo Pi Negre, The Black Pine, which has been instrumental in creating the Natural Park of the High Pyrenees – are all just echo chambers for that emptiness.

Yet we persist in our faith that something else might be happening, or be about to happen.

We went with Jordi Viñas and other friends from Farrera to the annual gathering at the Romanesque church of Santa Maria de Biuse with which the town of Llavorsí marks its boundaries. After the Mass the priest blessed a barrel of wine. He prayed over paper sacks of small loaves with crosses on them. We had the bread tucked under our arms and *porrons* of the wine in our hands as we went to sit in the field outside, with its view of Llavorsí in the valley below and the mountains all round. We made a fire to cook sausages and meat on a piece of slate. Over the burnt offerings, blessed bread and holy wine, we persuaded Javier Rodríguez to run again for mayor of Farrera in the local elections that were to be held shortly afterwards. Jordi reminded him that he had only lost by three votes the last time. He was still the best candidate we had. This time, with more of our people registered to vote, he was sure to win.

As soon as Javier had declared his candidacy there was a campaign meeting in Andrew's Hay Barn. The official list of voters, printed out on sheets of old-fashioned computer paper, was gone over name by name, family by family, house by house, village by village. Certain houses could be counted on to vote en bloc against the incumbent, for reasons that were discussed in detail. They would be the first to be visited by our man.

The imponderables were Marsal, who had his own allegiances as a fellow rancher with the Bernats; the postal voters who lived in Andorra and other places; and elements of the German contingent, who were likely to vote contrary, as they were contrary. Carles Carbó and others of the second-homers of Farrera would come up from Barcelona for the day just to vote for Javier.

We helped Javier to prepare a one-page manifesto addressed, in the respectful, formal *vosté*, to all the voters. As well as having open meetings of the council every three months, as the law obliged, Javier, if elected, would form a governing *junta* with one or two representatives from each village in the municipality. This *junta* would draw up and implement an Action Plan and see that it was executed with the support of everyone.

He went to every house in the four inhabited villages to give them his manifesto. Most of them were cagey, he said, and did not commit themselves.

Jordi de Bernat did not do any canvassing. He just drove round on his big blue tractor, as he always did.

On polling day, on my way back from voting in the Burg schoolhouse, I met Marsal on his way down with Perrico. Perrico was smiling, as if he were going to vote too.

By the time I went down again in the evening the count was nearly over. It was being checked one last time. All our people had red faces.

Javi got thirty-two votes. Jordi de Bernat got fifty-three.

Outside the schoolhouse, I made sure to congratulate Jordi de Bernat, his wife, his mother, his father, his brother, his three uncles, his two aunts, and his son, Sergi, who has a great look of his father about him, at the age of thirteen.

The next day, when I met Marsal working in one of his gardens, I asked him how he had voted.

— I couldn't deny him my vote.

I knew which him he meant.

Next time we will put our man or woman up on a tractor to drive round all day.

I promptly retired from local politics, everything – the *ajuntament*, the board of El Centre d'Art i Natura, village meetings – because I have come to realize that I am sometimes a dry drunk of impatience, intolerance and intemperance, no worse than many others, perhaps, but still not quite all the person I would like to be. For one thing, I need to go for more long walks on my own. For another, I have four volumes of Proust's *In Search of Lost Time* still to read, which Colm ordered for me from Amazon.com, knowing they would be delivered to the door of John's Haggard by Joan the postman, the son of Juanito, the postman and taxi man of a quarter of a century ago.

Besides, we had to finish our house. As we would, we hoped, with the help of the Mother of God, and legacies from our parents: our very own patrimony, that rock upon which middle-class Catalonia is built.

And if we have it finished by then, for the *cercavila* of the *festa major* in August we will set out candles on the path past Andrew's Hay Barn, round the back of the house, through the garden and down into the patio, where I will sing 'The Foggy Dew' without a single mistake and Mary will sing 'The Blacksmith', as she used to do:

> A blacksmith courted me, nine months and better,
> He nearly won my love, wrote me a letter,
> With his hammer in his hand, he looked quite clever,
> And if I were with my love, I'd live for ever.

We will invite everyone into the house to admire the work. Marsal, as father of the village, will make a speech. He will say that we are part of the family of Farrera, for openers, and then, no doubt, set out on a divagation through how long he has known us all, how much we will miss him and appreciate him when he is no longer there, and all he has done for Farrera, like the time that he saved the church of Saint Eulàlia in Alendo from burning down in a brush fire that swept up the mountain, and how Richard Betts appeared out of nowhere like an angel carrying two shovels with which they beat out the flames. He will stop when we ask him to sing a song.

Maeve and her boyfriend, Paul Geraghty, a scaffolder by trade and a steady, level-headed man in every other way, want to come in September to have a non-religious betrothal in the church of Santa Eulàlia, officiated by Michael Harding, now laicized, who performed the first act of exorcism on our demons all those years ago.

Afterwards Mary, Eoin and I plan to visit friends in Burgundy, Zurich, Lago Maggiore, Turin and the Côte d'Azur. Then Eoin will go back to Dublin to study environmental management, which he has discovered is his bent. He thinks part of his interest in matters ecological may come from me. I find that enormously gratifying.

By then I will have finished this book, whose writing has helped me to reclaim the past: for myself, for Mary, and, most of all, for our children, our beautiful, brave children, who at one time wanted to obliterate the past in order to kill the bully who loomed through it.

With our children, we have had to learn that we are as we are now, not as we might have been.